GRACE, POLITICS AND DESIRE

GRACE, POLITICS AND DESIRE: ESSAYS ON AUGUSTINE

Edited by H.A. Meynell

University of Calgary Press

© 1990 H.A. Meynell. All Rights Reserved

ISBN 0-919813-55-0

The University of Calgary
2500 University Drive N.W.
Calgary, Alberta, Canada T2N 1N4

Canadian Cataloguing in Publication Data

Main entry under title:

Grace, politics and desire

Includes bibliographical references.
ISBN 0-919813-55-0

1. Augustine, Saint, Bishop of Hippo. I. Meynell,
Hugo A.
BR65.A9G72 1990   270.2'092   C90-091072-0

Cover design by Rhae Ann Bromley

Printed in Canada

CONTENTS

INTRODUCTION

This volume consists of papers delivered at the University of Calgary from 30 October to 1 November 1986, to celebrate the sixteenth centenary of Augustine's conversion to Christianity.

On any list of the half-dozen or so most influential thinkers in the Western world, Augustine would have to figure. His thought dominated the early and central Middle Ages, and the fashion for Aristotle which affected intellectuals in the thirteenth century provoked a powerful Augustinian reaction. While the optimism characteristic of Renaissance humanism was certainly a countervailing influence, the two greatest Reformers, Luther and Calvin, were both conscious and enthusiastic followers of Augustine, especially in respect of this conviction of the absolute necessity of divine grace for salvation, and the utter moral impotence of human beings when left to their own devices. The Enlightenment certainly provided a substantial corrective to Augustine's pessimism; but the latter may be said to have come into its own once more in reaction to the appalling events of the twentieth century.

Augustine makes his mark in many fields: as political philosopher, biblical exegete, theorist of culture, and spiritual autobiographer. This phenomenal range is reflected in the present collection of papers. Hugo Meynell argues that there are norms for authentic conversion—for applying oneself in a thoroughgoing way to knowing what is true, and knowing and doing what is good—and that these were set out with remarkable clarity and force by Augustine in some of the writings which followed soon after his conversion. He tries to show that denial of the existence of such norms, for example by empiricists and relativists, is self-destructive. It is argued by Harold Coward "that the two processes of memory and Scripture provide the essential dynamics for the understanding of Augustine's conversion experience." He traces their effects through Augustine's childhood and the rebellion of his adolescence to his conversion and the faith of his maturity, and finds Augustine's own psychological analysis of his conversion more profound than later speculations of authors such as James and Freud.

It is remarked by Richard Chadbourne that, while Augustine has often been compared with Pascal, this has seldom been in respect of their conversions. He summarises and compares the conversion experiences of the two men, emphasising that in each case the actual conversion should be seen as the climax of a long process of development. In Pascal's case, as in Augustine's, there was a considerable period when he was "convinced in his mind of the need to serve God more fully but untouched in his heart, unmoved in his will." However, the sin which loomed large for Pascal was not sexual disorder but pride. As Margaret Miles sees it, it is above all in the frantic insatiability of babies that Augustine sees the essence of that disorder of our desires which he calls "concupiscence"; as we become adults our anxious grasping does not change in itself, but merely becomes directed to different objects—from "tutors, school-masters, footballs, nuts and pet sparrows," to "magistrates and kings, gold, estates and slaves." She stresses that the attitude he evinces to all this "painful disorientation and joyless compulsiveness" is not primarily condemnation, but sympathy. She also demonstrates that Augustine's reputation as contemner and despiser of the body is largely undeserved, since for him "concupiscence is an agenda *perpetrated on* the body rather than *instigated by* the body."

Anthony Parel raises the question why Augustine thought that love rather than justice was the ultimate principle of civil union. The justice of the city, in Augustine's view, is deficient and ineffective, and unable to achieve what it sets out to do, just because there cannot be genuine virtues which are not with a view to God. And coercion in civil life is the inevitable result of the disorder in human desires which has come about as a consequence of original sin.

Augustine's view about classical literature and rhetoric have been copiously discussed; but, as Haijo Westra remarks, comparatively little has been written about his attitude to the Christian poetry of his time as practised by authors such as Prudentius and Paulinus of Nola. Augustine follows Plato in his deep suspicion of any aesthetic pleasure derived from the senses, as opposed to the exercise of the intellect. He agonizes over the question of what is legitimate enjoyment, and where the pleasure useful to knowledge and virtue ends and indulgence begins. He even goes so far as wishing to suppress the aesthetic element in the liturgy, and his enormous influence boded ill for the fate of

Introduction

Christian poetry in the immediately succeeding centuries. Gordon Hamilton clarifies the hermeneutical principles by means of which Augustine sought to discover the hidden meaning of Scripture; the fundamental criterion here was that the double love of God and of the neighbour should be enhanced. "Whatever appears in the divine Word that does not literally pertain to virtuous behaviour or to the truth of faith you must take to be figurative." He also emphasises the Christological focus of Christian biblical interpretation, and its role within the life of the Church.

William Jordan presents the central teachings of Augustine's treatise on music, and shows the importance it had for both the music and the philosophy of the later Middle Ages. It provided the theoretical framework for the rhythmic polyphony of the Ars Antiqua of twelfth-century Paris, and had a profound influence on the philosophical writings of Saint Bonaventure in the thirteenth century. The importance of Augustine in the history of rhetoric is emphasised by Christine Sutherland. Considering the reservations of Christians in late antiquity as to the acceptability of rhetoric, it is remarkable that it survived the passing of the Roman Empire and its culture; it is in large measure due to Augustine that it did survive, and indeed became a central component in later educational systems. But his firm insistence that content and style are inseparable has often been misunderstood, and the matter provides a bone of contention for scholars even now. Certainly there is a surface inconsistency in Augustine's tendency both to praise and to condemn "rhetoric"; but the fact is that when he attacks it, he always has in mind the kind, very prevalent in the world in which he grew up, that divorces style from content.

Timothy Barnes describes the manner in which research over the last twenty years or so has modified our view of the society in which Augustine came to maturity, was converted to Christianity, and worked as bishop and theologian. He argues that the eastern Roman Empire integrated the Christian church into its social and political fabric earlier and more effectively than did the western, partly due to the more urbanised structure of the former, partly due to lack in the latter of the common intellectual currency afforded by Neoplatonism in the east, until this was provided by Augustine himself. Professor Barnes gives a vivid overview of the turbulent politics, both secular and ecclesiastical, of the period. John Vanderspoel says that Augustine had come, by the time he wrote his *Retractions*, to regret his earlier dictum that "union with wisdom is not achieved by a single road"—as though there could be a way to wisdom which was other than Christ. It is little wonder, in the circumstances, that he devotes so much effort in *The City of God* to an attempt to refute Porphyry, who argued for religious pluralism on a Neoplatonist philosophical basis. In his early years as a Christian, the structural basis of Augustine's thought was largely Neoplatonic; but as time went on, and his education receded further into the past, he was led to repudiate important elements of his earlier position. The opposite point of view is represented by Themistius, who urged the Emperor Jovian to tolerate religious diversity; had not God himself shown that he delights in diversity by creating Syrians, Greeks and Egyptians so different from one another? Similar arguments are found in Symmachus, who was so vehemently opposed by Ambrose.

My thanks are due specially to Shadia Drury, without whose efficiency, energy and good humour neither would the conference have taken place, nor would this collection of papers have been published.

Hugo Meynell
University of Calgary

THIS BOOK HAS BEEN PUBLISHED WITH THE HELP OF A GRANT FROM THE ALBERTA FOUNDATION FOR THE LITERARY ARTS.

AUGUSTINE AND THE NORMS OF AUTHENTIC CONVERSION

AUGUSTINE AND THE NORMS OF AUTHENTIC CONVERSION

Hugo A. Meynell

The phrase "norms of authentic conversion" has a suspiciously sententious ring, but the matter which it alludes to does appear to be of some importance. When and why is that kind of basic reorientation in life which we call "conversion" right and appropriate, and when and why is it not? This question is slightly complicated by the fact that to call such a change in a person a "conversion" is often, perhaps usually, to approve of it. So far as this is so, one has to reformulate the question: When and why is a basic reorientation in the aims of a person's life and the assumptions underlying them a "conversion" properly speaking, and when and why is it not?

The psychologists have by this time provided us with a great deal of information about the nature of conversion, what its predisposing factors are, who is most liable to undergo conversion and at what age, and so on.[1] But on the question of the *norms* of conversion—its proprieties and improprieties, its rights and wrongs—they have given us little or no information. Nor would it be proper to expect this of them, since psychology, by its very nature, can shed no direct light on the matter. Psychologists as psychologists are in the business of *describing* the phenomena of human mental life, but they are not quite sticking to their last when they *evaluate* them.

Furthermore, it seems that people in general have a great deal less confidence about this matter than they had in earlier times. Once, if anyone were (say) a Christian or a Muslim, she would take it for granted that, if one were *not* already a Christian or a Muslim, the *right* kind of conversion would be to Christianity or to Islam; and that if one *were*, it would be a matter of changing

3

from a sinful to a righteous way of life as conceived by either of these faiths.[2] Since the Enlightenment, another view of what constitutes the proper basic reorientation of human life has been gaining ground. Intellectually, it is a matter of embracing the world-view of the sciences, and, commonly, of rejecting the irrational superstitions of traditional religion. Morally, it amounts to becoming a responsible member of one's society. But in the last few decades, a scepticism as to both these assumptions about the norms of conversion has become fashionable. When there are so many different conceptions of rationality, and of the good life, available in the world (as we find from the work of historians and anthropologists), is it not arbitrary and presumptuous to accept some as better than others, let alone one as uniquely and absolutely true and valuable? Is *any* orthodoxy, whether religious or scientific, anything more than one's own doxy?

One might say, very crudely and schematically, that before the Enlightenment the norms of authentic conversion were supplied by one's own religious tradition; and that, since then, they have been apt to be supplied by secular rationality. But does not a thorough psychological and sociological analysis show that all such alleged "norms" are arbitrary? Each of us is socialised into a set of beliefs and values; what is "authentic conversion" *for us* will be a change *from* another set of beliefs and values *to* our own. But others have been socialised into very different sets of beliefs and values, so what is authentic conversion for them will differ accordingly. If someone has been brought up to a set of beliefs and values A, and becomes "converted" to a set of beliefs and values B, then A will supply what are for her the norms of authentic conversion before the change, and B will do so afterwards. One may well conclude, and many in our time have concluded, with the sceptical or relativist view that there *are* no objective norms by which systems of belief and value, and consequently the "authenticity" or otherwise of conversion as in accordance or lack of accordance with such norms, can be established.

Of the thinkers who have attended to this problem, I believe Augustine to be one of the most brilliant and profound. I hope in what follows to show that his reflections on this matter have a special relevance to our own almost uniquely confused and disoriented times. After Augustine's disappointment with Manichaeism, he flirted for a while with scepticism, with the view that properly speaking one can know nothing. It was in meditating on scepticism that he made two discoveries which I think are of fundamental importance: (1) that there are after all absolute norms both of cognition and of evaluation, and (2) that one has to look inside oneself in order to apprehend what these are and to justify them.

Evidently "conversion" is a term with many meanings; for our purposes it seems necessary to distinguish three: (1) change of religious (including

irreligions or anti-religious) affiliation;[3] (b) change of basic orientation of life;
(c) following-through of objective cognitional and moral norms. On
Augustine's own account, his embracing of Christianity was conversion in all
of these three senses. According to many of our contemporaries and to some of
his, conversion in sense (c) (let us call it "conversion-c") is impossible, since
such norms simply do not exist. Clearly conversion-a and conversion-b often
go together; but equally often they do not. Many people belong nominally to
religious institutions, and indeed participate in their rites and give assent to
their doctrines, in a somewhat lukewarm and automatic way; but, either at once
or over a period of time, come enthusiastically to pursue the ideals and promulgate the doctrines of these institutions. Such persons could be said to undergo
conversion-b but not conversion-a. A sociologist who conducted a survey of
American "converts" some years ago concluded (to use my terminology) that
none-tenths of these who underwent conversion-a did not experience conversion-b, or, even on their own account, conversion-c. The minority who did
were labelled by the author "authentic converts." Of the majority who were not
"authentic" in this sense, most gave as their motive for conversion marriage to
a partner of the denomination concerned; "unity of the family in all matters, including religion," was often given as the desired goal.[4] To quote one "convert"
in the survey: "After all, I'm a Christian and I always was. By joining the
Greek Orthodox Church I am still a Christian, but now I'm the kind that my
husband and his parents like most. So that is reason enough for conversion."[5]
The author, himself a Rabbi, noted with regret that the spouse for whose sake
one was thus "converted" frequently had "little more than a passing interest in
the religion of his ancestors."[6]

II.

So much for some facts about conversion. But are there any non-arbitrary
norms by which such conversion might be judged to be more or less authentic?
I shall sketch Augustine's answer to sceptical claims about cognitive and moral
norms, mention some objections, and then add some comments of my own.
Augustine imagines someone doubting whether there is any truth at all, or
whether one can be certain of anything whatever. But in this case, he insists, at
least he can be absolutely certain of the fact that he is doubting. "Every man
who recognizes that he is doubting recognizes a truth, and he is certain of this
fact which he recognizes; therefore, he is certain of a truth. Therefore, every
many who doubts whether truth exists carries in himself a truth why he should
not doubt." To be conscious that one is doubting is to be conscious that something is really so, and thus to know a truth. Some sceptics, says Augustine,
have argued that while we may recognize some statements as truth-*like*, as
having verisimilitude, we cannot apprehend truth itself. But he retorts that
having this is absurd; if we had no inkling of truth *itself*, how could we

possibly recognize anything as truth-*like*? It is as though one were to say, "I do not know his father at all, nor have I learned from rumour how much this boy resembles his father. Nevertheless, I think he resembles him."[8]

Even for us to doubt, in fact, we must have some apprehension of truth; and without some grasp of truth we could have no grasp even of the seeming truth that many sceptics are prepared to concede. And reflection on the nature of many truths, according to Augustine, soon leads us to acknowledge the truth of the existence of God. We find that there are many truths which exist prior to and apart from any human mind. "With all due modesty, I maintain that I know this..., the fact that three times three are nine...this is necessarily true, even if the whole human race were asleep."[9] Granted the not implausible assumption, that you cannot have truths where there is no mind to apprehend them as such, the existence of eternal truths seems to be evidence of the existence of an eternal Mind *for* whom they are true. "You can in no way deny that there is an immutable truth, containing all those things which are immutably true, which truth you cannot say to be your own or mine; nor can you say that it belongs to any man, but that it is present, and in wonderful ways exhibits itself in common as an unseen and universal light to all that discern things immutably true."[10]

Similar interior norms to the ones we find in the cognitive sphere can be found, as Augustine sees it, in the sphere of value as well. "Will you not acknowledge that it is most true that we ought to live most justly; that things less excellent are to be subordinate to the more excellent...; that to every one is to be given what belongs to him; and that the evidence of the foregoing is common to me and to you and to all who see it?"[11] Augustine stresses both the divine origin of these cognitive and evaluative norms, and the fact that they are to be found within ourselves. "Wherever you turn yourself, wisdom speaks to you by certain marks which she has impressed upon her works; and, when you fall back upon outward things, by the very forms of the outer she recalls you to that which is within."[12] The same moral is to be drawn from aesthetic value, and from the amenability of nature to mathematical and causal reasoning. "Whatever is delightful to you in a body, and attracts through the senses of the body, you can see is subject to number, and you can ask whence it comes, and you can understand that you cannot approve or disapprove that which you touch by the senses of the body unless you have in you certain laws of beauty, to which you refer whatever things beautiful you see without."[13]

III.

A good deal of water has gone under the philosophical bridge since Augustine's time, and it cannot be said that his notion that we have within ourselves norms of cognitive rationality and of evaluation, and his account of how these are to be identified and vindicated, are at present much in favour.

There are at least two important opposed views—opposed, that is to say, not only to Augustine's position but to one another—which one may label the empiricist and the relativist view. According to the empiricist view, the criterion of knowledge is extroverted experience rather than internal norms. A true judgment is one that tends to be confirmed by such experience, a false one one that tends to be refuted by it. Thinkers like Augustine, along with other swine of the Platonist herd, are apt to set store, as we have seen, by the propositions of mathematics and value judgments. Mathematical propositions may be accounted for either as very generalised judgments of experience, or as reducible in the last analysis to a matter of the meanings of their terms. Thus "three times three equals nine" might be taken in either or both of two ways. First, it tells us about a vast range of observable facts such as the following—that when we put three sets of three pebbles into a previously empty tin, and no pebble is removed or added in the meantime, we will subsequently find that there are nine pebbles. Second, it follows from the meaning of the terms "three," "times," "nine," and "equals," that three times three equals nine; someone who denies this proposition has not worked out the meaning of what he is saying, any more than one who says that she is acquainted with a married bachelor or (in the strict sense at least) a masculine cow. Value judgments, whether in ethics or aesthetics, are not really judgments at all; they are, so far as they are not disguised judgments of fact—"a good husband" and "a good sonnet" are respectively a man and a poem which have empirically specifiable characteristics—, either expressions of emotion or devices for social control. This if I say "sexual discrimination is wrong" or "Haydn is a great composer," I am evincing distaste for sexual discrimination and enthusiasm for Haydn's music; or I am contributing my mite to discouraging sexual discrimination or to enhancing Haydn's reputation.[14]

It is of interest that a relativist might well take issue with the empiricist position, largely because it presupposed an element of Augustine's view which had not been fully transcended. Empiricists are quite right, she would say, in their accounts of mathematics, logic and value judgments; but it is only through inconsistency that they can maintain their superstition that there are objective facts out there. Does not the underlying conviction, that we are able at least in principle to get at such facts, depend surreptitiously on the essentially Augustinian assumption that there *are* after all norms within us *by means of which* we can get at them on the basis of sense-experience? In any case, she would add, the notion of pure sense-experience, divorced from socially-imposed assumptions and interests, is a delusion. We cannot possibly, as social beings, transcend such conceptions of "truth," "validity" or "goodness" as may be imposed by our various human social milieus, to get at any supposed truth, validity or goodness which are independent of these milieus. A "true" judgment is in the last analysis one which is affirmed, or at least will soon be affirmed, by the most influential members of our society; a "valid" pattern of argument is one which is accepted and encouraged by them. The subjectivity and relativity which empiricists ascribe to "value-judgments" really apply to all cognitions whatever, even those which go by the proud title of scientific. For the scientist is no more able than the layperson is to transcend her social viewpoint so far as to achieve knowledge of whatever "real world" there might be.[15]

So much for empiricism and relativism. My summaries of these positions is certainly simplified—we have no time or space for a book-length exposition of either—but I would deny that they were *over*simplified. I believe that they describe fairly faithfully what empiricism and relativism come to when spelt out articulately as positions, rather than merely used as the source of dialectical maneuvers for undermining opposed viewpoints. What is the Augustinian to do when faced with two such large and entrenched armies of opponents? Must she capitulate, or resort in academic fashion to a smokescreen of learned obscurities? Not a bit of it; she has an answer which, so far as I can judge, can and ought to carry complete conviction. She can agree wholeheartedly with the relativist, that the empiricist is dependent on norms to which he cannot admit, and which are a relic of those which she (the Augustinian) holds herself. But she may further urge that both empiricists and relativists are confronted by an intolerable dilemma. Do they claim that their positions can be supported by argument and appeal to evidence, or not? If they do *not claim* it, their positions are mere dogmatisms, not to be taken seriously. But if they *do* maintain that there is such argument and appeal to evidence, by means of which empiricism or relativism may be shown to be true, or at least more likely to be true than the positions opposed to it,[16] then they are appealing implicitly to a norm—to the effect that one tends to make true judgments about what is so, so far as one submits to evidence and follows arguments. Thus cognitive norms are essential for anyone who wants to establish any position whatever, even the position that all positions are relative (which could not itself be relative, since that would imply that there was some other in principle equally sound position according to which some positions were not relative).

Someone might say that there is all the difference in the world between being committed to cognitive norms and being committed to evaluative ones; we may be objectivist in science, and subjectivist in ethics and aesthetics. There was or was not a big bang, however anyone feels about it; but its being wrong to torture the innocent for fun *is* merely a matter of how we feel about such behaviour. However, it is quite easy to show that cognitive norms do presuppose evaluative norms. It is of the essence of cognitive norms, so far as they amount to anything, that it is good to follow them and bad to neglect them.[18] If truth, and to aim at the truth, are not positive values, there is an end of all appeal to evidence and to argument. People very often argue for victory, or for the sake of picking a fight, or to hurt or degrade or humiliate; but the moment they set this out clearly as the principle underlying what they are at, they sabotage their own efforts. One thinks of the child who always concluded an argument with her younger brother by saying, "Well anyway, your face is dirty." An argument must be supposed to work just as an argument, and it must further be assumed that one is under some obligation to assent to the conclusions of an argument which works, if it is to be of any use for the nefarious purposes just alluded to.

Let me be a little more concrete. It is not very useful to begin an academic paper, of however recondite a nature, by saying or implying, "I never say anything for good reason, or because it is liable to be true, and certainly not in the present publication." Nor is it very impressive to start a public address with the remark, "I have never performed a responsible action, least of all in offering the following observations to this distinguished audience." We cannot abandon the norms of rationality and evaluation which, as Augustine says, we find within us, without implicitly disqualifying every statement we make. The only self-consistent sceptic was Cratylus, who, when visited by his pupils for a seminar, said nothing at all, but just sat wagging his finger from side to side.[19]

It may be objected at this point that standards of right reasoning are essentially public, and not to be got at by the kind of introspection which Augustine appears to demand. I would answer that a distinction has to be made between two senses of "public," in one of which the norms of reasoning are not public, and in the other of which they are. They are *not* public in the manner that perceivable external objects—tables, chairs, trees and flowers—are so; even the best textbook on reasoning envisaged just as a public object in this sense, is nothing but a bound-together sheaf of rectangular bits of white paper with black marks on them. They *are* public in the sense that every intelligent and reasonable being has access to them by virtue of, if only occasionally, conceiving intelligently and judging reasonably. These mental acts are in a sense private to us, and we can attend to our performance or non-performance of them; that they are not private to us in exactly the same manner as a toothache or a sensation as of blue does not affect the issue. Confusion on this matter may well be felt to have lead to a fair amount of trouble in contemporary reflections on reasoning. To quote from a recent paper by John Burbridge:— "Reasoning is not merely a stream of consciousness. It is a process that has certain norms, which can serve to justify the conclusions reached. And these norms are convincing, not only to the individual who generates the sequence of ideas, but also to others, who think about the way one idea leads to the next. It is this normative character of reasoning that led Frege to reject psychologism. But in so doing he rejected reference to all mental operations whatever. And this produced the arbitrary conventionalism of modern logic."[20]

It may also be objected that the mental operations I have alluded to, so far as they really bear on knowledge, can be reduced to logic, which is by now a very precise, sophisticated and well-formulated science such as need have no truck with such messy entities as mental acts or operations. But "logic" is ambiguous; the term can be understood either in a wider or in a narrower sense. In the wider sense, it amounts to an articulation of the norms of cognition as such; in a narrower sense, it amounts to a part, albeit a very important part, of this. As has been notorious since the work of Hume, for example, the move from the observation of particular instances to the formulation of a general hypothesis, which is a central feature of all actual reasoning whether in ordinary affairs or in the sciences, cannot be reduced to logic in the narrower sense. Nor, as has more recently been made clear, can one make any deductions which go the whole of the other way, in any mature science. From the hypothesis that some celestial object is a planet and not a star, one may be able validly to infer that it will have moved perceptibly over a certain period; but there is no strict logic by which one may prove that an observed smudge on a long-exposed photographic plate is evidence of such motion.[21]

But a least, it may be said, even if we concede to Augustine that there are cognitive and evaluative norms within each of us, we need not follow him in his dreadful suggestion that these norms, when fully articulated and followed through, tend to lead to faith in God. Is it not a fundamental assumption of the modern mind, too deeply entrenched to need clear articulation, let alone defence, that the God of theism, so far from being a necessary postulate of the scientific reason, is in permanent and ignominious retreat before its advance? But alas, even here I have no comfort to offer. If we maintain, as we must if we take science seriously, that reason can in principle compass the world; if we assume, as we cannot but do if we are to believe what radio-astronomers and cosmologists tell us, that nature to the utmost bounds reflects the structure of our minds; is not this a very strong hint at least that there must be something like reason at the basis of things to account for the fact? If rational consciousness were a mere sport within the cosmos, it would not have been capable of the mighty achievement which science is. I have not the space or time to argue here—I have tried to do it a length elsewhere—that other ways of explaining that amenability of the universe to rational explanation on which science depends, or pretexts for refusing to explain it, are all arbitrary, or incoherent, or fraught with consequences which hardly anyone would accept.[22]

So if I am right, in spite of subsequent developments in philosophy and in intellectual fashion, there is still a great deal to be said for Augustine's view, that we have within us sound norms of cognition and evaluation, and that these when followed through lead us to a conception and affirmation of God. But one might well wonder whether to follow Augustine thus far is to be committed to what one might call the dark side of Augustinism. Do we have to take on board Augustine's deep distrust of human nature, his treatment in effect of virtually all material enjoyments as merely a snare for the authentically converted, and his dismissive attitude towards natural science as presupposing an undue preoccupation with the physical world at the expense of spiritual things?[23] I do not see why this need be so. Here, one feels that it was essentially Augustine's discipleship to Plato that led him astray.[24] For Plato, the world of intelligible forms, which is the proper object of human concern, is *apart from* the physical world, rather than, as in effect for Aristotle and for modern science, to be discovered *within* and *through* it. Thus, from the Platonic point of view, study of the physical world may well seem a distraction from one's proper human vocation. Again, a proper concern that sensual enjoyments should be kept in their place may easily twist, for the Platonist, into the conviction that one should not engage in them at all. It is a truism, but for all that still worth careful pondering, that Augustine's attitude to material things and to sensual enjoyments shows that he had never fully got over the Manichaean dualism of his youth, and in fact was basically at odds with his brilliant defence of the Christian doctrine of creation, that the material world is through and through the good work of a good God, however much our attitudes to it are distorted by sin, and however powerful our tendency to become obsessed with what, for the sake of spiritual delight in other people and in God, should always be a subordinate source of pleasure. It is also difficult to reconcile with what Augustine rightly saw to be a corollary of creation, the so-called *privatio boni* doctrine that evil is nothing in itself, but constituted by a failure, or lack, or absence of proportion in what is essentially good.[25] It is ungrateful to God not to enjoy what God has given us in the material world. And it is at least indirectly an aspersion on God if we spurn the material creation as an object of study, running down the practice of science as a distraction from that pilgrimage towards God which, as would be agreed on all hands by theists, is the proper business of our lives.

I conclude that Augustine has provided norms that are permanently viable for authentic conversion, or for conversion properly speaking; cognitional and moral principles that are stable over the changes of time, culture and fashion. Authentic conversion is a matter of following through the norms of cognition and evaluation to be found within us; whereas inauthentic conversion, or "conversion" improperly speaking, is a radical change in one's life which either violates such norms, or is irrelevant to them. For example, if I became a Nazi or a Communist or a Catholic to save my skin, or further my career, or indulge my tendencies to sadism, this would amount to inauthentic conversion. If I did so on the grounds that, on mature reflection, it seemed the reasonable and responsible thing to do, I would be authentically converted. An authentic conversion could in principle be to a mistaken view of things at this rate, or even be to some scheme of ideas which was objectively evil; but it would at least be liable not to be, since the true and the good are what we tend to approach so far as we follow through our cognitional and evaluative norms. And one may believe in these norms, and their liability to issue in theism, without falling foul of what may be called the dark side of Augustine. On the contrary, properly to follow them through is to be enabled to see where Augustine himself may have distorted the real implications of the Christian theism of which he was such a splendid champion. Such a grasp at once of the genius and of the limits of Augustine may well be thought to be one of the main tasks on the ethical and theological agenda of the contemporary Church.[26]

Dr. Hugo Meynell, was educated at Eton College and King's College, Cambridge, where he took a B.A. in music and theology, and afterwards a Ph.D. in philosophy of religion. He was appointed to the University of Leeds departments of Philosophy, and of Theology and Religious Studies, in 1963; and to the Religious Studies Department of the University of Calgary in 1981. He is author of the following published books: *Sense, Nonsense and Christianity* (1964); *Grace versus Nature* (Studies in Barth's *Dogmatics*) (1966); *The New Theology and Modern Theologians* (1967); *God and the World* (1971); *An Introduction to the Philosophy of Bernard Lonergan* (1976); *Freud, Marx and Morals* (1981); *The Intelligible Universe* (1982); *The Art of Handel's Operas* (1986); *The Nature of Aesthetic Value* (1986); *The Theology of Bernard Lonergan* (1986). He has edited *Religion and Irreligion* (1985), and (with G.F. McLean) three volumes of papers for the International Society for Metaphysics.

NOTES

1.   For a useful survey of the state of the question up to the late nineteen-fifties, see G.W. Allport, *The Individual and His Religion* (New York: Macmillan, 1959), 33–35.

2.   The *Concise Oxford Dictionary* will have it that "conversion", in a "theological" sense, is "change from sinfulness to holiness"; and that to "convert" is to "cause to turn, bring over (to opinion, party, faith, etc.)."

3. It is surely just about as proper to say that someone is converted to Marxism or to secular humanism as to Buddhism or Catholicism.

4. Albert I. Gordon, *The Nature of Conversion* (Boston: Beacon Press, 1967), 265.

5. Ibid., 256.

6. Ibid., 266.

7. Augustine, *De vera religione*; quoted R. Arbesmann, "Introduction" to "Answer to Sceptics" in *Writings of St. Augustine*, vol. 1, ed., L. Schopp (New York: Cima Publishing House, 1948), 96.

8. Augustine, *Contra Academicos*; Schopp, *Writings*, 154.

9. *Contra Academicos*; Schopp, *Writings*, 92.

10. *De libero arbitrio*; Schopp, *Writings*, 95.

11. *De libero arbitrio*; Schopp, *Writings*, 92.

12. The translation has been very slightly emended.

13. *De libero arbitrio*; Schopp, *Writings*, 93.

14. The classic of empiricism is David Hume's *A Treatise of Human Nature* (Glasgow: Collins, 1962); though Hume does not, at least consistently, infer all these conclusions. A well-known book which does so is A.J. Ayer's *Language, Truth and Logic* (London: Gollancz, 1958).

15. Relativism is adumbrated in L. Wittgenstein's *On Certainty* (Oxford: Blackwell, 1969), P. Winch's "Understanding a Primitive Society" *(American Philosophical Quarterly,* vol. 1, 1964), and T.S. Kuhn's *The Structure of Scientific Revolutions* (Chicago: Chicago University Press, 1962); though the authors do not set out the position quite as I have presented it, many of their principles appear to lead to it. For a more thoroughgoing exposition, cf. David Bloor, "Popper's Mystification of Objective Knowledge" *(Science Studies* 3 [1973]). Many sociologists appear to take the position more or less for granted.

16. But cf. Augustine's argument cited above, that the notion of truth-*like* is parasitic (to use modern philosophical jargon) on the notion of true. We cannot have any conception of truth-likeness, unless we presuppose a conception of truth.

17. Cf. B. Lonergan, *Method in Theology* (London: Darton, Longman and Todd, 1972), 16–17.

18. The point is neatly illustrated by the remark of T.H. Huxley, to the effect that, if he thought that science was destructive of morality, he would regard it as his duty to say so. I am afraid I neither know the source of this remark, nor am able to quote it accurately.

19. The late Ayn Rand can have been no friend to Augustine, but on these points they do seem to see more or less eye to eye. 'We know that we know nothing,' they chatter, blanking out the fact that they are claiming knowledge. 'There are no absolutes,' they chatter, blanking out the fact that they are uttering an absolute...An axiom is a proposition that defeats its opponents by the fact that they have to accept it and use it in the process of any attempt to deny it" *(Atlas Shrugged* [New York: New American Library, 1957], 965). One might cavil at Rand's eccentric use of the term "axiom," but otherwise her points seem well taken.

20. A paper submitted for the 1986 meeting of the Canadian Philosophical Association.

21. For a number of papers dealing with this and related matters, see I. Lakatos and A. Musgrave, eds., *Criticism and the Growth of Knowledge* (Cambridge: Cambridge University Press, 1970).

22. *The Intelligible Universe* (New York: Barnes and Noble, 1982). for a briefer account, cf. "On the Reasonableness of Theism," H. A. Meynell, ed., *Religion and Irreligion* (Calgary: University of Calgary Press, 1985). A similar argument is propounded by C.S. Lewis, *Miracles* (Glasgow: Collins, 1960), 3.

23. Michael Polanyi wrote that Augustine "destroyed interest in science all over Europe for a thousand years," because for him science "contributed nothing to the pursuit of salvation" (M. Polanyi, *Personal Knowledge* (Chicago: Chicago University Press, 1962), 141; cited Matthew Fox, *Original Blessing* (Santa Fe: Bear and Company. 1983), 11).

24. It should be noted that this applies to the Plato of the early to middle dialogues, such as the *Phaedo* and the *Gorgias*, and not to such later dialogues as the *Timaeus* and the *Philebus*.

25. For Augustine on use and enjoyment, creation and evil, see respectively: E. Gilson, *The Christian Philosophy of Saint Augustine* (London: Gollancz, 1961), 166; Augustine, *Sermon 50*, 5, 7 (J.P. Migne, *Patrologia Latina* (Paris: Lutetiae, 1844-64; PL in subsequent references) 38, 329). Gilson, *Christian Philosophy*, 143–144, 189–190; Augustine, *De natura boni.*, 1 (PL 42, 551); *Confessions* XI, 5, 7 (PL, 32, 811–12). Gilson, *Christian Philosophy.*, 144–145, 313–314; Augustine, *De natura boni*, 3

and 4 (PL 42, 555–554); *Confessions* III, 7, 12 (PL 32, 688); *Opus imperfectum contra Julianum* III, 206 (PL 45, 1334).

26. For a trenchant putting of the case against this aspect of Augustine, see Fox, *Original Blessing*.

MEMORY AND SCRIPTURE IN THE
CONVERSION OF AUGUSTINE

MEMORY AND SCRIPTURE IN THE CONVERSION OF AUGUSTINE

Harold G. Coward

"How, then, Lord, do I seek you?"[1] These words present the fundamental question to which Augustine's life answers. The turning point in Augustine's answer is his conversion experience, an experience best understood in terms of the dynamics of memory and scripture. Unlike our modern education with its reliance on printed books rather than memory, Augustine was immersed in a traditional education which stressed the memorization of texts.[2] The aim of his education was to produce an orator who could cite texts from memory and explain the meaning of the text word for word. Throughout his life, with varying degrees of intensity, Augustine was exposed to the contents of the Christian Scriptures. That the Scriptures became firmly ingrained in his memory and consciousness is evidenced by the fact that throughout the *Confessions*, scriptural citations are woven into the fabric of Augustine's writing.[3] Indeed, in reading Augustine, one finds oneself "bathed in scripture." The thesis of this essay is that the two processes of memory and scripture provide the essential dynamics for the understanding of Augustine's conversion experience. We will examine the roles of memory and scripture first in Augustine's childhood experience of religion, second in his adolescent rebellion, and finally in his conversion and mature religious experience.[4]

I. Childhood Religion

Peter Brown's biography helps us to see Augustine growing up as a boy in a Christian home receiving a classical Latin education. The culture in which he lived was very oral—it was full of voices:

Augustine's world is full of sounds: the chanting of the Psalms, songs at harvest time, and, most delightful of all, the entrancing speech of his fellow-men. 'The face of a man: regular features, a glowing complexion, a face lit up with good spirits'; and, of course, 'A speech, imparting its message with charm, well-tuned to touch the feelings of its hearers; the melodious rhythms and high sentiments of a good poem.'[5]

Augustine grew up in a culture which valued the spoken word and he was educated to become a master of it. Like his friends, Augustine learned much of Vergil and Cicero by heart. Socrates' counsel against relying on the written word "least it implant forgetfulness in their souls...[and] they cease to exercise memory..."[6] was still being observed in Augustine's schools. Living with his devout mother Monica he would have heard the psalms and other passages of scripture chanted repeatedly. Although exposure to the Christian scriptures would have been lacking in his formal education, the intimate influence of his pious mother would have assured exposure to the scriptures even before his mind was filled with the Latin poets of his school curriculum.[7] Her early influence seems to have sensitized the young boy to a spiritual depth that could not be satisfied by the content of his classical education. Thus he was different from the other boys in that as he grew up he was dissatisfied with the classics, even though they continued to influence him. There was within him a restlessness which he later described as "a heart which is restless until it finds its rest in Thee."[8]

As a child Augustine seems to have uncritically adopted the patterns and teachings of his mother's Christianity and classical Latin education. The deep impact produced by his mother's Christianity, although not fully manifested until later, seems to have been interiorized by Augustine in his earliest years.[9] Indeed, when he reflects back to those years in the *Confessions* he sees in addition to his mother that God was also present within him.[10] "As a boy," says Augustine, "I began to pray to Thee, my Help and my Refuge, and by invoking Thee I broke the knots which bound my tongue."[11] Augustine also became a catechumen in the Catholic Church, which would have also involved him in the study and memorization of scripture passages. In the *Confessions* he laments that so much of his time and talent as a boy was wasted on dramatic recitations from the classics—so much smoke and wind. Instead, he says, my tongue might have been better exercised on "Thy praises, as found in Thy Scriptures" which "would have propped up the tender growth of my heart...."[12]

All in all, the picture we have of Augustine's childhood is of a bright boy nourished in infancy by a pious Christian mother, exposed to the rigours of a classical education, memorization and recitation of both Latin poets and passages of scripture, a remembrance of praying to God and the awareness of a spiritual searching from within. The conscience he developed was strongly influenced by the values of his mother and the Church in which he was a catechumen. It was in this period that the capacity for memory was nourished within him and filled with many contents both secular and sacred. Only later in life were these contents appropriated into his experience in terms of their meanings and spiritual significance.

II. Adolescent Religion

Commenting on adolescence the psychologist Gordon Allport says, "At this period of development the youth is compelled to transform his religious attitudes...from second-hand fittings to first hand fittings of his personality. He can no longer let his parents do his thinking for him."[13] Often this involves a period of rebellion in which the youth shifts allegiance to a religious institution different from that of childhood. Such rebellion often culminates in a conversion experience. In its broad outline Augustine's life pattern seems to have gone through these "normal stages" typical of adolescent religion. Augustine's guilt and shame for some of his teen-age exploits is fully chronicled in the *Confessions*. Our interest is not in the theft of pears by he and his friends or in their sexual exploits, but rather in his intellectual search. Leaving home for Carthage gave him freedom to try out different philosophical perspectives. In the course of his studies he came upon a book, *Hortensius*, by Cicero. Its exhortation to search for wisdom deeply moved the young Augustine leading him away from the "vain hope" of worldly fame and pleasure. However, he was disappointed not to find the name of Christ there, for "this name of my saviour...my youthful heart had drunk in piously with my mother's milk and until that time had retained it in its depths; whatever lacked this name could not completely win me, howsoever well expressed, and polished and true appearing."[14]

Responding to this disappointment, Augustine turns his critical but awakened and searching eyes to the Christian scriptures of his youth. But they did not speak to him. Instead he found them veiled in mysteries and, in matters of style, unable to measure up to the standards of Cicero.[15] Turning his back on scripture, Augustine then converted to become a follower of Mani whose teaching rejected the unspiritual Old Testament with its immoral stories and embraced Christ not as an incarnation but rather as a principle of Wisdom.[16] What especially attracted Augustine was that Manichaean thought seemed to have an answer to the problem of evil. In the Manichaean dualistic view evil came not from a good God, but rather from an invasion of his "Kingdom of Light" by a hostile force of evil, equal in power, the "Kingdom of Darkness" which remained externally separate.[17] From a philosophic point of view this position seemed superior to that of Christianity. It enabled Augustine to win arguments with Christians who tried to stand up for their faith and led him into a successful career as a teacher of rhetoric and philosophy. This career finally took him to Milan where he encountered Bishop Ambrose and was led to give up Manichaeism for the Greek philosophy of Plotinus and Ambrose's preaching of Christianity. Once Manichaeism was given up "the submerged bedrock of his ancestral religion—the Catholicism of Monica" was available for rediscovery by Augustine.[18] His decision to become a catechumen of the Church of Milan was an indication that he was moving in this direction.[19]

Adolescence for Augustine was marked by a brief period of rebellion against the standards of parents and society followed by an intellectual rejection of his childhood upbringing as a Christian. This included a rejection of the Bible in favour of the teachings of the Manichaeans. He remained a follower of the Manichaean teachings for several years until his move to Milan. There he became sceptical of the Manichaean teaching, began to study Platonic philosophy and reopened the door to the study of Christian scripture under the influence of Ambrose.

III. Conversion and Mature Religion

Maturity gives up egocentricism of youth, pays less attention to environmental pressures and opens the way for a further development of the religion of childhood which had been arrested during adolescence. The criteria for mature religion, says Allport, include transcending immediate biological impulses, becoming insightful about one's own life and realizing a unifying philosophy of life.[20] Conversion is often the first step in the development of such an integrated personality pattern. In the case of Augustine, scripture and the processes of memory played a major role in this psycho-spiritual integration.

Before examining Augustine's conception of memory and the role it played in his conversion, let us briefly set the stage. In Milan Augustine's study of the philosophers was leading him to glimpses of the goal, but such glimpses left him dissatisfied because they failed to show the way to that goal. Nor did they furnish the personal strength required to undertake the journey. Yet Augustine viewed this study of philosophy to have been part of God's plan for him—if only to see the limits of the philosophers.

> You willed, I believe, that I should come upon those [Platonic] books before I came to consider your scriptures, so that it would be stamped upon my memory how I had once been affected by those books. It was your will that later, when I would become responsive amidst your books, you would touch my wounds with your healing fingers. Then, as you willed, I would learn about and mark clearly the difference between those who see that a journey must be made and yet are blind to the way and those who see the way leading to the beloved homeland, a land to be dwelled in as well as perceived within the mind.[21]

Although the philosophers could help to prepare the mind, it was only through God's book, the Scriptures, that the way home would be made clear. Thus

Augustine comes to see the need for scripture where reason fails. What Augustine found lacking in the life of philosophy was the Hebrew dimension of *leb* or heart and the need for humble submission to God's authority and grace.

> Of all this, those writings say nothing...Therein no one sings: Will not my soul be submitted to God? From him is my salvation. Indeed my very God and my savior, my defender: no more shall I be moved. In those books, no one hears someone calling: Come to me you who labour. They disdain to learn from him, for he is meek and humble of heart. For these things you have hidden from the wise and prudent and have revealed them to the little ones.[22]

And so Augustine finds himself turning from the contemplation of the Greek mind to the submissive will of the Hebrew heart, from the vision of eternal truth to the hearing of God's saving voice. This shift is never complete. Augustine's psychology and spirituality retains elements of both the Platonic and the Hebraic. In contrast with Plotinus, who takes the soul to be its own light, Augustine finds that God's Word (John 1:1-5) supplies an inner spiritual light to the human soul that enables truth to be known. And it is God who moves Augustine with "interior pricks" until God is revealed in Augustine's inner experience.[23] How all of this takes place provides the main body of Augustine's recounting of his conversion in the *Confessions*.

William James in his *Varieties of Religious Experience* suggests that conversion experiences range between sudden spontaneous conversions which seem to "come out of the blue," and gradual conversions in which there is a preparing of the way by careful cultivation. But even in the gradual cases, says James, there will be some moment at which there is a sudden forward movement usually associated with a conscious self-surrender.[24] Augustine's conversion would seem to be closer to the latter type. Cultivation was certainly going on. He was busy studying the Christian scriptures with diligence.[25] He heard the stories of the conversions of other great men, Victorinius, Anthony and Paul—stories which challenged and inflamed Augustine with a desire to follow their experiences.[26]

Each story turns Augustine back upon himself. Entering into his innermost psyche, Augustine sees with the eye of his soul God's immutable light. This Platonic vision causes him to tremble with awe and is accompanied by a Hebraic hearing in his heart of God's voice saying "I am who I am."[27] Augustine falls back from this powerful experience of God, due to the strength still present in his previous behaviour patterns. But something within keeps drawing him inward to powerful glimpses of God. That "something" is identified by Augustine as "Thy memory within me."[28] In Augustine this memory of God within seems to be innate. It functions spiritually through the Holy

Spirit[29] and psychologically in a manner that prefigures Jung's notion of the individuation of the God archetype.[30] Augustine says:

> Recognize in yourself something which I want to call within...Leave behind what lies outside, leave behind your clothing and your flesh. Descend into yourself; go to your secret place, your mind...for not in body but in mind has human being been made after the image of God.[31]

Within Augustine's personality the struggle continued between "this memory of God within" which had been nourished in his childhood and the weight of his attachment to his previous philosophic way of life. His philosophic tendency to think of Christ as a wise man rather than as the word made flesh kept him from surrendering himself to the memory within. Finally, however, the psychological power accumulating around "the memory of God within" equals the force of habit that is keeping Augustine attached to his Platonic ways and the stage is set for the moment of conversion.

The Conversion Analyzed

Speculations by psychologists such as James and Freud as to the exact processes involved at the moment of conversion have not proved very convincing. Augustine's own psychological introspection and analysis offered in Books VIII to X of *The Confessions* seems more profound. It is framed in terms of an interplay between scripture and memory. The memory of God within, an active memory which elsewhere Augustine identifies with the Holy Spirit,[32] continually pricks at Augustine from within. Added to this innate memory of God are memories from childhood of the chanting of prayers and scriptures with his mother and in church. Such early memories engrave themselves deeply upon one's childhood consciousness and, like the poem learned in grade 4 or 5, remain with one for life always capable of bubbling up with meaning and power from the subconscious. We are also told that during this period Augustine is immersing himself in scripture—especially the Apostle Paul's writings. The demand for personal decision coming from both within and without so provokes Augustine that he rushes in upon his friend Alypius and cries out:

> What is wrong with us? What does this mean, this story you heard? Unlearned men are raising up and storming heaven, while we with our teachings which have no heart in them, are tumbling about in flesh and blood. Is it because they have led the way that we are ashamed to follow...?[33]

In an agitated state they go out into the garden and Augustine bursts into tears over the internal conflict going on within himself. He urges himself to make a decision feeling the two parts of himself to be locked in conflict.[34] He hears a voice chanting over and over, "Take it, read it!" He stops his tears, takes up the scriptures, opens them and reads the first passage that he finds, "Not in revelry and drunkenness, not in debauchery and wantonness, not in strife and jealousy; but put on the Lord Jesus Christ...immediately...all the darknesses of doubt were dispersed, as if by a light of peace flooding into my heart."[35]

Two things seem to have come together in this moment to have caused the conversion experience of Augustine: memory and scripture. The memory of God within, which in recent days had been gaining power, and the words of scripture from without. How these two could come together so powerfully is given psychological explanation by Augustine as follows. First there is Augustine's presupposition that the mind, even though it has become impaired and disfigured by loss of participation in God, still retains an image of God in memory.[36] Thus, says Augustine, "I should but hide Thee from myself, not myself from Thee."[37] The problem is how to bring that *a priori* image of God in memory into conscious awareness—how is God to be remembered? Augustine's answer is deceptively simple and one that we can all verify from our own experience. The way we "remember God" is just like the kind of exercise we all go through when we are trying to recall someone's name which we say is "on the tip of our tongue." We ask that various names be presented to us aloud, "John," "George," "Jim," etc., for, we say, when the right name is said we will recognize it immediately as the name for which we are searching. This presumes, of course, that we already have the person's name present in our subconscious. As Plato points out in *Meno*, we cannot look for anything absolutely new for how would we recognize it when we found it unless it were already present in memory.[38] The image of God, said Augustine is already present in our memory. Augustine's search for the name of God, prompted by its *a priori* presence in memory, had led him to try the names embodied in the teachings of Cicero, Mani and Plotinus but without success. No transforming flash of recognition had occurred. Only when, at the right moment, the New Testament is opened and the name of the Lord Jesus Christ is spoken does it "click" or "fit" with his inner subconscious memory of God and his conversion takes place. The "outer" expression of God's word in Scripture powerfully joins with the "inner" expression of God in memory and the perfect fit triggers a transformation of Augustine's consciousness. It is the joining together of scripture with memory that makes Augustine's conversion possible. Scripture alone without the image of God in memory would not result in recognition or verification. And the image of God in memory, without the revealing word of scripture, would have no way of being made present to conscious experience. We would be left unable to discover the name "on the tip of our tongue" because no one would be in possession of the name of Jesus Christ to present to us and so trigger recognition, remembrance and revelation. In *De Trinitate* Augustine identifies the will as having the function of bringing together name and memory so that recognition occurs.[39] The other side of the coin to the discovery or remembrance of God is the discovery of oneself as being in relation with God.

This explanation, however, presents us with a problem. Why was there no remembrance of God when the scriptures were previously experienced by Augustine as an adolescent? The answer is given in *De Trinitate*, Book XI. It is the function of the will to bring together and unite sense perceptions with the corresponding likenesses to be found in memory.[40] Indeed, this is exactly what happened in Augustine's conversion. The sense perceptions of the words of scripture were united with the memory of God. The will played an active role in this uniting process in that it was actively seeking a resolution to the conflict in which Augustine was embroiled. Why did this not happen earlier when after reading *Hortensius* and being disappointed in not finding the name of Christ there Augustine actively turned back to the Scriptures? The answer is found in the *Confessions*. Augustine reports that in matters of style he found the Scriptures unable to measure up to the standards of Cicero and so he turned away from the scriptures.[41] At this point in his life Augustine is more interested in matters of style than decisions of the heart. Thus his will is directed to other things and consequently remembrance of God does not occur.

A psychological analysis of such a situation is offered in *De Trinitate* where Augustine points out that as well as uniting sense perceptions with memory the will also has the power to divide and separate them.

> The will turns away the memory from the sense when it is intent on something else, and does not allow things that are present to cling to it. This can easily be established; for, when someone is speaking to us and we are thinking of something else, it often appears as if we had not heard him. But this is not true; we did hear, but we did not remember, because the speaker's words slipped immediately away from the perception of our ears, being diverted elsewhere by a command of the will which is wont to fix them in memory. And therefore, when something of the kind occurs, it would be more correct to say, "We did not remember," rather than "We did not hear."[42]

Augustine did not remember God in his adolescence because the attention of his will was not centered on memory but was directed elsewhere. Rather than attending to the voice of God in the scripture and its corresponding resonance in memory, Augustine's will was directed to a comparison of the literary style of the scriptures with the style of Cicero's *Hortensius*. Consequently no remembrance or conversion took place.

It might be remarked in passing that this is exactly what seems to take place in much contemporary study of scripture. Attention is focused on an intellectual analysis of the literary structure of scripture and this results in the will separating the hearing of God's word from the memory of God within. No remembrance takes place, no transforming power is experienced. The problem is not with scripture, for it still contains the name of Christ, nor with memory, for the memory of God is still innate within us. The problem with us, as it was with the adolescent Augustine, is that our wills are directed elsewhere to matters of style rather than substance and so obstruct the uniting of scripture with memory.

IV. Conclusion

A study of Augustine's own writings in *The Confessions* and *De Trinitate* has provided an effective psychological analysis of his conversion experience. In this analysis conversion depends on the memory of God within, which Augustine finds to be innate, being evoked by the presentation of the name of Christ in scripture. The will is seen as having a decisive role in either attending to and fostering this uniting process of sense and memory, or by directing attention elsewhere, obstructing the process. In the case of Augustine his adolescent fascination with matters of rhetorical style obstructed his experience of God through Christ. Turning away from scriptures his deepening search led to the hearing of the teachings of Mani and Plotinus. Neither of these succeed in uniting with his unconscious memory of God—the driving force in his spiritual search. Only later in his maturity, when matters of style have lost their appeal, does his will again turn itself with full attention to the Christian scriptures. Then, in the garden, when the name of Christ is spoken it powerfully resonates and fits with the memory of God within resulting in a flash of recognition or "remembering" and his conversion.

The question with which this essay began, "How, then, Lord do I seek you?" has been answered by Augustine. As he puts it in Book XI of the *Confessions*,[43] the voice of God speaks to us in scripture restoring us to the source from which we came. He has remained there everpresent in our memory awaiting our return. All that is needed from us is an attentive will that opens the way to the hearing of his voice and unites that voice with his memory within. Then remembrance of God occurs and our restless search is ended.

Dr. Harold Coward is Professor of Religious Studies at the University of Calgary and Director of the Calgary Institute for the Humanities,

University of Calgary. He received his Ph.D. in Religious Studies from McMaster University. Among his publications are: *Sphota Theory of Language*, Delhi: Motilal Banarsidass, 1980; *Jung and Eastern Thought*, Albany, N.Y.: State University of New York, 1985; *Pluralism: Challenge to World Religions*, Maryknoll, N.Y.: Orbis Books, 1985; *Sacred Word and Sacred Text: Scripture in World Religions*, Maryknoll, Orbis Books, 1988 and *The Philosophy of the Grammarians*, Princeton: Princeton University Press, 1990.

NOTES

1. The Confessions of St. Augustine, Rex Warner (Toronto: Mentor-Omega, 1963), Bk. X, Cp. 20, p. 229.

2. Peter Brown, *Augustine of Hippo* (London: Faber & Faber, 1967), p. 36. From his modern "literate" perspective Brown describes Augustine's education as "servile and myopic" imposing a "crushing load on the memory" (p. 36). This paper, however, argues that far from being "crushing", the classical emphasis upon memory was crucial to Augustine's conversion experience and his ability to compose the *Confessions*.

3. *Saint Augustine, Confessions*, Vernon J. Bourke (Washington: Catholic University of America Press, 1966), "The Fathers of the Church" Series, vol. 21, 3, n. 1. (All later references are to this translation.)

4. In adopting these three stages in Augustine's religious development, we are influenced by the psychological theory of Gordon Allport in his *The Individual and His Religion* (New York: Macmillan, 1978).

5. Augustine of Hippo, 36.

6. *Phaedrus* 275 in *The Collected Dialogues of Plato*, edited by Edith Hamilton and Huntington Carins, (Princeton: Princeton University Press, 1969), 520.

7. *Augustine of Hippo*, 29–31.

8. *Confessions*, I:1.

9. *The Individual and his Religion*, 100.

10. *Confessions*, I:2.

11. *Confessions*, I:9.

12. *Confessions*, I:17.

13. *The Individual and His Religion*, 36.

14. *Confessions*, III:4.

15. *Confessions*, III:5.

16. *Augustine of Hippo*, 43.

17. Ibid., 47.

18. Ibid., 81.

19. *Confessions*, V:14.

20. *The Individual and His Religion*, pp. 59–60.

21. *Confessions*, VII:20.

22. *Confessions*, VII:21.

23. *Confessions*, VII:26.

24. *William James, The Varieties of Religious Experience* (New York: New American Library, 1958), Lectures IX & X, "Conversion."

25. *Confessions*, VIII.

26. *Confessions*, VIII:1 & VII:21.

27. *Confessions*, VII:10.

28. *Confessions*, VII:17. Augustine here reminds us of Jung's notion of the innate God archetype within.

29. *The Trinity*, XI:22.

30. See "Mysticism in Jung and Yoga," in Harold Coward, *Jung and Eastern Thought* (Albany: SUNY, 1985), Cp. 7.

31. *Tracts on the Gospel of John*, XXIII:10.

32. *The Trinity*, XV:22.

33. *Confessions*, VIII:8.

34. *Confessions*, VIII:10 & 11.

35. *Confessions*, VIII:12.

36. *The Trinity*, XIV:8.

37. *Confessions*, X:2.

38. *The Collected Dialogues of Plato*, ed. Edith Hamilton and Huntington Carins (Princeton: Princeton University Press, 1969), "Meno" 80 d, 363.

39. *The Trinity*, XIV:8.

40. *The Trinity*, XI:7.

41. *Confessions*, III:5.

42. *The Trinity*, XI:8.

43. *Confessions*, XI:8.

TWO CONVERTS:
AUGUSTINE AND PASCAL

TWO CONVERTS:
AUGUSTINE AND PASCAL

Richard M. Chadbourne

In homage to my wife,
Gisela Chadbourne (1920–1986)

We ought to praise God on
earth because our joy in eternity
will be to praise Him, and no one
can be ready for this eternal
occupation if he or she does not
practice it here in time.
(Saint Augustine,
Commentary on Psalm 148)

I. Introduction

To associate the names of Augustine and Pascal is far from a novel idea.[1] The proponents of the Catholic reform movement of which Pascal was a follower in the seventeenth century were called "Jansenists" by their enemies, the Jesuits, the name being derived from that of Jansen, Bishop of Ypres, whose theological treatise in Latin, the *Augustinus*, was a chief source of the movement. But they considered themselves simply as "defenders of Saint Augustine" or "Augustinians."[2] For Pascal himself, in his *Ecrits sur la grâce*, they were "les disciples de Saint Augustin."[3] The Christian faith that any one of us knows about or believes in is inevitably conditioned and rendered concrete by our moment in history. For Pascal, Port-Royal, another name for the movement which grew out of the reformed Cistercian abbey of that name in Paris, was "the milieu in which [he] came to know the Christian tradition,"[4] Its faith, and consequently his, was profoundly Augustinian in nature.

As for comparisons between the two writers, the first may well have been made as early as 1670, only eight years after the death of Pascal, by the historian Le Nain de Tillemont. In a letter to Pascal's brother-in-law, Etienne Périer, he claimed that Augustine might have equalled but could hardly have surpassed the power of thought revealed in the fragments of an Apology for the Christian religion first published in 1670 as the *Pensées*; he further claimed that only Pascal could sustain such a comparison with Augustine.[5]

Since Pascal's time, his and Augustine's names have often been linked, but for the most part in passing and with little reference to them as converts. Nigel Abercrombie's chapter on the two thinkers in his *Saint Augustine and French Classical Thought* (1938) is the first extended examination of the subject and is still useful though in need of updating. The eminent Augustine scholar Pierre Courcelle explored certain aspects of the Augustine-Pascal relationship in his critical edition of *L'Entretien de Pascal et de Sacy* published in 1960. The text of this "entretien" or "conversation" between Pascal and the Port-Royal spiritual director and confessor Sacy is not by Pascal but reflects his thought accurately enough, having probably been based on notes taken of the exchange, presumably in 1655, by Sacy's secretary, Fontaine. Courcelle returned to the subject a few years later in his brief article, "De Saint Augustin à Pascal par Sacy." It was not until 1970 that the first full-fledged scholarly study of the subject was published, in the form of Philippe Sellier's doctoral dissertation, *Pascal et Saint Augustin*. No one, after reading Sellier, can doubt the massive extent to which Augustine's thought influenced Pascal's.

The justification for the present paper is twofold. First, although much has been written on the separate conversions of Pascal and Augustine, almost no attention has been given to comparing them. And second, existing studies, even Sellier's with its careful distinctions, tend to overstate Pascal's debt to Augustine and to neglect their sharp differences, with the resulting underestimate of Pascal's originality. My secondary aim is to correct what I believe to be such distortions of perspective.

My plan is first to summarize the conversion-experiences of the two writers, including Augustine's influence on Pascal's, and then to compare them. In the first section, I shall dwell in somewhat more detail on Pascal, both because of my greater competence in the subject and because I assume that most readers are less familiar with the Pascalian than with the Augustinian terms of my comparison.

II. Summary of Conversions

As many misconceptions exist about Augustine's as about Pascal's conversion. Each is a much more complicated "event" than it appears to be on the surface.

The "popular" view, if I may call it that, of Augustine's change of heart is that he heard the mysterious command "Take, read" in the garden at Milan, opened the Scriptures to a passage of Saint Paul in which God seemed to speak to him personally, abandoned a life of "pagan" immorality, and accepted baptism as a Christian, going on to become a priest and bishop of the Catholic Church. In reality, of course, it is more exact to speak of the "conversions" of Augustine than of his "conversion," a distinction that also applies to Pascal. One must approach the mysterious events we are discussing with as much *esprit de finesse* as possible, for they occur, as Etienne Borne reminds us, "on the frontier between the human and the divine."[6] Although both conversions can be viewed as dramatic turning points, recalling in some ways St. Paul on the road to Damascus, each also reveals a complex of factors at work over an extended period of time.

The Augustinian conversion that occurred sixteen hundred years ago in the Milan garden was in reality the climax of such an extended process. The "pagan to Christian" image of the event is a myth, as is the image of a Pascal the worldly scientist who discovered God and renounced science as well as the world. The young Augustine was a Christian catechumen hardly ignorant of the Christian faith and possessed of a deep respect for the human figure of Christ. What drove him forward was the search for truth, for wisdom; and what remained long a problem for him was how to shake off the lust of the flesh that he believed prevented his attaining truth and living as a wise man should. The discovery of Cicero's *Hortensius*, a work since lost, with its invitation to embrace the life of wisdom, is in the opinion of some Augustine scholars the first of his conversions, preparing the way for his eventual discovery of Christian wisdom. Unable to accept Christian revelation for several reasons, not the least of which was his rhetorician's contempt for the style of the Bible, his search for a God in whom he could believe caused him to embrace Manicheism, a second conversion that was in reality a stage on the way to the climactic and definitive one. His disillusionment with the Manichees and his discovery of the Neo-Platonic philosophers, Plotinus and Porphyry, and of the affinity of the Neo-Platonism he so admired with the doctrine of the Word in John's Gospel, led him finally to accept the Christian faith, a move in which the sermons and example of Bishop Ambrose of Milan, the discovery of the monasticism of St. Anthony, and his finding a way to accept the Old Testament as an essential part of Christian revelation, all were contributing factors.

Blaise Pascal, on the other hand, was born and baptized into a Catholic family—the first contrast with Augustine to note—whose practice of the faith was nevertheless based more on respect for outward form than on depth of conviction. The whole family was to be swept up in the great spiritual renewal of Counter-Reformation France of the 1640s, in this case the spiritual movement within the Catholic Church emanating from Port-Royal. It was a question, as Henri Gouhier has expressed it, of one of those periodical "discoveries of Christianity by Christians."[7] For Pascal there was no devout mother to learn the faith from, no Monica in his life, for Madame Pascal died when the children—Blaise, a younger sister Jacqueline, and an older sister Gilberte— were very young. It was their father, Etienne Pascal, a magistrate and intellectual, who brought the children up in the not uncharacteristic piety of the *noblesse de robe* of the period, an atmosphere in which faith was strictly separated from reason and what I have called respect for Christian duty was maintained.

Such at least was the situation until the family was visited in 1646, in Rouen where they were living—Blaise was then twenty-three years old—by two gentlemen bonesetters attending on Etienne Pascal who had sustained an injury to his leg. What they brought was not only physical healing for the father but spiritual healing, spiritual renewal, for the whole family, and foremost for young Blaise who took the lead in "converting" the others. The link with Augustine is clear: the Frères Deschamps (the healers) were disciples of the curé de Rouville (a town near Rouen), who was a disciple of the abbé de Saint Cyran, the chief disseminator in French of the Augustinian doctrines of grace of his master, Bishop Jansen.[8]

It is this event in Pascal's life that is referred to as his "first conversion." Such conversions were common in Counter-Reformation France, especially in the milieu of Port-Royal. Note, however, that the term was then used to describe, not the passage from unbelief to belief, but the "renewal and deepening"[9] of a faith already subscribed to. Pascal, as Sellier has shown, was already well acquainted with Augustine's thought, since his father "had instructed and guided him in the reading of the Bible, the Councils and Fathers of the Church, and ecclesiastical history." This conversion in 1646, as Sellier goes on to point out, "merely reenforced the whole family's interest in the study of theology and of what was then considered its richest source, the work of Augustine."[10] Just as there is no evidence whatever that Pascal was at any time an unbeliever, there is not the slightest implication in his first conversion of any transformation from a morally dissolute to a morally reformed way of life. The great sin from which Pascal had to struggle most of his life to free himself was not sexual disorder but pride, *libido dominandi*. Here a sharp contrast with Augustine presents itself: the stress which the author of *Confessions* places on sins of the flesh; the complete absence of such emphasis either in Pascal's spiritual writings or in his defense of the Christian faith. More on this point later.

In his first conversion, then, Pascal received the call to "live only for God and to have no other purpose in life but him," as described by Gilberte in her *Vie de Monsieur Pascal (à ne vivre que pour Dieu et à n'avoir point d'autre objet que lui*).[11] By taking the lead in encouraging his family he showed the first signs of that gift for the spiritual direction, indeed the conversion, of others that will remain characteristic of him. Yet curiously enough, a much deeper chord was touched in his sister Jacqueline, who conceived at that time the idea of truly overcoming worldliness (a goal stressed in Jansenist piety) by entering a religious order, and who later did so by becoming Sister Sainte Euphémie in the convent of Port-Royal. Pascal showed greater zeal at the moment, perhaps, but it was short-lived. His mind had been touched, indeed troubled; his heart, less so. H.F. Stewart remarks that his first conversion was in fact "very like St. Augustine's, touching the head rather than the heart"[12] (he is referring to the progress made between *Confessions*, V, 13-14, and VIII, 12). Strong attachments to the polite society of his time and to his scientific and mathematical pursuits (*not* abandoned, as Gilberte erroneously claims) prevented his responding more fully to the divine call. One would be tempted to dismiss the experience of 1646 as *une conversion manquée* except that the seed had been planted, nothing was really lost.

The second conversion of Pascal occurred eight years later, in 1654. Unlike the first, it affected him alone, was divulged to no one during his lifetime, and took place as a single dramatic event within a precisely defined time limit. Our knowledge of this mysterious event is based on the extraordinary document know as *Le Mémorial*.[13] Here, in a manner perhaps unique in the history of mysticism as well as in literary history, a great writer who was also a great scientist and mathematician recorded with as much precision as he could command the mystical experience, immediately after the event itself occurred. The document in question is a piece of parchment bearing a text arranged in some thirty single lines, like a poem in free verse; a copy of it (the original is now lost) was found sewn into Pascal's clothing after his death, suggesting that he wished to carry it with him at all times.

I shall quote only the first few lines of the text [14] and summarize the rest:

> The year of grace 1654.
> Monday, 23 November, feast of Saint Clement,
> Pope and Martyr, and of others in the Martyrology.
> Eve of Saint Chrysogonus, Martyr and others.
> From about half past ten in the evening until half past
> midnight.

> Fire (*Feu*)

> 'God of Abraham, God of Isaac, God of Jacob,' not
> of philosophers and scholars. (*Dieu d'Abraham, Dieu d'Isaac,*
> *Dieu de Jacob, non des philosophes et des savants.*)
> Certainty, certainty, heartfelt, joy, peace
> (*Certitude, certitude, sentiment, joie, paix.*)

God of Jesus Christ
God of Jesus Christ (*Dieu de Jésus-Christ*).

The reference to God's appearance to Moses in the burning bush (Exodus III, 6) is obvious. In the remainder of the text Pascal quotes Jesus to Mary Magdalen, "My God and your God" (John XX, 17), Ruth to Naomi, "Thy God shall be my God" (Ruth I, 16) a somewhat mysteriously used quotation which perhaps refers to Pascal's willingness to embrace fully the God acknowledged by his sister Jacqueline. He states that God is to be found only by the ways taught in the Gospel, affirms "the greatness of the human soul" (*la grandeur de l'âme humaine*—a phrase some critics find too "unBiblical" to fit in with the rest, although it is hardly out of keeping with God's creating man "in his own image" of *Genesis* I, 27); he refers to Jesus' fear of being forsaken on the cross, to his own fear of being "cut off" from Jesus, and to his remorse at having "cut myself off from him, shunned him, denied him, crucified him" in the past. He repeats the name of Jesus several times, as he also repeats the motif of "joy"— "Joy, joy, joy, tears of joy (*pleurs de joie*)." The text concludes with these lines:

> Total submission to Jesus Christ and my director [a reference to the seventeenth-century custom, especially adhered to by those of Port-Royal, of the devout Christian having a spiritual director].
>
> Everlasting joy in return for one day's effort on earth.
>
> 'I will not forget thy word' (in Latin in the original: *Non obliviscar sermones tuos*—Psalm 118, 16). Amen.

"The spark of 1646," observes Krailsheimer, "had become a consuming fire."[15]

Behind this event lay a whole chain of less dramatic contributory causes, the main evidence of which is to be found in the letters of Jacqueline and in Gilberte's life of their brother. Totally unaware of what has come to be called "the November night" (*la nuit de novembre*), they nevertheless were able to observe that their brother was going through a profound crisis that was changing him visibly. Jacqueline saw him almost daily prior to November 23 and spoke of a progressive maturing taking place within him, what she called a "growing" (*une croissance*), sufficient to make him a new man whom she barely recognized.[16] "In reality," observes Marcel Raymond, "the event of November 23 was the culmination, the sudden emergence in time of a slow labor of spiritual preparation."[17]

This "lent travail de préparation spirituelle" can be summed up as follows. The zeal aroused by Pascal's first conversion having subsided, he remained convinced in mind of the need to serve God more fully but untouched in his heart, unmoved in his will (a phenomenon with which Augustine, and Paul before him were only too familiar). He had not yet verified by personal experience the truth of his own *pensée*, "How far it is from the knowledge of God to loving him" (*Qu' il est loin de la connaissance de Dieu à l'aimer*),[18] with its inspired antithesis between abstract noun and concrete verb.

In the years between 1652 and 1654, leading up to the *nuit de novembre*, Pascal had thrown himself with a kind of frenzy into both scientific-mathematical activities and worldly contacts, the latter largely in the form of those polite conversations so loved by seventeenth-century courtly and cultivated bourgeois society. It was his physicians who had recommended this social life as a means of easing the strain which his otherwise uninterrupted intellectual activity was placing on his health.[19] Such worldliness was, paradoxically, both a hindrance (at least in his own eyes) to the spiritual perfection he was seeking and a marvelous means of widening his horizons as a preparation for the unique synthesis that was to be his Apology for the Christian Religion. Hardly any "vices" were involved in such worldliness, for, as Gilberte pointed out, "God preserved him from vices;" but still, she added, "it was the atmosphere of the world, very different from that of the Gospel."[20] More and more disillusioned with the "world," yet lacking any taste for the things of God, he had experienced, on the eve of his second conversion, a dark night of the soul. "He had found the void in nature," writes Morris Bishop referring to his experiments as a physicist, "he had found a greater void in his own heart."[21]

The closeness between Blaise and Jacqueline at this moment and earlier in their spiritual lives recalls that between Augustine and Monica, except that the brother-sister spiritual kinship is marked by a symmetry lacking in the other. It was Pascal who had been the chief human instrument of grace converting his sister in 1646 and preparing the way for her religious vocation. Now it was his sister who counseled her brother and helped open his heart to receive the grace of his second conversion.[22]

True conversion reveals itself in fruitfulness of works. In Pascal's case, his public writings on behalf of the Christian faith were supplemented by private ones, consisting largely of letters to his friends the Duc de Roannez and Charlotte de Roannez, the Duke's sister, for both of whom he served as a spiritual adviser, as he also did in conversation with many others.[23]

If true conversion reveals itself in works, it also reveals itself in the fact that it is merely the beginning of a life-long process. To be truly converted is to seek to be further converted. Jeanne Russier, one of the most perceptive interpreters of Pascal's faith, links this aspect of his experience with Augustine. "One of Saint Augustine's fundamental ideas," she writes, "which neither Pascal nor the *Messieurs de Port-Royal* overlooked, is that the fact of having found God—and this applies not only to *certain* Christians but to *all* Christians—obliges one to continue searching for him."[24] No "born-again

Christian," Pascal, with Jesus found and that's the end of it! If nothing else, Pascal's Jansenism, particularly his concept of grace and election, would have prevented such naive overconfidence. The Jansenists stood in extreme fear of losing the grace they had once received, though one should add that such healthy fear is hardly alien to the central Christian tradition. Even in the midst of certainty and joy the *Mémorial*, we remember, records, "I have cut myself off from him...Let me not be cut off from him forever." This motif is taken up again in Pascal's meditation on Jesus' agony in the garden, the extraordinary prayer-poem known as *Le Mystère de Jésus*,[25] a kind of monologue in which the image of Christ's presence is projected with such force that the effect becomes one of a dialogue with the suffering Lord. "The constant danger of losing what one has received," writes Raymond, "is also a part of Pascal's faith...It meant that the fiery certainty of the moment's vision of God was something quite different from permanent certainty."[26]

In considering the consequences of the momentous event of 1654, as J.H. Broome has pointed out, "it would be wrong to think of Pascal's life as having undergone an abrupt and total transformation."[27] His scientific and mathematical labors and his various inventions, which continued until almost the end of his life, as well as his worldly contacts (through which he sought to penetrate the psychology of the unbeliever, *le libertin*), were to be incorporated into his Apology. Yet a great struggle was taking place within him to overcome his "intellectual pride." The affair of the cycloid, as Alban Krailsheimer points out, "shows that as late as 1658, four years after his conversion, Pascal had not succeeded in exorcising this pride, amounting to arrogance, which his precocious exploits as a boy had made his besetting sin."[28] It was *libido dominandi* more than *libido sciendi*, though the latter played some role also. Courcelle believes that his increasing awareness of the "vanities of the mind" was reenforced by the reading of Augustine's *Confessions* recommended to him by M. de Sacy.[29] "Unless you change and become as little children ..." (Matthew 18: 3). With what immense effort, we can only surmise, this proud young intellectual overcame his pride and became, as Gilberte and others bear witness, ever more humble and, in the best Gospel sense, childlike.

In this still further spiritual growth, which is referred to as Pascal's "third conversion," his illness played a decisive role. Since the age of sixteen, Gilberte tells us, her brother had never spent a day without some physical pain.[30] From 1658 until his death in 1662 he experienced ever more intense physical suffering which—and here is the important point—he welcomed as the opportunity to grow spiritually and to share more fully in the redemptive suffering of Jesus. Gilberte quotes him as saying, "La maladie est l'état naturel des chrétiens" ("Illness is the natural state of Christians"),[31] meaning, I think, not so much that Christians should recognize their sinfulness as illness, but that all

Christians should emulate the total trust in the Lord which the seriously ill, especially the fatally ill, depend on for their day to day survival. In his great essay, "The Death of Pascal" (*La Mort de Pascal*), Daniel-Rops has written movingly of this last phase of Pascal's life, a life which he describes as one of continual ascent toward "the supreme achievement whose other name is total renunciation of self."[32] "Lord, I give you all" (*Seigneur, je vous donne tout*) we read in *Le Mystère de Jésus*.[33]

The key document for this "third conversion" is the *Prière pour le bon usage des maladies*, which Mesnard dates from early 1659 when Pascal's deepening illness caused him to question once again his whole life and ask himself "if he had not once again failed to respond to the grace that had been given him."[34] Sellier calls the *Prière* "the *Confessions* of a man preparing to die" and compares it to Augustine's *Confessions*, not, of course, in its much smaller scope (it is what the French call an *opuscule*), but in its fervor as an "act of adoration of 'eternal providence'."[35]

Daniel-Rops records with wonderment the fact that in the *Prière* Pascal prays not for the healing of the body but for the grace of conversion![36] Perhaps this grace was granted to him, the same writer speculates, in the form of a "fourth and last conversion, a conversion to charity."[37] Mesnard also refers to "une suprême conversion, presque aux portes de la mort."[38] Whatever the case, in his last weeks of life on earth Pascal fulfilled still another Gospel admonition, "Sell what you have and give to the poor" (Matthew 19: 21, and others)—divesting himself of many possessions, reserving for the poor the profits from the system of public transport he had invented, selling all but a handful of books and giving the proceeds to the poor (a sacrifice that we, as scholars, will be quick to appreciate), sharing his home with the poor, or, as he put it, "communicating with Christ in his members" when illness forbade his receiving Christ in the Eucharist.[39] (Among the few books he retained were the Bible and Saint Augustine. . . .)[40] Such love of the poor, reminiscent of his contemporary Saint Vincent de Paul, brought this "genius attempting sainthood" (Bishop's phrase)[41] indeed to the threshold, if not into the very realm, of sainthood. His last recorded words on his deathbed were an echo of the *Mémorial*: "May God never abandon me" *(Que Dieu ne m'abandonne jamais).*[42]

III. Comparison of Conversions

Having considered the conversions of Augustine and Pascal for the most part separately, I turn now in the final section of this paper to a general comparison of the two as converts, first, in their conceptions of what conversion is, and second, in their experiences of it.

Given Pascal's indebtedness to Jansenist sources for his conception of conversion, and the Jansenists' indebtedness in turn to Augustine, one would expect the Pascalian view to follow closely the Augustinian, and such is the case. The key to Pascal's view is found in the following fragment of the Apology:

> 'If I had seen a miracle,' they say, 'I should be converted.'. . .They imagine that such a conversion consists in a worship of God conducted, as they picture it, like some exchange or conversation. True conversion consists in self-annihilation (*la conversion véritable consiste à s'anéantir*) before the universal being whom we have so often vexed and who is perfectly entitled to destroy us at any moment, in recognizing that we can do nothing without him and that we have deserved nothing but his disfavor. It consists in knowing that there is an irreconcilable opposition between God and us, and that without a mediator there can be no exchange.[43]

Conversion is renewal in response to the gratuitous gift of grace. It is to acquire a new heart (*un coeur nouveau*), a new vision of things, to see all things in a new light (*une lumière nouvelle*).[44] It must be nourished further by prayer, the reading and meditation of Scripture, and the Eucharist. Far from being a final stage, it demands continuation and perseverance, for it commits the convert to further seeking, further perfecting of the life of grace.

Absent from Pascal's conception of grace, however, is any reference to the creature's first creation as set forth by Augustine in the *De Trinitate*. David Hassel has discussed Augustine's views in his paper, "Conversion-Theory and *Scientia* in the *De Trinitate*." Augustine hypothesizes three principal moments of conversion: "The creational first moment wherein the creature issues from God's creative hand," the second moment in the same creative act "when the creature is impelled to turn back towards God, that is, to convert to God" and is thereby "formed out of formlessness," and the third moment, belonging only to spiritual creatures and alone depending on their cooperation, the "freely chosen and progressively more perfect imaging of God."[45] Of these three moments or stages of conversion, only the third concerns Pascal, whose interest in, and perhaps gift for, metaphysical speculation fall short of Augustine's.

Between the Augustinian and Pascalian experiences of conversion there are interesting parallels but perhaps ultimately even more significant divergences.

With both writers, conversion was a gradual process, reaching a decisive moment of renewal after which nothing was the same as before, followed by a periodical renewal thereafter as they sought ever greater union with God. Each knew several individuals who served as the instruments of the divine grace that converted them: with Augustine it was his mother, Ambrose, a few friends; with Pascal, the followers of Port-Royal, his sister Jacqueline. Sellier compares Augustine's relationship to Monica with Pascal's to Jacqueline.[46]

Philosophy played a key role in both conversions. Augustine worked his way to a Christian philosophy using first Manicheism and then Neo-Platonism as stepping-stones, assimilating whatever he could of the pagan philosophers into his Christian vision. Pascal, prodigiously gifted as scientist and mathematician (no equivalent for this in Augustine) and living, unlike Augustine, in one of the great ages of physics and mathematics, was less inquiring as a philosopher, narrower in his philosophic outlook. The whole of philosophy for him in *L'Entretien avec M. de Sacy* is reduced to an antithesis between Stoics and Skeptics; the pre-Socratics, Plato, Aristotle, the Epicureans, are barely recognized; the philosophical scope of the Apology is hardly much wider. Pascal was interested above all in establishing the limits of philosophy (and of reason), of using philosophy as a springboard for the leap of faith he calls on us to make. Yet he would never have undertaken his Apology had he not progressed beyond the simplistic fideism taught him by his father to a more refined view of the relationship between reason and faith. Sacy congratulated him on using philosophers in such a way as to make "remedies" out of "poisons."[47] Pascal, however, repulsed tactfully but firmly Sacy's efforts, based on a distorted reading of Augustine, to convince him that philosophy was dangerous for Christians.

Yet in the end one returns to the pivotal discovery Pascal made in November 1654—a negative finding so far as philosophy is concerned—that the God who revealed himself to him was the "'God of Abraham, God of Isaac, God of Jacob,' not of philosophers and scholars." It is doubtful that Augustine, the disciple of Plotinus and Porphyry in a way that Pascal was the disciple of no philosopher, would have subscribed to such a statement or seen the Biblical God as necessarily excluding the other. The irony of this situation is that the chief philosopher whose claim to arrive by way of reason at certainty about God so exasperated Pascal was none other than that other great seventeenth-century French disciple of Augustine (especially of the "ur-Cogito" found in Augustine)- René Descartes![48]

Other divergences, sharper than those already hinted at, divide the two converts.

Augustine the catechumen came to baptism later than Pascal and was blessed with good health and a very long life in which to grow toward conversion and to produce its fruits. Pascal the baptized Christian was allowed by the same Providence, despite ill health and death at an early age, to telescope, as it were, his spiritual growth, his fruits of mind and spirit, into a brief span of life spent entirely within the Catholic Church. It is instructive to remember that Augustine was thirty-two at the time of his conversion in Milan and died at age seventy-six, whereas Pascal was twenty-three when first converted, thirty-one at the time of his second conversion, and only thirty-nine when he died.

Another important difference is that from Pascal's first conversion on, his spiritual life was focused intensely on the person of Christ. The *Mémorial*, the *Mystère de Jésus*, the Apology are all profoundly Christocentric. Contrasting with this emphasis is Augustine's theocentricity. The person of Christ, as Marc Lods has shown, played surprisingly little role in Augustine's conversion. It was not until after his baptism that he began in earnest his discovery of Christ.[49]

Illness, as we have already seen, was a key factor in Pascal's spiritual growth, especially in his third conversion; it was at most a minor one at any time for Augustine. What effect did this difference have on their approaches to the theology of the body? It would be simplistic as well as medically uninformed to argue that Augustine's robust health contributed to the strong sexual desire we hear so much about (too much, perhaps) in the *Confessions*; or that Pascal's illness reduced his libido if not deprived him of it altogether. The evidence is lacking to give us definite answers to the questions of whether Pascal was ever in love or ever contemplated marriage. The very little he said about sexuality—in the Apology he writes, "Sneezing absorbs all the functions of the soul just as much as the sex act" (he uses the pejorative term *la besogne*, "the chore," for the latter);[50] the reference to marriage as "the lowest Christian condition"[51]—would hardly lead us to single him out as a forerunner of a more positive theology of Christian sexuality. What does distinguish him sharply from Augustine is his total lack of commitment to or celebration of celibacy as a superior Christian state or a condition of union with God. Nor in his development of the "triple concupiscence" theme, which Augustine before him had expanded on from John's First Epistle, does he emphasize either the lust of the flesh or the struggle between flesh and spirit.

Indeed, in the highly original concept which Pascal the mathematician—theologian worked out of the "three orders" (*les trois ordres*), a concept that has no precedent in Augustine and is a keystone in the edifice of the Apology, the body has its order of greatness, that of worldly power, a greatness exceeded in turn by the greatness of the mind (Archimedes, symbol of scientific learning), and this higher order in turn is exceeded only by the greatness of love (the order exemplified by Jesus Christ).[52] A *pensée* alluding to "the Pope" has him not lusting in secret after the flesh but, from within his order of the flesh or worldly power, "hating and fearing scholars who are not vowed to his obedience."[53]

The streak of "angelism" that made Augustine, the erstwhile disciple of the Manichees and the Neo-Platonists, appear at times to regret having a body has no parallel in Pascal who, in fact, condemns such yearning after spiritual purity in one of the sharpest of his *pensées*: "Man is neither angel nor beast, and it is unfortunately the case that anyone trying to act the angel acts the beast"

(*L'homme n'est ni ange ni bête, et le malheur veut que qui veut faire l'ange fait la bête*).[54]

In comparing the works that were the fruits of the two writers' conversions, one finds a similar pattern of affinities and divergences, the latter, in the end, more significant.

The brilliant polemicist who produced *Les Lettres provinciales* is close in spirit to Augustine the religious polemicist, even to the point of fighting similar causes; in this case, for Pascal, "Pelagian theses" in a new, Jesuit-inspired form. In justifying his use of irony, as a Christian, in the *Provinciales*, Pascal cites Augustine himself as his authority.[55] Ironically enough, in that work he was *defending* those accused of heresy in his day, whereas the Bishop of Hippo was *attacking* the alleged heretics of his. How providential for Augustine, observed Pascal, that he had appeared in an earlier age, for in the seventeenth century he would have been accused of heresy like the Jansenists who defended his teaching![56]

As for Pascal's Apology, despite the many Augustinian qualities that Sellier and others have shown it to possess, it has no real parallel in Augustine's *oeuvre*. It is clear that in the finished work Pascal would have continued to reject the orderly logical procedure from one principle to another associated with the Cartesian method, in favor of what he calls "the order of the heart" (*l'ordre du coeur*), an order he found exemplified in the Bible and in Augustine.[57] On the other hand, as a critic of rhetoric, or more exactly, as a proponent of the anti-rhetorical rhetoric that had gained favor in France since Montaigne's time, he is wary of what he considered to be the "false beauties" (*les fausses beautés*)[58] of Augustine's style in the latter's more oratorical moments.

Other divergences go deeper than matters of form, into substance itself. A child of an era still recovering from the trauma of the Wars of Religion, Pascal is less willing than Augustine (often cited by churchmen of his day as an authority for the use of force in "conversion") to use such force; in fact, he rejects it altogether,[59] as he rejects Augustine's argument from the numbers of believers as a proof of the truth of Christianity. "It is your own inner assent and the consistent voice of your reason rather than that of others which should make you believe."[60] Pascal's appeal to the psychology of the *unbeliever*, whom he understood with rare insight, is (as Thérèse Goyet, Paul Ricoeur, and others have pointed out) without parallel in the history of Christian apologetics.[61] Compared with Augustine's sensitivity to the presence of God in the physical universe,[62] his awareness of history, and his exploration of the inner world of memory and of what we now call the subconscious, Pascal's apologetic method seems austere at first, until one discovers how varied are the kinds of evidence he cites, appealing not only to the intellect but also to the will and the "heart," according to his own logic of converging probabilities.

The boldness of his apologetic approach (it puzzled and alarmed most of his friends at Port-Royal) would, I think, have seemed strange to Augustine. But even more strange, to him, as an embodiment of clerical authority and power, would have been the fact that it was a *layman* defending the Christian religion in this manner. Henri Gouhier, in his *Commentaires sur Pascal*, has argued in a way I find convincing, the thesis that the project of the Apology grew out of Pascal's zeal, as a convert, to convert others, a zeal that first exercised itself on the members of his own family, then extended to his friends the Roannez and others, and finally assumed the form of an attempt to convert unbelievers as well as lukewarm Christians "at large."[63] It was as a layman that he trained himself in theology,[64] engaged in religious polemics, became a spiritual director of many, and undertook his Apology. With all his respect for the clergy (he questioned the Papal abuse of authority but remained faithful to the Church of Rome), it is becoming more and more clear today that Pascal is not only a child of the post-Reformation era, when the religious competence of the laity asserted itself; he is also, as a Catholic, a little-recognized precursor of the apostolate of the laity as affirmed by Vatican Council II.

Great converts themselves, Augustine and Pascal retain the power to convert others. In writing of them (if I may be allowed a personal remark in conclusion), I am pleased to be paying a debt I owe to both—to Pascal, the reading of whose *Pensées* in college raised salutary doubts in my mind about the confident atheism I was then professing and prepared the way for my own "first conversion"; and to Augustine, the reading of whose selected writings in Vernon Burke's *The Essential Augustine* helped renew my faith at almost sixty, after many years during which it lay dormant. In my attempt to repay this debt, I am very conscious of my foolhardiness in venturing into the Augustinian field, and I hope that what Job said to the Lord of his own presumptuousness is not entirely applicable to my situation: "I have been holding forth on matters I cannot understand, on marvels beyond me and my knowledge" (Job 42: 3).

I close with a tribute to Augustine and Pascal paid by another of their readers, whom neither succeeded in converting but whose life was deeply touched by their work and for whom they represented the "highest achievements" (*les sommets*) of Christian thought—I refer to the late Albert Camus. Responding to a journalist's question about the problem of evil, he refused to be baited into a facile condemnation of what the journalist implied was the Christian "cop-out" (*une démission*) in the face of this awesome problem. "I would think carefully," said Camus, "before suggesting that Christian faith is a cop-out. Can one really apply this term to a Saint Augustine or a Pascal? To be intellectually honest, one must judge a doctrine not by its by-products but by its highest achievements."[65]

Dr. Richard Chadbourne, B.A. Brown University, M.A. and Ph.D. Yale University, has taught French at Fordham University, the University of Colorado, as Visiting Professor at Notre Dame University and the University of California, Los Angeles, and presently is Professor of French at the University of Calgary. He has published several books and numerous articles on French literature (the essay; nineteenth-century French authors) and Quebec literature (Gabrielle Roy, Michel Tremblay, and others). His interest in Pascal stems from courses he has taught on that author and dates back to his M.A. thesis on Pascal's influence on Ernest Renan. He is currently preparing studies of the French essay and of the theological implications of selected imaginative works by Quebec authors.

NOTES

1. I have used as the point of departure for my study "Pascal and Saint Augustine" in Nigel Abercrombie's *Saint Augustine and French Classical Thought* (New York: Russell and Russell, 1938), Pierre Courcelle's "De Saint Augustin à Pascal, par Sacy," in *Pascal présent, 1662–1962*, 2nd edition (Clermont-Ferrand: G. de Bussac, 1963); the same author's "Les 'Confessions' entre Pascal et Sacy," in his *Les Confessions de Saint Augustin dans la tradition littéraire, antécédents et postérité* (Paris: Etudes Augustiniennes, 1963), and above all, Philippe Sellier's *Pascal et Saint Augustin* (Paris: Armand Colin, 1970). For the conversions of Saint Augustine and Pascal, I have relied especially on the following: Gerald Bonner, *Saint Augustine of Hippo, Life and Controversies* (London: SCM Press, 1963); Pierre Courcelle, *Recherches sur les Confessions de Saint Augustin* (Paris: E. de Boccard, 1968); David J. Hassel, "Conversion-Theory and *Scientia* in the *De Trinitate*," *Recherches Augustiniennes* II (1962): 383–401; Marc Lods, "La personne du Christ dans la 'conversion' de Saint Augustin, "*Recherches Augustiniennes* XI (1976): 3–34; Robert J. O'Connell, *Saint Augustine's Confessions: the Odyssey of Soul*

(Cambridge, Mass.: Belknap Press and Harvard University Press, 1969); John O'Meara's "Augustine and Nco-Platonism," *Recherches Augustiniennes* I (1958): 91–103; the same author's *The Young Augustine: an Introduction to the Confessions of Saint Augustine* (London and New York: Longman, 1980); Henri Gouhier, *Blaise Pascal, Commentaires* (Paris: Vrin, 1966); Alban Krailsheimer, *Pascal* (Oxford, Toronto, Melbourne: Oxford University Press, 1980); the same author's *Conversion* (London: SCM Press, 1980); Jean Mesnard, "Les Conversions de Pascal," in *Blaise Pascal, l'homme et l'oeuvre, Cahiers de Royaumont* (Paris: Les Editions de Minuit, 1956); Marcel Raymond, "La Conversion de Pascal," in his *Vérité et poésie, études littéraires* (Neuchatel: Editions de La Baconnière, 1964).

2. Abercrombie, 91.

3. Blaise Pascal, *Oeuvres complètes*, ed. Louis Lafuma (Paris: Seuil, 1963), 312. Hereafter referred to as *Oeuvres*.

4. Jeanne Russier, *La Foi selon Pascal* (Paris: Presses Universitaires de France, 1949), II, 238. Translations from the French are my own, unless otherwise indicated.

5. Le Nain de Tillemont is quoted by Louis Cognet in *Cahiers de Royaumont*, 27.

6. Etienne Borne, "De Pascal à Teilhard de Chardin," in *Pascal, Textes du Tricentenaire* (Paris: Arthème Fayard, 1963), 366.

7. Gouhier in *Pascal présent*, 84.

8. My principal source here: Mesnard, "Les Conversions de Pascal," in *Cahiers de Royaumont*.

9. Hugh M. Davidson, *Blaise Pascal* (Boston: Twayne, 1983), 7. Davidson cites Saint Cyran on this point.

10. Sellier, 13.

11. In Pascal, *Oeuvres*, 20. Gilberte's account is reliable on this point, but in some other respects must be used circumspectly.

12. H.F. Stewart, *The Holiness of Pascal* (Cambridge, Eng.: Cambridge University Press, 1915), 60. See also Morris Bishop, *Pascal, the Life of Genius* (New York: Reynal and Hitchcock, 1936), 181: "Saint Augustine, one of Pascal's closest spiritual companions, had also a philosophic, intellectual conversion at nineteen, and a later emotional one." (The choice of the adjective "emotional" hardly does justice to the depth of either convert's experience).

13. In Pascal, *Oeuvres*, 618.

14. In Krailsheimer's translation, Pascal, *Pensées* (Penguin Classics), 309.

15. Krailsheimer, *Pascal*, 9.

16. Jacqueline Pascal, quoted in Gouhier, *Cahiers de Royaumont*, 305.

17. Raymond, "La Conversion de Pascal," 13–14.

18. Fragment 377, in Pascal, Oeuvres, 546.

19. Gilberte Périer, in Pascal, *Oeuvres*, 21.

20. Ibid.

21. Bishop, *The Life of Genius*, 80.

22. Gilberte brings out this symmetry beautifully: "God who was asking of him [my brother] greater perfection did not wish him to remain long in the world [*le monde*, in the Biblical sense of what is opposed to the Gospel] and made use of my sister to withdraw him from it, as He had once used my brother to draw my sister away from her commitments to the world" (*Oeuvres*, 21).

23. See, in *Oeuvres*: *Sur la conversion du pêcheur, Abrégé de la vie de Jésus-Christ, Ecrits sur la grâce, Comparaison des chrétiens des premiers temps avec ceux d'aujourd'hui, Les Provinciales, Pensées*; and for the letters to Roannez, 265–270. Pascal's rôle as spiritual advisor is discussed by Gouhier, *Blaise Pascal, Commentaries*, 117–118.

24. Russier in *Cahiers de Royaumont*, 143.

25. In *Oeuvres*, 619–621. Lafuma dates the *Mystère* from early 1655.

26. Raymond, 21. "We must work unceasingly," wrote Pascal to Charlotte de Roannez two years after his second conversion, "to preserve within us the joy that tempers our fear, and the fear that tempers our joy (*cette joie qui modère notre crainte...et cette crainte qui modère notre joie*), Oeuvres, 269.

27. J.H. Broome, *Pascal* (London: Edward Arnold, 1965), 37.

28. Krailsheimer, 14. Pascal promoted an international competition to solve the geometrical puzzle of the cycloid, or "path traced by a peg, fixed on the circumference of a moving wheel" (p. 10). He had already found the solutions himself. Bishop puts the matter with characteristic wit: "In later years, [Pascal] interrupted his quest for humility to defy Europe to find out his solutions for the cycloid" (p. 57).

29. Courcelle in *Pascal présent*, 143.

30. Gilberte Périer, in *Oeuvres*, 20.

31. Ibid., 32.

32. Daniel-Rops, in *Pascal, Textes du tricentenaire*, 11.

33. *Oeuvres*, 621.

34. Mesnard, "Les conversions de Pascal," 60.

35. Sellier, 375–377.

36. Daniel-Rops, 13.

37. Ibid., 14.

38. Mesnard is quoted by Cognet in *Cahiers de Royaumont*, 23.

39. Gilberte Périer, in *Oeuvres*, 32–33.

40. Stewart, 100.

41. Bishop, 353.

42. Gilberte Périer, 33.

43. Fragment 378, in *Oeuvres*, 546.

44. Sellier, 359. See also, Guitton in *Pascal, Textes du tricentenaire*, 318, and Gouhier, in *Pascal présent*, 82.

45. Hassel, 384.

46. Sellier, 159.

47. *Oeuvres*, 297.

48. See Abercrombie, Ch. III, "Saint Augustine and the Cartesian Metaphysics." Pascal's attacks on Descartes occur in a number of well known fragments of the *Pensées*, see *Oeuvres*, numbers 84, 553, 887, 1001, and 1008.

49. Lods, "La Personne du Christ dans la 'conversion de Saint Augustin.'"

50. Fragment 795, in Oeuvres, 601.

51. Quoted in Sellier, 321.

52. Fragments 308 and 933, in *Oeuvres*, 540, 624. For further discussion of this significant difference between Augustine and Pascal see Krailsheimer, *Conversion*, 66.

53. Fragment 677, in *Oeuvres*, 590.

54. Fragment 678, in *Oeuvres*, 590.

55. *Onzième Lettre Provinciale*, in *Oeuvres*, 421.

56. Fragment 517, in *Oeuvres*, 577.

57. Fragment 298, in *Oeuvres*, 539.

58. Pascal quoted in Sellier, 558.

59. Fragment 172, in *Oeuvres*, 523.

60. Fragment 505, in *Oeuvres*, 574.

61. Thérèse Goyet in *Méthodes chez Pascal, actes du colloque tenu à Clermont Ferrand, 10–13 juin 1976* (Paris: Presses Universitaires de France, 1979), 522; Paul Ricoeur and Alasdair MacIntyre, *The Religious Significance of Atheism* (New York and London: Columbia University Press, 1969), 12–13.

62. See Jacques Maritain on this divergence: "The proof of the existence of God from the sensible world has with Saint Augustine (from whom Pascal deviated widely on this point) its full value: 'Behold heaven and earth have a being, and they cry out that they were made, etc.'"—In M.C. D'Arcy and others, *Saint Augustine* (Cleveland and New York: Meridian Books, 1957), 82.

63. Gouhier, *Blaise Pascal, Commentaires*, 117–119.

64. Any lingering doubts about Pascal's competence as a theologian have been dispelled by Jan Miel in his fine book, *Pascal and Theology* (Baltimore and London: John Hopkins Press, 1969).

65. Albert Camus, *Essais* (Paris: Gallimard and Calmann-Lévy, 1965), 380.

THE BODY AND HUMAN VALUES IN AUGUSTINE OF HIPPO

THE BODY AND HUMAN VALUES IN AUGUSTINE OF HIPPO

Margaret R. Miles

Augustine, bishop of Hippo in the North African province of Numidia at the end of the fourth century, was the first Christian author to begin his thinking and writing with an analysis of human experience. In place of beginning as the pre-Socratic philosophers did, with speculation about the physical world, or as Plato did with a cosmological scheme, or yet with Aristotle's question about the behavior of people and things, Augustine began by examining the human condition, in particular his own human condition—the texture, the subjective color of the fabric of his life. In doing so, he was amazed that his starting point was so distant from the characteristic interests of most people:

> And people go abroad to wonder at the heights of mountains, the huge waves of the sea, the broad streams of rivers, the vastness of the ocean, the turnings of the stars—and they do not notice themselves. [1]

Augustine began, then, by noticing himself. "I came to understand," he wrote, "through my own experience." [2]

When you examine human nature as it is, Augustine said, the first thing you notice is that things are not as they should be: a puzzling and terrifying disjunction lies between every person's concerted efforts to be happy and the overwhelming pain human beings experience.

Everyone, whatever his condition, desires to be happy.

> There is no one who does not desire this, and each one desires it with such earnestness that it is preferred to all other things; whoever, in fact, desires other things, desires them for this end alone...in whatever life one chooses...there is no one who does not wish to be happy. [3]

Why, then, Augustine asked himself, looking around, did he see so little happiness in others and in himself? He recognized that part of the problematic nature of human life lies in a vast amount of involuntary suffering, a constant and lifelong vulnerability to an almost infinite supply of pains. In the *City of God* XXII.21, he described the evidence he saw that there is too much pain in the world, far more, that is, than one can learn from. He listed a long catalog of woes which range from the discipline one must undergo as a child in order to be socialized and educated[4] to the "pains that trouble all humankind": the human and non-human sources of pain, terror and death, the harshness of weather—storms, tempests, floods, earthquakes—political upheavals, the danger of being crushed by falling buildings, or of being attacked by animals: "anyone walking anywhere is liable to sudden accidents,...the assaults of demons, and diseases for which the treatments and medicine themselves are instrument of torture." The list goes on and on: restless dreams, fear itself.... But it was not the involuntary pain experienced by human beings that Augustine was most interested in, but the apparently voluntary way that human beings seemed to dismantle their own happiness as fast as they build it. The *Confessions*, Augustine's own story, both illustrates this observation and tries to explain it. To an extent unexampled in his predecessors, Augustine insisted on setting his ideas in the context of his life and invited his readers to do so also.

Augustine, newly elected bishop by congregational acclamation at the age of forty, wrote a journal in order to understand his own experience. The *Confessions* is therapy, not only in the modern sense of introspection and reconstruction of one's personal past, but also in the much broader ancient sense described by Plato when he called the practice of philosophical exploration *therapeia*—therapy, the attempt to locate and orient oneself not only within the events of one's own life, but also within time and space, history and the cosmos, the larger arena of human existence. Also, the *Confessions* is a case history that Augustine shared with other interested people, not his private "journal." Part of Augustine's motivation in telling the story of his life was his reader's perennial interest and stimulation in hearing about someone else's "journey."   .

Augustine described the events and circumstances of his life as episodes in a frenzied struggle for happiness, accompanied by the cumulative disillusionment that eventually brought him to the burned-out condition in which he learned a new way of being and living. He wrote of his life as a prize-winning public speaker and popular teacher of rhetoric in Milan:

> I panted for honors, for money, for marriage...I found bitterness and difficulty in following these desires... How unhappy my soul was then!...I got no joy out of my learning... I was eaten up by anxieties.[5]

Let us look at this subjective "tone" of Augustine's experience more closely. Augustine called his anxiety, his habitual grasping at every object that crossed his path in the fear that something would be missed, concupiscence. He saw it operating most nakedly, most undisguisedly, not in sex—contrary to his "press"—and not even in promiscuity. Rather his paradigm of concupiscence was the newborn infant. Taking his paradigm of concupiscence seriously helps to illuminate what Augustine meant by the often misinterpreted word "concupiscence." Augustine stripped off the rose-colored glasses through which adults romantically view babies and revealed the infant's behavior as anxious behavior. From the perspective of the infant's subjectivity, the world seemed at once very hard work and terrifying. The classical world, the world of Augustine's education, had seen old age as the time of human life that most deserved sympathy; Augustine wrote: "Who would not tremble and wish rather to die than to be an infant again if the choice were put before him?"[6] Compare the behavioral psychologist Jean Piaget's description of infant behavior in order to get a sense of what Augustine saw in the behavior of the infant:

> It is striking to observe...how the nursling, when its mother...is getting it ready for its meals, counts very little on her for obtaining the object of its desires; it makes a great fuss, becomes impatient, tries to grasp the breast or bottle...but is not at all content to await the natural course of events. It all happens as though it depended only on itself to attain its goal.[7]

Moreover, Augustine saw in the behavior of the infant the form of all future concupiscence; as the infant grows up, his anxious grasping is not so much eradicated as extended, given different objects and wider scope. The anxiety of infancy gives way to the anxieties of childhood, adolescence and adulthood:

> For it is just these same sins which, as the years pass by, become related no longer to tutors, school-masters, footballs, nuts, and pet sparrows, but to magistrates, kings, gold, estates, and slaves.[8]

What impressed Augustine was the continuity of the structuring role of anxious grasping, or compulsiveness.

Concupiscence pervades and organizes human life, from the first moment of the infant in which he grasps breath, to the adult's pursuit of sex, power and possessions. It is not, we must notice, a pleasant aspect of human experience. To interpret the element of concupiscence in human life as zestful and energizing, giving interest and motivation to life, is to misinterpret in the most fundamental way. To demonstrate this, Augustine gave his reader a long and sometimes excruciatingly detailed exposition of his experience—experience he consistently presents as painfully disoriented and joylessly compulsive. The conclusion at which he arrived was that the appropriate attitude toward concupiscence is sympathy. He marveled that "no one is sorry for the children; no one is sorry for the older people; no one is sorry for both of them."[9] Augustine called concupiscence "sin," but he did not use the word judgmentally to cast blame or to convoke personal guilt; rather, Augustine understood concupiscence as a sickness or wound, the result of an ancient fall which radically and disastrously debilitated human nature. No one, Augustine said, gives concupiscence the sympathy it deserves.

Augustine's account of the reinforcement of the habit pattern of concupiscence also insists on the unsatisfying nature of this compulsive behavior. From the perspective of the self-knowledge he had gained in his experience of conversion—the breaking of that ancient pattern—Augustine said that concupiscence is not, in fact, "nourished" by its objects, even in attaining them. The objects are, Augustine insisted, good in themselves; but they are nevertheless consistently unsatisfying to the person who pursues them concupiscently. Instead, the person, repetitiously following the grasping pattern of concupiscence, experiences an increasing lack of real nourishment: "For those who find their gratification in external things easily become empty and pour themselves out on things seen and temporal and, with starving minds, lick shadows."[10] The finite object's ultimate incapacity to provide infinite satisfaction, however, curiously only seems to prompt human beings to redouble their efforts to secure gratification, efforts which spin them deeper and deeper into the ruts of habitual behavior. Augustine summarized his cumulative experience of "enslavement" in his description: "From a disordered will came concupiscence, and serving concupiscence became a habit, and the unresisted habit became a necessity. These were the links—so I call them a chain—holding me in hard slavery."[11]

The pseudo-"nourishment" of the habit of concupiscence is the gratification of a repetition compulsion: in Augustine's vivid language, "scratching the itching scab of concupiscence"[12] rather than happy enjoyment of objects. Suffering from malnutrition, the psyche sinks into a state in which lethargy and anxiety are combined, [13] a state which assimilates the inertia of the sleepwalker with frenzied activity. The quality of relationships with other human beings in this mode is dramatically presented in Augustine's image of "eating one another up, as people do with their food."[14] The behavior of the infant at the mother's breast is disguised, but structurally unaltered in adult behavior. Augustine's real sympathy was not with the victim of this greedy use of another human being, but with the victimizer; Augustine knew by experience that the role of victimizer is at least as unpleasant—and perhaps more so—than that of the victim. "And no one is sorry for both of them...."

Two questions emerge from Augustine's graphic, even lurid, description of human life as organized by the frantic pursuit of objects. First, what is the body's role in this pattern of anxious grasping? Is concupiscence really a happy enjoyment of bodily pleasures—at least until Augustine's guilt reinterpreted these pleasures as detrimental to the soul? The second question is, how has Augustine's account of human nature reached forward in time to affect twentieth-century people?

Let us consider first the relationship of concupiscence to the human body. Is Augustine responsible for the dualistic, body-denying ideas that have influenced the history of the West in both its most fundamental cultural and institutional forms and in the most private and intimate experience of the individual?

We began by speaking of Augustine's sharp, perhaps, to us, exaggerated, sense of the inevitable pain and suffering of human life; we need to recall Augustine's neuresthenic sense of the pervasiveness of human pain in order to understand the body's role as Augustine did. Beginning as he did with personal experience—not with received ideas, whether metaphysical or scriptural— Augustine interpreted human suffering as part of the evidence that the human race as a whole exists in a "state of punishment." Augustine found concupiscence and death the two clearest and most poignant pieces of evidence of such a state. Human life with its gratuitous suffering was unintelligible to Augustine without understanding suffering as a punishment: "What else is the message of all the evils of humanity?" This conclusion must be carefully and sensitively interpreted. Many twentieth-century people think it pessimistic to interpret human life as seriously and permanently damaged, weakened, and disoriented because of an ancient fault. A theory of original sin may, however, be a far gentler interpretation of concupiscence than personal responsibility.

Death was an even more conclusive evidence to Augustine than concupiscence that human life is a "state of punishment." In strong contrast to earlier Christian authors who urged their readers to "despise" or even happily to "embrace" death, Augustine had no such minimizing interpretation of this "greatest of human evils."[15] To his own question, "Is death, which separates soul and body, really a good thing for the good?" Augustine answered: "The death of the body, the separation of the soul from the body is not good for anyone...it is a harsh and unnatural experience."[16]

Like concupiscence, death's most obvious effect appears in the human body. Did this mean to Augustine that the body caused these evils? No, Augustine said; concupiscence is caused by the soul's insubordination from its creator, by the soul's unrealistic attempt to exist in isolation from its source of being. The body is not responsible for concupiscence, nor for death, but is, rather, a "helpless victim" of the soul's—the psyche's—ruthless pursuit of objects. Unlike earlier Christian authors and classical authors who understood the body as insignificant, merely the "lowest" of the series of stacked components that compose human being,[17] Augustine recognized the permanent integrity of the human body in human being and attempted to describe a theological anthropology that highlighted this cornerstone of human nature. He objected to the late classical commonplace of referring to the body as a prison:

> You consider the flesh as fetters, but who loves his fetters? You consider the flesh a prison, but who loves his prison? No matter how great a master of the flesh you may be, and no matter how great may be the severity toward the flesh with which you are kindled, I am inclined to think that you will close your eye if any blow threatens it.[18]

Involuntary behavior contradicts flowery disclaimers of the value of the body, Augustine said. He also understood that the Christian doctrines of creation, the Incarnation of Christ, and the doctrine of the resurrection of the body all imply that the body has a high metaphysical status and is an integral and permanent part of human being.

In Augustine's painstaking rehabilitation of the body's public image, there are some curious and significant implications. We have seen that Augustine understood the pattern of concupiscence as resulting from the soul's presumptuous self-absorption with its own powers; as a result of this disorientation, the body, in turn, refuses to serve the soul. Augustine's primary example of the body's insubordination to the soul reveals his assumption that "the body" is male. Impotence, which reveals an embarrassing disconnection between the soul's desire and the body's ability to act on that desire, exemplified insubordination to Augustine. In spite of his rejection of philosophical anthropology in which the body was pictured as insignificant because of its position as the lowest aspect of human being, he still maintained a hierarchy of human being. The body is supposed to serve the soul—but sometimes does not—and the soul is supposed to serve its creator, and does not. The resulting disorientation and disequilibrium pervade the whole human being and all his activities. What appear to be bodily desires, then, are in fact the soul's desires which use the body as a tool (*organon*) for the soul's agenda of self-promotion and deficit gratification.

This is Augustine's proposal for rehabilitating the body, for clearing its "good name," for affirming its goodness as created, and its permanence and integrity in human being. Did it work? It is time to go on to the second of our questions: What has Augustine to do with us? Why does his almost compulsive "confession" simultaneously so attract and repel us? Why does his philosophical and theological affirmation of the human body strike us as less compelling, less pungent, than his intense and colorful description of what he experienced—or at least what he recounted twenty years later—as vivid but unpleasurable erotic experience? These are questions that put us in touch with some problems that were not only Augustine's problems, but may also have reverberations in the twentieth century.

Concupiscence, in Augustine's description, is an agenda perpetrated on the body rather than instigated by the body. It includes all the debilitating forms of anxious grasping—whether it pursues the objects of power, possessions or sex. Yet there was still, for Augustine, a close association of concupiscence, the body and sexuality; sexuality defines a person; sexuality is a key to personality. For twentieth-century people as for Augustine, sexuality is important; for us, as for Augustine, there is often a bewildering sense of disjunction between different levels of the person, revealed most pointedly and poignantly in our sexual feelings and activities. It was probably Augustine, more than any other single person, who bequeathed to the West the notion that sexuality is, as Peter Brown has written, a uniquely resonant, because symbolically precise, clue to our personhood.[19] This does not immediately appear to signify anything but a recognition of the importance of sexuality, yet the implications of identifying sex as the key to who a person is has had some far-reaching, and often oppressive and repressive, repercussions in western individuals and societies. The "effective history," as Hans-Georg Gadamer calls the history of the influence of an idea, must be considered a central part of the significance of Augustine's ideas on sexuality. Augustine's description of the special status of sexuality has been more influential in the Christian West than his project of redefinition of the body's meaning and value.

Augustine spoke of sexuality from the perspective of his own experience, and his experience was unfortunate, not only for himself, but also for those who have inherited the effective history of his ideas of sex. While involved in sexual relationships, Augustine felt unfree, driven, compulsive. When a religious resolution occurred in his life, its first result was that it was a solution to his sexual compulsiveness—renunciation of all sexual activity, accompanied, he insisted, by feelings of relief and freedom. We can, of course, acknowledge and appreciate Augustine's unprecedented honesty and openness in recounting for us so much of his experience. But his more or less silent inference that, in fact, his experience is universal, mythically formulated in the story of Adam and Eve, and reenacted, to a point at least, by every human being, has led to a problematic effective history. The power of language to create the reality it claims merely to explain, if never before recognized, could be amply demonstrated by Augustine's example. Augustine's conversion was to continence, as he had know it would be. His famous prayer, "Give me chastity, but not yet," expresses both his recognition that sex was his special problem area, and his awareness that, for him an integrated sexuality was impossible. Augustine, I think, was keenly and humbly aware that one who is compulsive in a particular area may not be able to manage an integration of "goods" that someone who is not compulsive can enjoy with freedom and gratitude. There are persons for whom the only alternative to addiction is total abstinence.

It was not Augustine's universal recommendation of his resolution of sexual compulsiveness that was influential for centuries in which celibacy was valued as the highest form of Christian life in the West. Augustine did not urge his resolution on anyone else. But he did describe his experience of freedom and relief in such a vivid way that it was easy for his readers to forget hat he was talking about a personal resolution that emerged from—and responded to—his own particular experience, his own historically and geographically-located perspective. His ultimate rejection of sexuality appears to be contradictory to his lifelong and persistent effort to construct a new theological anthropology in which the body is affirmed.

What has Augustine to do with us? His identification of the unique religious significance of sexuality reaches to our time, to the way we imagine our lives, to the way we address questions of sexual preference, to the way we construe our responsibility to other human beings. This feature of Augustine's thought is not an entirely negative heritage; it is certainly, however, an ambiguous one. Perhaps no one can distinguish with clarity and precision the positive and negative effects of Augustine's construction of sexuality as significant, worthy of thought, responsibility and concern.

Secondly—and still asking, what has Augustine to do with us? How have his problems and resolutions become our problems and tools for interpreting and managing our lives? Augustine's model of human being as hierarchically structured—body controlled by soul, soul controlled by God—both reflected Roman society and, in turn, helped to produce western Christian society. Augustine extended his hierarchical anthropology so that it became his model for society. It was a model that featured the necessary and inevitable subordination of some people to others. In the slippery social world of the newly-sacked city of Rome, he specifically urged that a hierarchical model be accepted and reinforced as the lesser of the social evils. Social inequality, he wrote, is part of the evidence that human beings exist in a "state of punishment," the result of the anxious craving of a few for dominance over the many. But Augustine did not criticize this "order," but rather urged respect for dominance and subordination on every level of society, from kingdoms to families. Even though "God did not wish the rational being, made in God's image, to have dominion over any but irrational creatures, not human over human, but human over the beast," the "ordered harmony" that Augustine advocates begins in the household, where "the husband gives orders to the wife, parents to children, and masters to servants."[20]

Glorification of inequality is conspicuously missing from Augustine's program for "ordered harmony" under the permanently unsettled and unsettling conditions of this human pilgrimage. Yet Augustine could not envision social arrangements in which dominance and subordination would not be necessary for peace. Unknowingly, Augustine provided the rationalization which has been used throughout the history of the Christian West to justify dominance and subordination. The one who gives orders, Augustine said, must consider himself the "servant," caring for the needs of those to whom orders are given; he must act from "dutiful concern," not from "lust for domination."[21] Few medieval tyrants failed to appropriate Augustine's rhetoric of servanthood.

Society was, for Augustine, a macrocosm of the human being; both are complex organisms that require orderliness. In Augustine's anthropology, we have seen the body's lesser value in relation to the soul must result in its subordination to the soul even—or especially—when Augustine calls the body the "spouse" (*sponsa*)[22] of the soul. Likewise, in society Augustine understood dominance and subordination as inevitable. His anthropology did not—as it certainly might—provide him with a model of interdependence. Rather, in society as in the body, slavery is inevitable; classicism and sexism is taken for granted.

Augustine, of course, had a very strong doctrine of original sin, a vivid sense of the dark undertow—not explainable by individual sin and guilt—of all human existence. If he had thought that people were basically good he might have been much more perplexed by his own experience and by what he saw about him in the last years of classical civilization. The story of his conversion in Book Eight of the *Confessions*, whether we take it as a literal or as a literary account of an event, illustrates Augustine's respect for the incremental, monumental weight of the habit of concupiscence, the result of an ancient and pervasive flaw in human nature. Conversion, for Augustine, was not simply the conscious reversal of intellectual decisions, but an overwhelming experience of coming—being led, he said, in retrospect—to the bitter end of his own agenda and resources. He was brought to the decisive experience in the garden at Milan that was to decide the whole future course of his life by following with all his energy the course in which he was most completely mistaken. Augustine never seemed to recognize, and never acknowledged, that the way—the journey—painful, damaging, and destructive as it was to himself and other human beings around him, was nevertheless, for him, a process of coming to what he described as a highly satisfying and productive synthesis in his life. Augustine is typical of many religious leaders who do not advise their readers to follow their path in order to come to understand what they have understood. Rather they express nothing but regret for and rejection of their experience as if it had nothing to do with their "seeing the light." They require their readers to learn from their "mistakes," to accept their conclusions, not their process.

But let us return, for a moment, to Augustine's conversion, the vivid emotional experience in which a new synthesis emerged. Augustine's respect for the inertial weight, the bottom—heaviness of the habit of relating to the world "concupiscently" is illustrated in his story. The moment of conversion occurred when Augustine realized that the objects he had so strenuously pursued and attempted to possess had instead, in effect, possessed him: and "a slave can't enjoy that which keeps him enslaved."[23] The event Augustine described as his conversion—a conversion not of the mind but of the will—began with a painful but illuminating vision of himself:

> But you, Lord, were turning me around so that I could see myself; you took me from behind my own back, which was where I had put myself during the time when I did not want to be observed by myself, and you set me in front of my own face so that I could see how foul a sight I was—crooked, filthy, spotted, and ulcerous. I saw, and I was horrified, and I had nowhere to go to escape from myself.[24]

He recognizes this psychic "place"; from the perspective of "facing myself" he realizes that he has neither moved nor grown since his infant relation to the world, a relation characterized by anxious grasping—concupiscence. Then he became aware of a childish voice chanting, "Tolle, lege": take and read! His response was obedience, the trusting acceptance of the message as directed to him. It is this response that he must hereafter remember and reinforce; around this new and incredibly fragile response he must begin to organize a new relation to the world. The response of trust must replace the child's first instinct to grasp breath and life. Augustine's message to his readers was that real change is possible, although it is not easy, and, of course, real change occurs by the initiative of the grace of God. It was God who took him from behind his own back. The point of the *Confessions* is that change is possible; that is what Augustine's first readers were interested in hearing about.

What has happened to human values in Augustine's thought? We can now draw some observations by way of conclusion. First, as we have seen, the human body does well in Augustine's account. Sexuality, however, does not receive a similarly productive interpretation. The body—men's and women's bodies—can and will participate in Augustine's explicitly imaginary vision of the perfection and completion of human nature—the resurrection of the body. He described the resurrection of the body in the last book of the *City of God* and his vision is inclusive, sensual, and exuberant. We need to interpret Augustine's understanding of human life from the perspective afforded by this magnificent vision of the goal and fulfillment of human nature—what human nature is capable of—if we are to understand the problems he identifies in the present condition of human being.

Human bodies, sexually differentiated, "risen and glorious," will be the "ultimate fulfillment" of whole persons. But although there will be sexes in the resurrection, since sexes are not an "imperfection," *there will not be sex*. For Augustine, the absence of sex in the resurrection of the body is decisive.

Although Augustine insisted on the presence of men and women in the resurrection, it was the male body he envisioned and described. His vision of the resurrected body preserves the male body intact and entire—nipples, beards, teeth and sexual organs—in the interest of beauty, but not of use. Augustine did not fail to draw from the absence of sexual activity in his vision of physical perfection the inference that since present sexual activity cannot be understood as a foretaste of this reward, it must therefore be a part of the present "state of punishment" of humankind. In Augustine's thought, human actualization and fulfillment is postponed to another time and space, beyond human life and beyond the sensible world. To understand what Augustine valued, we must look at his fantasy of the resurrection of the body, based on, but not defined by, scripture, to see what appears. Equality among human beings appears; "all injustice disappears, and God is all in all."[25] Equality among all the aspects of human beings also appears; the body appears, all its senses raised to a heightened and intensified pleasure that even now may be "glimpsed" in brief, strong synesthetic experiences:

> There where the greatest peace will prevail, nothing will be unsightly, nothing inharmonious, nothing monstrous, nothing offend the eyes, but in all things God will be praised. For it now, in such frailty of the flesh and in such weakened operation of our members, such great beauty of body appears that it entices the passionate and stimulates the learned and thoughtful to investigate it...how much more beautiful will the body be there...where there will be unending eternity, and beautiful truth, and the utmost happiness?[26]

The picture Augustine painted is enticing, but it is important to ask, not only about the intent of Augustine's description of the resurrection of the body, but also about the effects, observable in the Christian West to our own time, of the indefinite postponement of full human actualization. Augustine's vision, exuberant and provocative as it is, did not have the effect of compelling Christians to work toward just social arrangements in the present, the equality of women and men in present life, and affirmation of, and gratitude for, the beauty and goodness of sexuality. We have seen that Augustine's personal experience and his religious commitments provide some of the reasons for the nature of his vision of human "perfection." And a strain of body-denying, world-rejecting Augustinianism in the Christian West can be deplored without blaming Augustine himself for it.

Nevertheless, any attempt to understand a historical author in the context of his life and times enables us to see once again the complexity of human beings, and therefore, of historical interpretation. Our mutual attempt—author and reader—to understand both the intent and the effect of Augustine's thought and teaching on the body and sexuality permits us, in the final analysis, to find Augustine not so much a formidable and threatening authority of the history of

Christian doctrine, but, as he asked and expected to be seen, in the context of his own struggles, our "fellow pilgrim."

Margaret R. Miles is Bussey Professor of Historical Theology at Harvard University Divinity School. Her most recent publications are *Image as Insight: Visual Understanding in Western Christianity and Secular Culture* (Boston: Beacon Press, 1985); *Practicing Christianity: Critical Perspectives for an Embodied Spirituality* (New York: Crossroad, 1988); and *Carnal Knowing: Female Nakedness and Religious Meaning in the Christian West* (Boston: Beacon Press, 1989). A forthcoming book to be published in Italian, will discuss Augustine's *Confessions* as a text fascinated with the maximization of pleasure in human life.

NOTES

1. *Confessions* X. 8; trans. Rex Warner (New York: Mentor-Omega, 1963).

2. Ibid., VIII. 5.

3. *Serm.* 306. 3.

4. *City of God* XXII. 21: "How is it that what we learn with toil we forget with ease?" trans. Henry Bettenson (Middlesex, England: Penguin, 1972).

5. *Conf.* VI. 6.

6. *City of God* XXI. 4.

7. Jean Piaget, *The Construction of Reality in the Child* (New York: Ballantine, 1954), 329.

8. *Conf.* I. 1.

9. Ibid., I. 9.

10. Ibid., IX. 4.

11. Ibid., VIII. 5.

12. Ibid., IX. 7.

13. Ibid., IX. 13.

14. Ibid., IX. 2.

15. *City of God* XIII.9.

16. Ibid., XIII. 6.

17. Michel Foucault has recently demonstrated, however, that late classical "strategies of the cultivated self" involved attention to the physical practices by which a self alternative to the socially-constructed self was achieved: *The Use of Pleasure* (New York: Pantheon, 1985) and *The Care of the Self* (New York: Pantheon, 1986).

18. *De utilitate jejunii*, 4.

19. Peter Brown, "Augustine and Sexuality," Colloquy 45 (Berkeley, Calif.: The Center for Hermeneutical Studies, 1983), 12.

20. *City of God* XIX . 14.

21. Ibid., XIX. 15.

22. Ibid., XV. 7.

23. *Conf.* VIII. 5.

24. Ibid., VIII. 7.

25. *City of God* XXII. 15.

26. *Serm.* 243. 8.

JUSTICE AND LOVE IN THE POLITICAL THOUGHT OF ST. AUGUSTINE

JUSTICE AND LOVE IN THE POLITICAL
THOUGHT OF ST. AUGUSTINE

JUSTICE AND LOVE IN THE POLITICAL THOUGHT OF ST. AUGUSTINE

Anthony J. Parel

The nature of the relationship of justice and love to civil society had always attracted the attention of political philosophers. The most famous treatment of this problem is perhaps that found in Plato's *Republic*. Aristotle is not less instructive: friendship, according to him, was the perfection of justice,[1] and justice, implied all other moral virtues.[2] Whereas both Plato and Aristotle saw the basic harmony of love and justice in civil society (in fact they called for the reinforcement of the one by the other), Augustine saw them in alternative terms; one is tempted to say, in exclusive terms. His attitude on this issue was such that he was obliged to redefine civil society as that which was held together not so much by justice as by love.

Why did Augustine judge justice to be an unsatisfactory basis of civil society? And why did he argue that love would be a more coherent principle of civil union? These are the two main questions which I wish to discuss here. Augustine's reflections on these issues amount to being a major reevaluation of one of the major postulates of classical political philosophy.

Ernest Fortin has remarked that *The City of God* is Augustine's "response" to Plato's *Republic*.[3] And if it might be said that he "responded" to Plato because in his case the light of faith illuminated natural reason, a further question arises: is the Augustinian "response" the only response possible that faith can make to reason, revelation to political philosophy?

I

Why does Augustine reject justice as the foundation of civil society? The short answer would be that justice of the city is deficient and ineffective: it does not, and it cannot, achieve what it sets out to achieve, without violating the principle of justice which is that one should give each one his or her due.

Augustine's critique of justice begins with a consideration of Cicero's famous definition of the republic. A republic, Cicero had written, was a thing of the people. And a people was not just any multitude gathered for any purpose whatsoever, but a multitude gathered together by *consensus juris* and *utilitatis communio*: a consensus, a common sentiment as to what constitutes right, the just; and by a sharing, a communion, in the materially useful things.[4] In analyzing this definition, his attention focuses on the meaning of *jus*. He is not content with explaining it in juridicial terms; he is interested in the moral and theological implications of *jus*. For he notes that Cicero himself, elsewhere in the *Republic*, had interpreted just in a moral sense, in reference to *summa justitia*. A republic, according to Cicero, could not be well governed without the recognition of the relationship of government to *summa justitia*.[5]

However, at this stage Augustine's argument makes an important turn. He substitutes Cicero's *summa justitia* with his own *vera justitia*, and the rest of Augustine's argument in the *City of God* proceeds accordingly. In Augustine's view, then, to have a true republic there had to be a reference to *vera justitia*, without which, according to him, there could be no *consensus juris*.

It goes without saying that the success of our attempt to grasp Augustine's critique would depend on the prior understanding of what he means by *vera justitia*, and how *vera justitia* is related to human behaviour. True justice, according to him, implies more than the just relations between men. It presents a broader picture, an *ordo*, an order that establishes the proper relationship of the various forces within man, between men, and between men and God, an order that reflects in the final analysis, Divine Wisdom. And true justice can affect human affairs only when the will is illumined by the Divine Light. According to him divine illumination is necessary not only for cognitive activity but also for moral activity. Only with such illumination can virtues become efficacious, and without it virtues remain only quasi virtues. One becomes just by making one's soul conform to the immutable rules and lights of virtues dwelling eternally within the Truth and Wisdom common to all.[6] Thanks to divine illumination, the will becomes disposed to seek to live rightly and honourably, and to acquire what Augustine calls "good will." And whoever possesses "good will" is incapable of wishing evil for anyone. So it will follow that "he does not harm anyone, and this can be the case only if he gives to each man his due."[7]

Augustine rejects as false and vain the view that there can be genuine virtues without reference to divine illumination. He writes: "For although some suppose that virtues which have a reference only to themselves, and are desired only on their own account, are yet true and genuine virtues, the fact is that even then they are inflated with pride, and are therefore to be reckoned vices rather than virtues."[8] Thus only that virtue which is illuminated by divine light can establish the proper order within each individual, "so that the soul is subject to God, the body to the soul, and consequently both soul and body to God...."[9] "Hence, when a man does not serve God, what justice can we ascribe to him, since in this case his soul cannot exercise a just control over the body, nor his reason over the vices? And if there is no justice in such an individual, certainly there can be none in a community composed of such individuals."[10]

Given this notion of true justice, and given also the condition for its effective realization, namely divine illumination, it is not surprising that Augustine should find the republic of Rome wanting. "Rome never was a republic," he writes, "because true justice had never a place in it."[11]

And what was true of Rome was true of civil society as such: it made no difference whether the civil society in question was Christian or non-Christian. According to the criterion of true justice, there could only be one truly just society, and that is none other than the city of God. "But the fact is, true justice has no existence save in that republic whose founder and ruler is Christ...."[12]

In support of his contention Augustine offers two proofs, both taken from the example of the Roman state: its polytheism and its imperialism, and he finds both to be in violation of true justice.

A considerable part of *The City of God* (the first ten books) is taken up with a critique of pagan religion—its mythologies, its addiction to astrology, divination, and its civil theology. Paganism, he argued, was the work of imagination: its divinities did not have real existence. Besides, it was fraudulent in the sense that civil authorities had first invented it and then used it for their own political ends, as reinforcement of the state's chief aim, viz., temporal felicity. Civil authorities "persuaded the people, in the name of religion, to receive as true those things which they themselves knew to be false; in this way, as it were binding them up more firmly in civil society, so that they might in like manner possess them as subjects."[13]

But in Augustine's judgement the worst aspect of polytheism was not its mythical or fraudulent character, but its injustice towards the true God: for it gave to false gods that reverence and worship which belonged only to the true God. By implication every civil society has the tendency to practice injustice of this sort, insofar as it attempts to develop a civil theology and to see religion as a secular phenomenon, and an *instrumentum regni*, a means of temporal felicity.

The case of Roman imperialism fared no better. Augustine endorsed Cicero's view that it was "unjust for some men to rule and some to serve"; yet the imperial city to which the republic belonged could not rule her provinces without having recourse to this injustice.[14] The empire was an undeniable sign that Rome was not built on *consensus juris*. Had true justice been the basis of civil society, asserts Augustine, "all kingdoms would have been small, rejoicing in neighbourly concord; and thus there would have been many kingdoms of nations in the world, as there are very many houses of citizens in a city. Therefore to carry on war and extend a kingdom over wholly subdued nations seems to bad men to be felicity, to good men necessity."[15] Rome at its best was moved by the desire for temporal glory, at its worse by the desire for domination over fellow men, and that was why what began in the name of liberty had gradually degenerated into an imperial republic of wars and conquests.[16]

Generalizing on this theme he is moved to wonder whether there is any real moral difference between civil society and organized brigandage. "Justice being taken away, then," he asks, in a much quoted passage, "what are kingdoms but great robberies? For what are robberies themselves but little kingdoms?"[17] The difference between the justice of civil society and that of a band of robbers, it seems, was not one of substance but of scale.[18] The band of robbers is made up of men; it is ruled by the authority of the leaders; it is held together by the compact of confederacy; and the booty is divided according to rules agreed upon. If the band becomes large, and establishes itself on a broad territory, "it assumes more plainly the name of a kingdom, because the reality is now manifestly conferred on it, not by the removal of covetousness, but by the addition of impunity."[19] He uses with obvious relish the alleged reply of a pirate to Alexander the Great. When the great conqueror asked the pirate what he meant by keeping the hostile possession of a certain harbour, he answered with "bold pride,'What thou meanest by seizing the whole earth; but because I do it with a petty ship, I am called a robber, whilst thou who dost it with a great fleet art styled emperor.'"[20]

The explanation of why civil society—any civil society—is not founded on true justice now seems at least consistent. Civil society cannot render to God nor to fellow human beings nor to other civil societies what is their respective due. On the other hand it conceals this very injustice under the cloak of what it calls civil justice and civil religion (which in current terminology may be translated as political ideology).

II

But Augustine does not want to leave the matter as it were in a definitional limbo: it was quite absurd to suggest that there was no Roman state, simply on the ground that it did not meet his definition of true justice. So the search begins for a new definition:

> But if we discard this definition of a people, and, assuming another, say that a people is an assemblage of reasonable beings bound together by common agreement as to the objects of their love, then, in order to discover the character of any people, we have only to observe what they love. Yet whatever it loves...it is reasonably called a people; and it will be a superior people in proportion as it is bound together by higher interests, inferior in proportion as it is bound together by lower. According to this definition of ours, the Roman people is a people, and its weal is without doubt a commonwealth or republic.[21]

Augustine is not content to limit his analysis to the case of Rome: he wants to universalize his discovery: "What I say of this people and of this republic I must be understood to think and say of the Athenians or any Greek state, of the Egyptians, of the early Assyrian Babylon, and of every other nation, great or small, which had a public government."[22]

This is one of the great passages, not only of the *City of God*, but also of political literature, one that has generated and continues to generate an endless stream of debate.[23] Did he mean to undermine justice? Did he really separate love from justice? Did he exalt the will at the expense of reason? Or is he saying that if justice is separated from true justice, if will is separated from the unchanging good, every assertion of will becomes tainted? Such a will may be thought to create values, but the values so created are necessarily flawed. These and related questions have been with us for long, and there is no point in rehearsing them here. Suffice it to say that he did not proffer the new definition in a fit of absentmindedness or enthusiasm. The textual evidence is loud and clear that he had mulled over the problem over a long period of time. Book II, where the problem of justice is first raised, promises that a new definition will be forthcoming. The promise is fulfilled only in Book XIX, and between the writing of these two books there had elapsed a period of twelve years,[24] so that we know that we are looking at a problem to which Augustine had applied his mind for over a decade.

Augustine's point is that we fully understand civil society only when we understand its loves and its hates. These give a better clue to its character than do its constitutions or systems of justice or formal declarations. No doubt, he is led to this insight not by moral philosophy, or jurisprudence, but by philosophy illumined by faith. Thus human realities are seen in a new light, in terms of love, because God is love. Applied to humans, this insight shows that they are what they love: "my love is my weight, I am carried by it wherever I am carried."[25] Thus when the self moves towards what it loves, there is desire (*cupiditas*); when it delights in what it loves, there is joy (*laetitia*); when it flees from its love, there is fear (*metus*); and when it actually loses its love, there is grief (*tristitia*). These four modes of love—desire, joy, fear and grief, alone or in combination—constitute the web of human existence.[26]

As for the objects of love, they are grouped by him under four headings: God, the self, other selves and things.[27] In what order must one place these four objects? This is the decisive issue in every human life.

Augustine fully recognized the fact that our love for ourselves is constitutive of us. But he also recognized that as creatures this constitutive love, by itself, would not be enough: a more basic love than that would be needed, for that is the lot of all finite rational creatures. And that love is none other than the love of God, the immutable love, in the possession of which all fear of losing it ceases, so that there is no grief...and the joy of possession is indestructible.[28] But a rational creature is also free, it is free to choose aversion or conversion, aversion from God or conversion to Him.

Augustine takes the fundamental position that we cannot love ourselves properly unless we are converted towards God. The same applies to our love for other selves, and of course to our love for things:

> he is the best man who turns his whole life towards immutable life and adheres to it with his affection. But if he loves himself on his own account, he does not turn himself towards God, but, being turned towards himself, he does not care for anything immutable. Therefore his enjoyment of himself is imperfect, for he is better, when he adheres to and is bound completely to the immutable good than when he lapses away from it, even towards himself. If, therefore, you should love yourself not on your own account but on account of Him who is most justly the object of your love, no other man would feel angry with you if you love him also on account of God. This is the divinely instituted rule of love: Thou shalt love thy neighbour as thyself....[29]

In this scheme of things original sin introduces the basic disorder in love. In Augustine's interpretation, original sin is the outcome of pride, that is aversion from God and conversion to ourselves: "the soul abandons Him to whom it ought to cleave as its end, and becomes a kind of end to itself."[30] The operative phrase here, it seems, is "a kind of end." For there is something unnatural and artificial in man becoming his own end, for that is to forget his true nature as creature, as a contingent being.

Augustine understands aversion from God partly in terms of freedom of will, and partly in terms of our origin from nothingness. Our will would not have been turned away from God, had we not been made out of nothing. Aversion from God has the implication of turning towards nothingness, towards nihilism. "...to exist in himself, that is, to be his own satisfaction after abandoning God, is not quite to become. a nonentity, but to approximate to it."[31] Once you are, you cannot will yourself out of existence. The nihilist must be fooling himself or herself if he or she thinks that turning away from God is the same as murdering God. The idea of the death of God, in Augustine's terminology, must appear as a pseudo idea, characterized more by self-delusion than by incoherence. For a God-averter cannot help being aware of what it is that he is averting.

Our interest here is not in the theological aspects of this aversion, but in its psychological and political consequences. Disordered love necessarily seeks to master others; it incessantly compels us to seek to do better than others, and to extract praise from them; it is driven by the love to possess and consume things, not for the sake of life (*uti*) but for the sake of exclusive delight (*frui*). The most serious of these implications concerns domination, or *libido dominandi*. The disordered love, as it were, transforms man's natural sociability into the will to dominate; it rebels against man's natural equality. The fallen man "endeavours to dominate those who are naturally his peers."[32] Disordered love "abhors equality with other men under Him; but instead of His rule, it seeks to impose a rule of its own upon equals. It abhors, that is to say, the just peace of God and loves its own peace...."[33]

Thus civil society, understood as an arena *of* domination and *for* domination, is not natural to man; but it is his actual lot. This, however, is not God's making; it is his own making.[34]

However, the deepest effect of disordered love is the discontent within the self. Paradoxically, pride is paralleled by weakness of will to control itself. What else is misery, asks Augustine, in a memorable passage, "but his own disobedience to himself, so that in consequence of his not being willing to do what he could, he now wills to do what he cannot?"[35]

If the Fall has introduced disorder in love, Augustine is careful not to press the matter beyond certain limits: our nature, insofar as it is created, is good and remains good; it is our will and our loves that have been impaired.[36] Thus even after the Fall, "vestiges" or "shadows" of true justice inhere in the soul,[37] thanks to which the fallen man is able to establish some kind of civil order. However, these vestigial traces of justice are at the mercy of disordered love to such an extent that whatever civil society achieves, it achieves only if one presupposes coercion. Coercion is, as it were, the price that one has to pay for self-love. As Peter Brown remarks, "Fallen men had come to need restraint. Even man's greatest achievements had been made possible only by a'strait-jacket' of unremitting harshness."[38] Augustine had a healthy respect for the achievements of reason, notes Brown, yet he was obsessed with the difficulties reason had to face to obtain knowledge, with the long and coercive process that intellectual life entails.[39] Thus, there is tension between what nature requires and what it is actually able to achieve. And in civil society the pressure from self-love is manifested in the struggle for domination, for consumption, for recognition. These are the objects of love of civil society, and that is why *consensus juris* cannot be its true basis. On the contrary, civil society manipulates the vestiges of justice and corrupts them. The justice of the city, accordingly, reflects the collective self-interest of those who constitute the city. Whatever it embodies, justice is not one of them. Instead of *jus* determining national interest, national interest determines *jus*.

However, Augustine recognizes the possibility of there being better states and worse states, depending on what they love. Thus there is a real difference between tyranny and constitutionalism; but these differences ought not to hide the common denominator of all states—whether they be Christian or pagan, Jewish or Islamic, Hindu or Buddhist, Marxist or liberal—and that common denominator is the collective love of those who compose them.

Critics have noticed a certain ambiguity in Augustine's attitude towards civil society: on the one hand, it is an organized system of self-assertion, yet on the other, it does contribute something positive, without which man, in the present conditions, cannot manage his affairs. His attitude towards Rome illustrates this ambivalence.

He regarded the ancient Romans, writes Peter Brown, with the same "intense ambivalence" with which modern Englishmen regard their Eminent Victorians. Both were idealized as models of behaviour, yet they were all, as it happened, transient men. They "refused to regard the'earthly' values they had created as transient and relative. Committed to the fragile world they had created, they were forced to idealize it; they had to deny any evil in its past, and the certainty of death in its future."[40]

Thus, notes Augustine, there were "genuine Romans," "ancient heroes," "moral bulwarks and ornaments of the city," who exhibited "wisdom and forethought."[41] This was particularly the case in the early republic, which had valued liberty more than domination. These heroes despised their own interests for the republic, they moderated their avarice for the public treasury.[42] That is to say, domination and avarice were not their dominant loves; their dominant passion was *love of praise*. "This was what they loved wholeheartedly; for this they lived, for this they did not hesitate to die; all other lusts they battened down with this overwhelming desire."[43] That is to say, at its best Rome was moved by the love of praise; at its worst it was moved by domination and the passion for consumption. "There is assuredly a difference between the desire for human glory and desire for domination," observes Augustine. However, "it is not true virtue which is slave to human praise."[44] The noblest of Romans were defective in that they did what was honourable only because they wanted others to praise them for it. Such virtues, the civic virtues, fall short of being true virtues.

In the final analysis, Augustine believed that his new definition took better account of the empirical realities of political life than did the definition he rejected. Even the best states, at bottom, exist to serve the competing loves of their citizens. Civic justice and positive law, when isolated from *vera justitia*, are merely human inventions that tend to reconcile, rationalize, coordinate these loves. Not a function to be despised, even by Augustine's standards; but neither must we think that it will lead us to the beatific vision.

Nothing brings out Augustine's awareness of the deficiency of human justice, and his anguish over it, better than his celebrated analysis of the "wise judge" who has to sanction torture.[45] The context of his analysis is the judicial system prevailing in the fourth century in his own society. But the issues raised have a wider significance. They underline the imperfect character of human justice always and everywhere, the necessity under which it operates, and our necessary dependence on such an imperfect instrument as positive justice. The root cause of the imperfection is the difficulty men have in judging the guilt or innocence of fellow human beings. The use of torture (we may compare the torture methods of the fourth century with our use of "detention" in remand centres before the accused is proved to be guilty) is an "unendurable" thing, notes Augustine, something "to be bewailed, and, if that were possible, watered with fountains of tears." In analyzing these "melancholy and lamentable" aspects of human judgement, his point is, it seems, not to endorse any moral evil, but to argue that "judges are man who cannot discern the conscience of those at their bar." Truth is hidden from them. The judge necessarily operates under an epistemological handicap. Despite this, he has no option but to render a judgement. Such "ignorance" of the judge often results in "calamity" for the innocent.

Augustine is not questioning the good faith of the judge. He concedes that he is applying torture in order that "he might not condemn the innocent." Yet the certitude he can reach even with torture is not absolute but only circumstantial and external. Even after the application of torture, the judge could "still be in ignorance of whether he has put to death an innocent or guilty person."

Knowing that he has to operate under such conditions of ignorance, under such "darkness" that shrouds social life, is the judge justified in rendering a verdict? Would it not be morally correct for him to resign from his office? "Will a wise judge take his seat on the bench or no?" asks Augustine. "Beyond question he will," is his answer. He is morally obliged to act, because not to act would be a greater calamity. Not to act would mean the dissolution of society into anarchy. Society would be in a worse condition without such judges than it would be with them. "For human society, compels him to his duty." He is bound by duty to society even if it means acting in "ignorance." Augustine recognizes that what the judge does is evil, (*male*), but he also points out that what is done is not done out of malice. Neither is it sin (*peccata*). For the "wise judge" does these things not from a will to harm but from the necessity of ignorance (*non enim haec facit sapiens judex noscendi voluntate, sed necessitate nesciendi*).

However that might be, the law of necessity does not explain the whole matter: other considerations enter in. The judge may not be guilty (*reus*), but he is miserable because of what he has done. Being without malice does not mean that he is "happy." He is pulled from all sides—from those of conscience, duty, necessity, misery, unhappiness. And he is aware of "the misery of these necessities" and if he is pious, notes Augustine, he would wish that he did not have to submit himself to it, and would ask God, "From my necessities, deliver Thou me." But these considerations do not absolve him from the necessity of having to render judgement for which he has no absolute certitude.

Thus human justice rests on a very imperfect foundation. On it falls the shadow of original sin. What the judge has to choose is between two evils, imperfect justice of society or social chaos, and, according to Augustine, he is justified in choosing the former. Indeed, he has an obligation to do so. Such in Augustine's view is the system of justice of the earthly city.

III

There is hardly any doubt that Augustine arrives at these conclusions about human justice because of faith illuminating reason. What we have before us is a theological critique of positive justice. What we find in Augustine is not a full blown political philosophy, but a reflection on the limits of politics. But a nagging problem enters here. If Augustine admits, as in fact he does, that nature is not wholly corrupted, why is it that nature is not able to act effectively in the civil sphere, which is, admittedly, its own sphere? Why is it that it always remains a prey to self-love? To say that we have a nature, and at the same time to say that it cannot act efficaciously without the assistance of grace, is to put strain on the doctrine.

This is not to say that Augustine's insight is not compelling. It tells us that we cannot expect much from the justice of this world. It invites us to take a critical look at our loves. And his realism points to a dualism between the city of man and the city of God, and on this point the difference between him and Machiavelli and Hobbes, with whom he is often compared, are fundamental. The realism of Machiavelli and Hobbes moves in the direction of an absolutism that brooks no rivals, whereas Augustine's realism puts the state, as it were, in its place. Also, Augustine gives a warning (for those who have the wits to heed it) that the quest for the best regime, understood as the quest for philosophy by philosophers, cannot be man's right quest if God and the city of God are left out of the picture. On all these and many other points Augustine's contributions are permanent and his eminence not threatened.

However, the implications of his doctrine of nature and grace for civil society are not without their difficulties. Could it be that he is forced to emphasize the role of grace in the sphere of nature because he had a deep insight into the condition of fallen men? In a very moving passage in the *Confessions* he writes: "I beheld other things below you and I saw that they were not altogether existent nor altogether non-existent; they are, because they are from you; they are not, because they are not what you are. For that truly exists, which endures unchangeably...(thus) if I do not abide in Him, neither will I be able to abide in myself."[46]

This altered vision of reality is no doubt one of the consequences of his conversion. He recognizes as fact that one cannot be oneself unless one knows oneself as related to God. This is Christian "self-knowledge." This self-knowledge, if we should call it that, cannot be revealed except by illumination by grace. Granted this, does it follow that to live the life of nature in the civil sphere anything more than natural reason and natural justice would be required? It is true that man's ultimate concern, namely conversion to God, is impossible without grace. But life in the city is not man's ultimate concern; and if that be so, would grace be necessary for politics?

Under these circumstances it is not surprising that St. Thomas Aquinas would feel obliged to criticize St. Augustine on this very point. As Etienne Gilson tells us, St. Thomas bases his criticism on his "new" concept of the relationship between the first cause and the second created cause. It is Thomas' position that even in fallen condition, the causality of the second created cause, that is, the natural causality of human nature, is not impaired.

> In St. Thomas, man receives from God everything he receives from Him in St. Augustine, but not in the same way. In St. Augustine God delegates his gifts in such a way that the very insufficiency of nature constrains it to return toward Him; in St. Thomas, God delegates His gifts through the mediacy of a stable nature which contains in itself— divine subsistence being taken for granted—the sufficient reason for all its operations. Accordingly, it is the introducing into each philosophical problem of a *nature* endowed with sufficiency and efficacy, that separates thomism from augustinism.[47]

This is hardly the place to discuss who is right, Augustine or Thomas. My point is simply that Augustine's position on nature invites cautious treatment, and criticism. And such criticism has relevance to the topic under discussion, the relationship of love and justice to civil society.

In the final analysis the answer will depend on how one estimates the causality of human nature, under fallen conditions, to be. The relationship of love and justice to civil society would be cast in favour of justice, if, with St. Thomas, one thinks that nature can act efficaciously in the civil sphere even in the fallen state. However, the relationship will be cast in favour of love, if, with Augustine, we think that nature needs grace to act efficaciously even in the civil sphere after the Fall.

Dr. Anthony Parel is presently Professor of Political Science at the University of Calgary. He has edited a number of printed works including: *Political Calculus: Essays on Machiavelli's Philosophy*; *Calgary Aquinas Studios*; *Theories of Property: Aristotle to the Present*, (edited with Thomas Flanagan); and *Ideology, Philosophy and Politics*.

NOTES

1. "...when men are friends they have no need of justice, while they are just they need friendship as well, and the truest form of justice is thought to be a friendly quality." Aristotle, *Nicomachean Ethics*, VIII. 1. 1155a 25ff. For the parallelism of civic friendship and civil justice, see Ibid., chs.9–11.

2. What Aristotle calls general or "legal justice" is not just part of justice but "justice entire." See *Nicomachean Ethics*, V.1. 1129b 12ff.

3. Ernest Fortin, *Political Idealism and Christianity in the Thought of St. Augustine* (Villanova: Villanova University, 1972), 4.

4. Marcus Tullius Cicero, De Republica, The Loeb Classical Library, no.213, Bk.I.25. *De Civitate Dei*, trans. Marcus Dods (New York: Random House, 1950), II.21; XIX.21 and 24 (Hereafter *DCD*).

5. Cicero, *De Republica*, Bk.II.42; the use of both *summa justitia* and *vera justitia* occurs in *DCD*, II.21.

6. Etienne Gilson, *The Christian Philosophy of Saint Augustine*, trans. L.E.M. Lynch (London: Victor Gollancz, 1961), 131. See also St. Augustine, *On Free Choice of the Will*, trans. Anna S. Benjamin and L.H. Hackstaff (Indianapolis: Bobbs-Merrill, 1979), Bk.II, ch.19.

7. *On Free Choice of the Will*, Bk.I. ch.13.

8. *DCD*, XIX.25.

9. Ibid., XIX.4.

10. Ibid., XIX.21.

11. Ibid., II.21.

12. Ibid.

13. Ibid., IV.32.

14. Ibid., XIX.21.

15. Ibid., IV.15. This passage makes it clear that Augustine preferred small states to empires, whether republican or monarchical.

16. Ibid., IV.12.

17. Ibid., IV.4.

18. See Christopher Dawson's appraisal of this passage, which follows here. Dawson, "St. Augustine and His Age," in *St. Augustine*, eds. M.C. D'arcy *et al.* (New York: Meridian Books, 1957), 63.

19. *DCD* IV.4.

20. Ibid.

21. Ibid., XIX.24.

22. Ibid.

23. A recent summary of these debates in the present century can be found in Jeremy Duquesnay Adams, *The Populus of Augustine and Jerome* (New Haven: Yale University Press, 1971), 123–135. Adams reviews the opinions of John Nevelle Figgis, Sergio Cotta, F.X. Millar, Herbert A. Dean, Ernest Troeltsch, Etienne Gilson and Domenico Pesce.

24. For the dating of the various books of *DCD*, see the chronological tables A-E in Peter Brown, *Augustine of Hippo, A Biography* (London: Faber and Faber, 1967).

25. St. Augustine, *The Confessions*, XIII.9.

26. *DCD*, XIV.7.

27. St. Augustine, *On Christian Doctrine*, trans. D.W. Robertson Jr. (Indianapolis: Bobbs-Merrill), 1.23.

28. See Karl Jaspers, *Plato and Aristotle*, ed. Hannah Arendt; trans. Ralph Mannheim (New York: A Harvest Book, 1957), 95.

29. *On Christian Doctrine*, I.22.

30. *DCD*, XIV.13.

31. Ibid.

32. *On Christian Doctrine*, 1.23.

33. *DCD*, XIX.12.

34. *DCD* XIX.15.

35. Ibid., XIV.15.

36. Ibid., XIV.13.

37. See Herbert Dean's classic *The Political and Social Ideas of St. Augustine* (New York: Columbia University Press, 1963), 97–99. Deane, as far as I know, is the first critic to point out the importance of *vera justitia* for the correct understanding of Augustine's position of civil justice.

38. Brown, *Augustine of Hippo*, 238.

39. Ibid.

40. Ibid., 308–309.

41. *DCD*, 11.2. Karl Jaspers writes: "To him (Augustine) Roman culture was both self-evident and indifferent; there was no other. In reading Augustine it is the ancient Roman world, not that of the Middle Ages, that we must bear in mind" (p. 115).

42. *DCD*, V.15.

43. Brown, *Augustine of Hippo*, 310.

44. *DCD*, V.19.

45. Ibid., XIX.6. What follows is an exposition of this chapter.

46. *The Confessions*, VII.11.

47. Laurence K. Shook, *Etienne Gilson* (Toronto: The Pontifical Institute of Mediaeval Studies, 1984), 397. As Shook points out, this was part of a short abstract of Gilson's seminar on Augustine offered in the University of Paris for 1921 and 1922.

AUGUSTINE AND POETIC EXEGESIS

AUGUSTINE AND POETIC EXEGESIS

Haijo J. Westra

When one thinks of Augustine in connection with poetry and literary aesthetics, certain topics come immediately to mind, such as his attitudes towards classical literature and rhetoric, as well as their implications for Christian literature, especially in the *De doctrina christiana*. In fact, these well-known topics have become commonplaces of Augustinian scholarship.

The situation is entirely different for a relatively little explored and problematic subject, namely Augustine's attitude towards the Christian poetry of his own times, practiced by authors such as Paulinus of Nola and Prudentius. As things stand now, there is, to my knowledge, no direct comment on Christian poetry as practiced by his contemporaries in Augustine's writings. Could this possibly be due to the accident of transmission? There are letters missing from the correspondence with Paulinus.[1] But Augustine's complete silence on the subject of his older contemporary Prudentius is most telling. The preface to the collected works of Prudentius has been dated to 404 – 405 and the individual works are likely to have circulated beforehand.[2]

In general, one can posit a basic distrust of artistic creation in the *De doctrina christiana*, combined with a progressive antipathy to secular literature on the part of Augustine.[3] At the same time, however, one can detect, from the earliest works and throughout Augustine's entire oeuvre, an inherent tension or ambivalence in his attitude towards *poiesis* and to one of its basic elements, aesthetic pleasure, which needs to be explored before his attitude towards the Christian poetry of his time can be properly evaluated. I shall begin with an examination of the negative pole in this tension-laden field.

The inherent ambivalence in Augustine's thought towards artistic creation and its reception through the aesthetic experience can be attributed in part to the Platonic legacy. Whereas Plato, in the context of Book Ten of the *Republic*, downgrades artistic activity because its mimetic product is twice removed from ideal reality and beauty, Plotinus already reduces that distance by claiming that Pheidias, when sculpting the image of Zeus at Olympia, must have had some inkling of the Idea of the divine for his stunning creation.[4] By the time of Proclus, Socrates' statement about the divine inspiration of the poets in the *Ion* (533E–535A) was read "straight" rather than ironically as it was probably intended in the context of that dialogue.[5] Add to this the statements about the divine inspiration of the prophet, the mystic and the poet as manifestations of divine madness in the *Phaedrus* (265A–B), as well as the exclusion of the traditional poets from the ideal state in the *Republic*, and the fundamental ambiguity of the Platonic legacy for Augustine, and for western civilization in general, is complete.[6]

Another reason for Augustine's ambivalence towards the aesthetic experience in particular lies in the nature of the experience itself which oscillates between the sensuous and the cognitive aspects of beauty. As a result, according to Jauss, "both the highest dignity and the most serious defect could be deduced...[The aesthetic experience] could be denied all cognitive use and all ethical seriousness and be roundly condemned when the negative functions of mimesis—second-order imitation, deception through sensuous experience, pleasure in a-moral objects—were adduced."[7]

Augustine's early treatise on aesthetics, *De pulchro et apto*, is lost, but it is evident that he distinguished between two kinds of beauty: that which is beautiful in and of itself, and that which is harmoniously related to other things. The following statement from the *Confessions* (2.5.10) evaluates these two *vis βàβ vis* each other:

> There is truly a sightliness in beautiful bodies, in gold and silver and all things. In the realm of tactual sensations, congruity is the most important. And in each of the other senses there is its own agreeable quality....Nevertheless, one must not depart from Thee, O Lord, nor deviate from Thy law, in all these objects of desire. Even the life which we live here possesses its own appeal, arising from a mode of beauty which is its own and from a suitableness in relation to all these lower things of beauty. So, too, friendship among human beings brings sweetness through the loving knots whereby from many minds a union is formed. Sin arises from all these and similar things, when because of an immoderate leaning to these lowest of goods, the better and higher are deserted.[8]

Underlying this view is the notion that the only perfect beauty is in God, and that it is only from the contemplation of the divine that true and legitimate

enjoyment are derived (cf. *Confessions* 10.27.38; *De libero arbitrio* 2.38.151).
Also, a formal criterion for earthly beauty is established, namely harmony. At
the same time, a basic fear is expressed, namely that earthly beauty is prone to
lead men away from God into error.

Fundamental to this lapsarian view of earthly beauty is a distinction between sensible and intelligible beauty. Already in the *De ordine* (2.14.38)
Augustine writes:

> *Desiderebat enim* [scil. ratio] *pulchritudinem, quam sola et simplex
> posset sine oculis intueri; impediebatur a sensibus.*[9]

Augustine, like Plato, is deeply suspicious of pleasure that is related to the senses, because it is likely to divert people from the contemplation of the divine
involving legitimate pleasure, even rapture, derived from cognition. In other
words, he does not eliminate pleasurable cognition or cognitive pleasure, but
he wants to separate it very strictly from sensuous pleasure. Of course, affective sense experience and cognition cannot be separated in this way, and
Augustine attempts to address this problem in the *Confessions* (10.33–35; cf.
De doctr. chr. 1.33.37) where *fruitio* or enjoyment is divided into a legitimate
and an illegitimate use of the senses, the one turned towards God, the other
towards the world. But even the legitimate enjoyment of the senses is always in
danger of sliding into self-enjoyment and of "abandoning itself to the aesthetic
attractions of a sensuous experience that is heightened by...means of the
arts."[10] Marrou speaks of Augustine's aversion to the "fallacious magic of aesthetic sensation" and his desire to "transcend" the aesthetic experience and to
"pass from art to science."[11] Marrou also notes the violent rejection of literature as an aesthetic activity in the *De doctrina christiana* when he remarks that,
to Augustine, the thought that literary form and beauty could be justified *per se*
was anathema. His judgement is accurate and incisive: *Nous retrouvons ici la
rigide subordination de toutes les manifestations de l'esprit βàβ la fin
religieuse qui domine toute la culture augustinienne.*"[12] Augustine even goes
as far as wishing to suppress the aesthetic element in the liturgy: "At times, in
fact, I could eagerly desire that all the sweet melody of the chants whereby the
Psalter of David is accompanied, were banished from my ears and from the
whole Church" (*Confessions* 10.33.50; but also cf. 9.6.14–9.7.15). Again, how
Platonic and how characteristic of the repressiveness of metaphysical con-
structs! In the same Platonic fashion, this outlook becomes the basis of
Augustine's vehement rejection of the traditional pagan poets, the foundation
of pagan culture which to him appeared empty in content and obsessed with
aesthetic questions.[13]

Against this repression we can adduce the notion of the aesthetic experience as a voluntary act: the very fact that philosophers, theologians and
other tyrants have tried—and failed—time and again to control the hearts and

minds of their fellow-men, including their aesthetic experience, is an historical proof of the basic voluntariness, inalienability and "refractoriness" of the aesthetic experience, and a clear demonstration of the failure of attempts to separate its objective and subjective elements.[14] The basic argument here is Kant's notion of "disinterested" pleasure.[15] "Pure" aesthetic pleasure need not necessarily be an abandonment of the self in sensuous pleasure, but rather involves the distancing of the aesthetic object from the self as something other. As Jauss mentions, it is Augustine who first introduced the notion of self-indulgence in the area of the aesthetic experience and cognition through his concepts of *voluptas* and *curiositas*, with far-reaching consequences for Christian culture.[16] And how Augustine agonizes over what is legitimate enjoyment and where pleasure useful to cognition ends and indulgence begins![17] This predicament hinges on his belief that man can achieve truth exempt from error, on condition that he seek truth not in the sensible, but in the intelligible realm.[18]

Of course, one also has to keep the historical context in mind. At the time, pagan culture still figured as a dangerous rival of the new religion.[19] This culture was carried by a literature that, in late antiquity, served as a spiritual refuge for the educated elite. In his attacks on this literature, Augustine first of all focuses on the fact that it features false gods rather prominently. Following Varro's euhemeristic approach, he "debunks" and ridicules the pagan gods at great length. He also attacks the immorality and obscenity of the playwrights. But, more fundamentally, he repeatedly refers to the fictions of the poets as *mendacia*, as lies. In addition to its nefarious aesthetic lure, pagan literature is found to be lacking in truth (*Confessions* 1.13.22). Learned pagans will admit, he says, that Aeneas never came to Carthage! Two issues are involved here: first, the old charge that the poets, including Homer and Hesiod, are liars, a claim that goes back to Heraclitus and to Plato; secondly, a profound misunderstanding of the nature of fiction on the part of Augustine. As is well known, the charges against Homer and Hesiod, which mainly rest on a lack of understanding of the primitive mythical material they dealt with, led to the allegorical interpretation of their writings as early as the sixth century B.C., a practice that ultimately turned them into crypto-philosophical gospels at the hands of the Cynics and the Stoics. Also, the fact that Plato himself used philosophical allegories or myths to express the ineffable raised the epistemological status of such fictions in late antiquity to exalted heights. Augustine's contemporary Macrobius can claim that the highest truths are, at one and the same time, concealed and revealed in these fabulous narratives. The ancient poets are actually called, and treated as, theologians. Their status, by late antiquity, had been raised to that of divinely inspired hierophants, prophets, conduits of divine truth, by analogy with the role of the priests of the mystery religions. The reverence for Vergil is a good example, and Augustine's attack on Vergil is not fortuitous. In the fourth century, the old charge of the mendacity of the poets must have sounded very deliberately sacrilegious. It further displays a profound, almost willful, misunderstanding of the poet's work on the part of Augustine, who, incidentally, totally succumbed to its aesthetic lure and its fictions as a youth. Indeed, the vehemence on this score noted by Marrou shows all the signs of the recent convert. O'Connell has suggested several reasons for Augustine's literalmindedness: the lingering, pejorative identification of poetry with *techné* or craft; his training in literature under the grammarians and their cerebral, mechanical dissection of poetic texts [*De ord.* 2.14.40]; but also his theory of signification. According to this theory, poetry, like prose, uses words to express meaning (*De ord.* 2.34), but "Augustine tacitly assumes that whether they occur in prose or poetry, words are words and there is the end of it."[20] Also in *De ordine* (2.14.13), Augustine would like to purge poetry of its ornaments, which he calls *nugae*, the very term he uses to characterize the "trifles" that keep him back from conversion (*Conf.* 8.11.26). He proposes the following: translate poetry into prose and everybody will agree that this ridiculous stuff is only good for the theatre (*De ord.* 2.4.13). Well, of course, but that is also precisely the point: poetry is not the same as prose. In other words, the fact that there may be a connection between form and content, medium and message, totally and deliberately escapes him here (but not, say, in the *De doctrina christiana*, Bk. 4). The closest Augustine comes to underwriting the classical dictum that poetic fiction should delight and instruct is when he says: *Fabula est compositum ad utilitatem delectationemue mendacium* in the *Soliloquies* (2.11.19; cf. *De ord.* 2.14.40). Philosophy is to be preferred (*Contra Academicos* 3.1) and he asks himself and his readers the leading question: *An forte Graeco Platoni potius palma danda est, qui cum ratione formaret, qualis esse civitas debeat, tamquam adversarios veritatis, poetas censuit urbe pellendos? (De civ.* 2.14.1; cf. *De civ.* 2.8).

This might be taken as the final word on the subject, the exclusion of the pagan poets from the Christian commonwealth. Yet there are two more aspects to this question, the first being the famous Augustinian notion that truth, wherever it is found, is God's truth:

> But we should not think that we ought not to learn literature because
> Mercury is said to be its inventor, nor that because the pagans dedi-
> cated temples to Justice and Virtue and adored in stones what should
> be performed in the heart, we should therefore avoid justice and vir-
> tue. Rather, every good and true Christian should understand that
> wherever he may find truth, it is his Lord's.[21]

Here we see Augustine at his most liberal, intent on saving from pagan culture, including its *poiesis*, whatever it had in terms of *utilitas ad salutem*. This *appears* to involve a dispensation, albeit severely restricted, of the cognitive element in the aesthetic experience of pagan literature. The second aspect involves Augustine's own preoccupation with establishing a Christian aesthetic in the *De doctrina christiana*. Together, these two aspects can be thought to constitute the positive pole in Augustine's ambivalence towards the aesthetic experience, to which we now turn.

In his creation of an aesthetic for Christian literature based on the Bible, Augustine inevitably had to come to terms with the same basic issues that arose from pagan literature, namely rhetorical artifice, fiction and aesthetic pleasure. First of all, and most relevant to the topic of this paper, is the fact that he does not mention non-liturgical Christian poetry at all in the *De doctrina christiana*. This in itself is an indication of the embarrassment it must have posed for Augustine. His own efforts in this area are restricted to very functional genres, namely a brief epitaph, the *Versus de S. Nabore*,[22] and the abcdarian *Psalm Against the Donatists*, a didactic poem in rhythmical rather than quantitative verse. In fact, Augustine only concerns himself with prose, and the entire discussion in Bk. 4 of the *De doctrina christiana* is put in terms of rhetoric. In itself, he argues, rhetoric is neither good nor bad: it depends on what use it is put to. If it serves the truth, it is legitimate. And if it is used in the service of error by the pagans, why should the Christian teacher forego the power of this artifice in the service of truth? Yet even in the right cause, the enjoyment of its use for its own sake leads to error.[23] The latter position is actually quite close to the classical notion expressed by Cicero at the beginning of the *De inventione*, namely that eloquence and wisdom need to be combined, an ideal that Martianus Capella is thought to have presented in the quasi-religious allegory of the marriage of Mercury and Philology.

Equally classical is the reference by the former teacher of rhetoric to the three *genera dicendi: docere, delectare* and *movere*. As Herzog has shown, Augustine is able to translate *docere* and *movere* without any problem into Christian terms as teaching the Gospel and moving the faithful to action in accordance with it; but *delectare* "leads to a barely concealed embarrassment."[24] In the *De doctrina christiana* (4.25.55) it is subordinated to the other two *genera*, and it is to be used "discreetly." For the role of *delectatio* in general, he only has scorn: "To the art of pleasing those whose pampered tastes truth does not satisfy, if it is presented in any other way than an agreeable one, no small place has been assigned in eloquence."[25] *Delectare* finally finds its subordinate place in oratory when Augustine asserts that the Christian orator, when he is urging that something be put into practice, must not only teach in order to instruct, and finally persuade in order to be victorious, but also *please* in order to hold the attention of his listeners (*De doctr. chr.* 4.13.29; cf. 4.2.3; 4.5.7). Augustine's horror of rhetorical fireworks, even in the service of the right cause, is particularly evident in one of his letters where he describes how once he got involved in a debate with the Donatist bishop of Thubursicum, Fortunius, and how most of the citizens crowded together not for their salvation, but as if for a gladiatorial battle between two great rhetoricians.[26]

Another problem was posed by the fact that "fiction" not only occurs in pagan literature, but in the Scriptures as well. For example, the parables are clearly intended as paradigmatic fictions, *not* as descriptions of historical events. This point seems obvious but it leads Augustine to distinguish between the legitimate (i.e., biblical) and illegitimate (i.e., secular) use of fiction, as follows: *Fictio igitur quae ad aliquam veritatem refertur, figura est; quae non refertur, mendacium est (Quaest. Evang. 2.51).* Then there was the problem of "difficult passages" in the Old Testament, where the literal or historical sense is barely defensible in the light of Christian charity. Here his solution was to make an aesthetic virtue out of an apparent vice by calling obscurity figurative discourse and by elevating it to a principle of beauty. The obscurity of the biblical text becomes the source of its fecundity, its richness of meanings, and its beauty. It is the pleasurable task of the exegete to extract its meanings through allegorical interpretation, *the* hermeneutic tool for real or supposed obscurity (Cf. *De Doctr. chr.* 2.6.7–8). In the hands of Augustine—and his predecessors—this type of interpretation becomes a creative activity that reconstitutes the biblical text cognitively, leaving the exegete quite rapturous in the process. As Marrou observes, the allegorical interpretation of the Bible is a form of poetry.[27] At the same time, this form of poetic exegesis of an authoritative but obscure text, yielding cognitive pleasure, is similar to the allegorical interpretation of Homer and Vergil: both are expressions of the same mentality.[28]

To sum up the positive aspects of Augustine's attitude towards the aesthetic experience, it can be said that, as for pagan literature, he would allow that some truth might be hidden beneath its fictions, artifice and sensory-affective quality, but this concession is immediately neutralized by his desire to strip this literature of precisely these elements. As far as the aesthetic element in Christian literature is concerned, it has been firmly subordinated to didactic purposes in preaching and it has been reduced to a supposedly purely cognitive affair in exegesis. But most important of all is the fact that the *De doctrina christiana* effectively suppresses Christian poetry by not mentioning it.

This state of affairs does not bode well for Augustine's attitude towards the flourishing Christian poetry of his own times, to which we now turn. The main problem, clearly, lay in the fact that Christian poetry was, by necessity, based on pagan models. Earlier naive (Proba) and iconconclastic (Commodianus) attempts had failed. The attitude of the Christian poets of the period themselves towards their classical models is perhaps best summed up in a letter from Paulinus of Nola to his brothers Jovius (*Ep.* 16.11, ca. 400 A.D.):

> Let it be enough to you to have taken from them their fluency of speech and verbal adornment, like spoils taken from enemy arms, so that stripped of their errors and clothed in their eloquence you may adopt to the fulness of reality the sheen of eloquence used by empty wisdom to deceive. Thus you may adorn not the empty body of unreality but the full body of truth, and ponder thoughts which are not merely pleasing to human ears, but also to the benefit of human minds.[29]

This position presents a Christian transformation of the classical dictum that literature should instruct as well as delight, supported by the Augustinian dispensation for rhetoric used in the right cause. The metaphor of the captive spoils is an adaptation of Augustine's own allegorical interpretation of the taking of gold and silver by the Israelites from their Egyptian captivity as a precept for salvaging what truth there is in pagan philosophy.[30] The clothing imagery used by Paulinus to characterize rhetoric as a veil of words conveying a more substantial, inner meaning is also very Augustinian. On the whole, then, the pagan models did not present a problem to Paulinus, if properly approached in accordance with Augustine's precepts. But there is an important difference with Augustine as well: the ready acceptance of the combination of the *dulce et utile*, the *delectare et prodesse*.

Augustine's precept—in the form of an allegorical interpretation—to take from pagan culture what is useful reads like an encouragement to practice allegorical interpretation of pagan literature and mythology in the manner of Lactantius. Initially, Augustine seems to have favoured the use of allegory to save what truth there is (*Contra Academicos* 3.5.6). He even encourages allegorical representation as a creative methodology in *De ordine* (1.8.24), where he urges the poet Licentius to transform the story of Pyramus and Thisbe into an allegory of pure love in which two souls, enhanced by learning and virtue, are joined in understanding through philosophy, thereby escaping death in the enjoyment of eternal life. In his *Retractions*, Augustine regrets having referred Licentius to the pagan Muses (*Retract.* 1.3.2). And in the *De doctrina christiana* (3.7.11—3.8.12), the turning point, Augustine explicitly rejects (pagan) allegorical poetry in reference to the following lines by an unknown poet:

> O Father Neptune, whose hoary temples crowned resound with
> the noisy sea, from whose beard eternally flows
> the vast Ocean, and in whose hair the rivers wander...

He goes on to characterize this gem as follows:

> This pod shakes rattling beans inside an agreeable husk.
> Yet, this is not food for men, but for swine.[31]

This represents not only a rejection of pagan allegorical poetry and its Christianizing interpretation, but also of an entire mode of communication. Again, this attitude did not bode well for Christian poetry based as it was on pagan models for its rhetorical artifice, mythological thematics and ornamentation, and its highly charged, late-antique, affective aesthetic.[32] The only exception may be when the poet Licentius is urged to abandon his worldly poetry and to learn humility from Paulinus of Nola (*Ep.* 26). Yet the reference is so general, that it could hardly be taken as an endorsement of Paulinus' poetry.

Herzog has shown how, in sharp contrast with Augustine, Jerome enthusiastically envisions the potential for a Christian poetic upon receiving the (lost) Theodosius panegyric sometimes attributed to Paulinus of Nola. Probably the most poetic of all prose genres, the panegyric inspires Jerome to the following vision (*Ep.* 48):

> O! If only I could lead natural ability of this kind not only amongst the Aeonian mounts and the summits of Helicon, as the poets say, but amongst Sion, Thabor and Sinai and the peaks of the Scriptures; if only it was given to me to teach what I have learned, and to deliver from my hands the mysteries of the prophets, there would be born to us something learned Greece never had!

And, recommending the veiled allegorical discourse of the Scriptures as a propaedeusis for poetic Christian discourse, Jerome goes on to say:

> If you had [the Scriptures] as your foundation or if [they] served as the finishing touch, we would have nothing more beautiful, nothing more learned, nothing more Latin than your books.

And finally, in a Christian transformation of the Ciceronian ideal of the combination of eloquence and wisdom, Jerome exclaims:

> If your prudence and eloquence were to be combined with a study or understanding of the Scriptures, I would see you in very short time occupying a place on the Capitol amongst our great poets...

Clearly, what Jerome envisions here is a combination of poetics and exegesis, of doctrine and esthetics.[33] He also envisions this new poetry as something totally original, dismissing the Vergilian centos of the biblical narrative as puerile (*Ep.* 53.7). However, settled permanently in Palestine since 386, he was less likely to have read Prudentius.

Given this reception by Augustine and Jerome, one is left to wonder about the impact of their widely diverging attitudes. In any case, it is clear that Jerome's vision did not win the day. The work of Prudentius, which represents the most complete integration of Christian doctrine and pagan rhetoric in its poetic transformation of patristic exegesis, was passed over in silence by Augustine, who clearly did read (pagan) poetry! In sharp contrast, as Herzog has demonstrated, the significant post-Augustinian poetic work of the fifth and sixth centuries involves Biblical paraphrases that make a clear distinction between the rhetorical *narratio* of the biblical narrative and the unadorned authoritative exegesis following it. In Sedulius and Arator the *dulce* and *utile, delectatio* and *aedificatio,* poetry and exegesis have effectively been separated.[34]

What are the reasons for this separation of poetic and exegetical functions? Is it possible that the poetic transformation of exegesis was perceived by Augustine especially as methodologically and even doctrinally unsound or, combined with its aesthetic appeal, as a potential rival to patristic *auctoritas?* Since there is no positive evidence, the answer to this question must be based on an argument *ex silentio.* However, the suggestion of a possible quarrel of the theologian with the poet may not altogether be unreasonable, especially because of the actual poetic use of exegesis. Prudentius provides the clearest case in point. Thoroughly familiar with patristic interpretations, the poet selects, combines and weaves them together for his own thematic, structural and esthetic purposes in creative works of Christian literature, modifying these interpretations in the process. One example will suffice, namely the poet's development of the figure of the devil in the *Hamartigeneia* (126–202). Already identified with the serpent of Genesis in patristic exegesis, the devil's appearance and nature are now expanded by the identification with Marcion's god of evil. Moving from the classical image of the snake-wreathed head of a Gorgon or Fury (*Ham.* 130; cf. *Aeneid* 7.445–51) to the devious trapper and hunter Nimrod (*Genesis* 10.8–9), the conception of the devil is made fully anthropomorphic. At the same time his metamorphosis into a serpent is explained through a correspondence in appearance before and after, in the manner of pagan physical allegory: Lucifer's originally tall, straight and smooth form is changed into the corresponding horizontal, base and slippery form of a snake as a result of his envy of mankind (*Ham.* 186–203). In this way, different elements of Scripture and exegesis are connected with each other through pagan imagery and pagan allegory, creating a truly new and original representation, but also a rather eclectic remythologization.[35]

Another possible reason for Augustine's displeasure may have been the way Prudentius perceived his role and that of his Christian poetry. In programmatic fashion, Prudentius combines two allegorical passages from the New Testament (John 14.2–3: my father's house has many mansions, etc., and 2 Tim. 2.20–21: in any great house there are not only utensils of gold and silver, but also of wood or earthenware) to represent and to characterize the role of the Christian poet in the *Epilogue* to his collected works:

> In the rich man's house there are many furnishings set in every corner; there is the shining golden cup, and the basin of bronze finely wrought is there, and the earthenware pot, and the heavy, broad tray of silver; there are pieces made of ivory, and some hollowed out of oak or elm. There is a use of every vessel that is fitted for the master's

service, for the house is furnished both with things that cost a great price and things made of wood. As for me, in his Father's house Christ fits me, as a poor, outworn vessel, for transitory services, and suffers me to keep a place in a corner. You see me do but the office of earthenware in the court of salvation; yet it is good to have rendered even the lowest service to God.[36]

This novel and daring use of Scripture to formulate poetic purpose fundamentally changes classical modesty topoi by combining a sense of self-worth and even pride in the service of God with Christian humility. However, the most striking presentation of the role of the Christian poet is to be found at the end of Prudentius' poetic hagiography of Eulalia, a saint of his native Spain (*Peristephanon* 4.197–200):

Cast yourself down along with me, noble city on the holy graves, you and all your people; then, when the saints' souls and bodies rise again, you and all your people will follow them.

Here the poet presents himself as the leader of the chorus offering a hymn at the martyr's grave, but also as a religious celebrant, since the tomb may also serve as an altar for the celebration of the Eucharist. Thus he leads the community of the faithful in a prayer for salvation, like a priest. Poetry has become a means of salvation, not just for the poet, but for mankind.

Against the background of the exalted status of the antique poet as *vates* or divinely inspired hierophant, Prudentius could be thought to present the Christian poet as a prophet or apostle delivering salvation through his art. Clearly, this view of the poet's role and of his poetry was not recognized in his own time. It would take another thousand years before this vision of salvation poetry was realized again by Dante.[37]

Dr. Haijo J. Westra studied at the Universities of Amsterdam, British Columbia and Toronto, graduating with a B.A. in Classics from U.B.C. and a Ph.D. in Medieval Studies from University of Toronto. His dissertation involved a critical edition of the commentary on Martianus Capella attributed to Bernardus Silvestris, subsequently published by the Pontifical Institute Press. He has also written on Prudentius and on a variety of medieval Latin texts. He has been teaching in the Classics at the University of Calgary since 1977.

NOTES

1. P. Courcelle, "Les lacunes de la correspondance entre Saint Augustin et Paulin de Nole," *Revue des Etudes Anciennes* (1951): 253–300.

2. For the date of the preface, see A. Cameron, *Claudian: Poetry and Propaganda at the Court of Honorius* (Oxford, 1970), 470–471; the first datable echo of the *Psychomachia* is in Cassian's *Institutions* (ca. 426); the first reference to Prudentius as a "classic" is by Sidonius Apollinaris, *Epistle* 2.9 (ca. 461–467). For the reception of Prudentius by Cassian and others in Gaul, Italy and North Africa in the fifth century, see E.B. Vest, "Prudentius in the Middle Ages" (Diss. Harvard, 1932).

3. "Augustinus," *Reallexikon ffüßr Antike und Christentum 1* (1950), 983; cf. *De doctrina christiana* 4.30–31.

4. *Enneads*, 5.8; cf. A.S. Preminger, et al., *Classical and Medieval Literary Criticism: Translations and Interpretations* (New York, 1974), 227–233.

5. See Preminger, *Classical and Medieval Literary Criticism*, 310–313, for a summary of Proclus' views.

6. See H.R. Jauss, *Aesthetic Experience and Literary Hermeneutics*, trans. M. Shaw with an introduction by W. Godzich (Minneapolis, 1982), 36–38.

7. Jauss, *Aesthetic Experience*, 38.

8. V.J. Bourke, trans., *Saint Augustine: Confessions*. The Fathers of the Church, vol. 21 (New York, 1953), 41.

9. *De ordine* 2.14.39, ed. W.M. Green, *CCSL* 29 (1970), 129.

10. H.R. Jauss, *Aesthetic Experience*, 24.

11. For Marrou's and other relevant evaluations, see R.J. O'Connell, *Art and the Christian Intelligence in St. Augustine* (Cambridge, Mass., 1978), 2.

12. H.-I. Marrou, *Saint Augustin et la fin de la culture antique* (Paris, 1938), 510.

13. See Marrou, *Saint Augustin*, 348; for Augustinian testimonia concerning hymns, see W. Bulst, *Hymni Latini Antiquissimi LXXV, Psalmi III* (Heidelberg, 1956), 161–172.

14. W. Godzich, introd. H.R. Jauss, *Aesthetic Experience and Literary Hermeneutics* (Minneapolis, 1982), xxxix.

15. I. Kant, *Critique of Judgement*, Section 1, Bk. 1, par. 2, par. 5 and par. 12; cf. Jauss, *Aesthetic Experience*, 14.

16. Jauss, *Aesthetic Experience*, 23–24.

17. See especially *Confessions*, 10.33.

18. Marrou, *Saint Augustin*, 234, n.2; 255–287.

19. Marrou, *Saint Augustin*, 345–350.

20. R.J. O'Connell, *Art and the Christian Intelligence in St. Augustine* (Cambridge, Mass. 1978), 30, 31, 36–37.

21. *De doctrina christiana* 2.18.28; cf. *ibid.*, 2.40.60.

22. Migne, *PL*, Suppl. 2, 356–357.

23. *De doctrina christiana* 4.5.7; cf. Marrou, *Saint Augustin*, 508–514.

24. R. Herzog, "Exegese—Erbauung—Delectatio: Beitrßäßge zu einer christlichen Poetik der Spßäßtantike," in W. Haug, ed., *Formen und Funktionen der Allegorie* (Stuttgart, 1979), 52–69, esp. 56.

25. *De doctrina christiana* 4.13.29, trans. J.J. Gavigan, *The Fathers of the Church*, vol. 2 (2nd ed., 1950), 195.

26. *Ep.* 44, 1 (1), *PL* 33, c.174; see *De doctr. chr.* 4.24.53 for the legitimate use of the grand style.

27. Marrou, *Saint Augustin*, 478–491, esp. 488–489; cf. H. de Lubac, *Exßéßgßèße mßéßdißéßvale. Les quatre sens de l'Ècriture*, vol. 1 (Paris, 1959), 119–128.

28. Marrou, *Saint Augustin*, 494–495.

29. *Letter 16: To Jovius*, trans. P.G. Walsh, *Letters of St. Paulinus of Nola*, vol. 1 (New York, 1966), 162.

30. Cf. *De doctrina christiana* 2.40.60–2.40.61.

31. *De doctrina christiana* 3.7.11, trans. J.J. Gavigan, in *The Fathers of the Church*, vol. 2 (2nd ed., 1950), 126; cf. Luke 15.16.

32. R. Herzog, "Exegese," etc., 60.

33. Cf. R. Herzog, "Exegese," etc., 55, n. 27, and 45.

34. See R. Herzog, "Exegese," etc., 58–62.

35. See R. Herzog, *Die allegorische Dichtkunst des Prudentius* (Munich, 1966), 94–96.

36. H.J. Thomson, trans., *Prudentius*, vol. 2 (Loeb, 1953), 373–375; but see also K. Thraede, *Studien zur Sprache und Stil des Prudentius* (Gßößttingen, 1965), 21–78, esp. 71–78; cf. R. Herzog, *Die allegorische*

Dichtkunst des Prudentius (Munich, 1966), 119–122; M. Smith, *Prudentius' Psychomachia: A Reexamination* (Princeton, 1976), 29–108.

37. Even if it could be demonstrated that Augustine most likely would not have known the works of Prudentius, the argument presented here could still stand on the basis of his silence on the subject of Christian poetry as such.

AUGUSTINE'S METHODS OF BIBLICAL INTERPRETATION

AUGUSTINE'S METHODS OF BIBLICAL INTERPRETATION[1]

Gordon J. Hamilton

Introduction

Augustine sets forth his basic hermeneutical principles, the theoretical under-pinnings of his methods of biblical interpretation in *On Christian Doctrine*. He used these principles as a key to decoding the hidden meaning of the scriptures. A large part of *On Christian Doctrine* is devoted to the training that a Christian exegete should have to discover this hidden meaning. However, it should be realized that Augustine believed that for any interpretation to be valid it must build the double love of God and of neighbor.[2] This purpose permeates both his hermeneutical principles and his exegesis of specific passages in other works. Thus, while Augustine gives both specific and general educational guidelines by which a Christian exegete might be trained so as to be able to in-terpret, these studies should be seen as tools or aids that must be reconciled to the basic purpose for the interpretation, that of helping a Christian to enjoy God more fully. In dealing with Augustine's methods of biblical interpretation it should also be realized that he was primarily a pastor, a bishop, a preacher and a Christian—and not an exegete at least in the modern sense of that word.[3] It is in this general context of the Christian community that Augustine must be situated. Bonner believes that Augustine's main hermeneutical contribution is this very emphasis on interpreting scripture within the ecclesial community.[4] The Christocentricity of all of Augustine's exegesis is apparent even in his general principles of interpretation. Bonner typifies Augustine's perspective in one sentence: "Christ is the guarantor and the interpreter of holy scripture, the witness from whom it derives its authority."[5] The importance of Augustine's hermeneutical principles, as developed especially in *On Christian Doctrine*, in the history of exegesis is enormous, especially in the Medieval Period.[6]

Augustine's Early Development

I believe that it is important at least to outline those parts of Augustine's formal classical education, his Manichaean period, his Neo-Platonist phase, and finally his early time as a Christian which had a direct bearing on the development of his mature interpretive principles.

Formal Education

Augustine's formal education is an important concern when dealing with his hermeneutical principles. It is in this phase that Augustine acquired his great knowledge of the Latin classics. He also acquired general techniques for the treatment of literature which he later applied to the biblical texts. His education "...placed its emphasis on literary style and valued learning as a means to embellishing an oration rather than as something of value for its own sake."[7] The effect of this literary training,"...which paid minute attention to style and concentrated upon the details of the language,"[8] is seen clearly in his exegetical works where he always focuses sharply on the exact form of the text, even in instances where we would have believed the text to have been so corrupt as to render it unintelligible. The other facets of Augustine's formal education must be seen as extremely weak and undeveloped. "History...was mainly a matter of historical anecdotes, natural science a collection of curious facts (*mirabilia*)....Philosophy...was mediated at second hand by popularisers like Cicero and Seneca."[9]

Manichaean Phase

One possible result of this formal training might be that it made Augustine's association with the literalist Manichees very easy. The Manichees "...were using literalism in order to discredit the patriarchs of the Old Testament, insisting on the immoralities which scripture imputed to them."[10] They also claimed that the New Testament had been interpolated by advocates of the Jewish Law.[11] However, as Augustine discovered after nine years as a Manichee, this movement could not supply an uncorrupt text of the scriptures. Grant writes: "Augustine already questioned the motives of his Manichaean friends, and he was psychologically prepared to receive the exegetical answer to his problems."[12] Many times in the rest of his life Augustine wrote against the literalism and materialism of the Manichees.

Neo-Platonist and Early Christian Period(s)

The Neo-Platonist phase is also an important stage in the development of Augustine's hermeneutical principles. The value of the Neo-Platonists "...was twofold: they helped destroy the last remnants of Manichaean materialism which haunted his mind, and they provided a metaphysic which appeared to harmonize with Christian revelation."[13] The Neo-Platonists also acted as a balance to his formal literary education.[14] The Neo-platonic and Christian phases of his life seem to overlap (many scholars would say that they were permanently married, in a Christian wedding, of course!). As Bonner has noted: "Under Ambrose's influence, Augustine's difficulties about the Bible began to be resolved, and the process was accelerated by his discovery of Neo-Platonic philosophy in which (he persuaded himself) he could find confirmation of much that was in the Gospel."[15] "The influence of Neo-Platonists upon Augustine's exegesis...cannot be over-emphasised."[16] They added another testimony for the need of an allegorical method of scriptural interpretation.

It was this allegorical method, coupled with the eloquence of Ambrose, that won Augustine over to the Catholic Church. To quote Robert Grant concerning the specific *raison d'être* of this conference: "Only when he discovered the allegorical method of interpreting the Old Testament was he able to become a Christian."[17] The degree of influence that Ambrose and others in Milan exerted on Augustine cannot be ascertained exactly, but clear signs of their influence can be seen long after he had abandoned the Neo-Platonists as theological guides.[18] Grant characterizes Augustine's use of allegory as follows:

> And yet the mind of Augustine could not rest in simple allegorism. Like other interpreters in the orthodox tradition, he continued his search for an all-inclusive principle by means of which he could determine what was allegorical and what was not. Moreover, in the course of his theological development he came to take more and more passages of scripture literally. The allegorical method was only a stepping-stone towards a final interpretation of scripture.[19]

Augustine makes use of this allegorical method for the first time in *On Genesis against the Manichees* in which he refuted the literal Manichaean view of the Old Testament.[20]

On Christian Doctrine

One of the problems in dealing with *On Christian Doctrine* is that it is both a relatively early work, begun in the years 396–97, and an example of a later period, 426–27, so that one would expect a great deal of development in Augustine's thought about his hermeneutical principles. The chronological break is at the thirty-fifth Chapter of Book III.[21] However, there appears to be no development or revision of his principles, and as such we must take *On Christian Doctrine* to be a work primarily written in his early period but given the seal of approval of his last years, thereby indicating that Augustine felt it stated his mature hermeneutical principles well. Indeed, we should note that even the typological interpretation, represented by his inclusion of the *Book of*

Rules of Tyconius, was included in the earlier section of the text and at the later date he simply continued to comment on the last three rules (and added Book IV, which is beyond the scope of our topic).[22]

Canon and Translations

It is also important to note which canon Augustine recognized and with which translations he worked. His canon included the so-called Apocryphal or Pseudepigraphical books of the Old Testament and is basically that of the Roman Catholic Church of our day. The Council of Carthage in 397, which Augustine attended, recognized this canon. Augustine, himself, lists the canonical books in Book III, Chapter 8, of *On Christian Doctrine*. [23] "Augustine was aware that in his day there was still some hesitation among Catholic Christians regarding the reception of certain books of the Bible, and laid down the general principle that the books which command the greatest measure of support enjoy the greatest authority."[24] Augustine advised: "In the matter of canonical Scriptures [one] should follow the authority of the greater number of Catholic Churches, among which are those which have deserved to have apostolic seats and to receive epistles."[25] It is significant that for Augustine the distinction between canonical and non-canonical books had to be made by the Church. Augustine treated this distinction very seriously, because only on the canonical books could doctrine be based. For example, in one controversy about whether an unbaptized person who had died was damned, Augustine "...was quick to point out that the *Passion of St. Perpetua* [to which some appealed] was not canonical and could not therefore be used to establish any point of doctrine."[26] The translations that Augustine employed and the authority that he gave to them had deep impact on many of his interpretations. He considered the Septuagint, the Greek version of the Old Testament, authoritative to the end of his life, even after Jerome's work on the *Vulgate*, partially based on the Hebrew scriptures, had been completed.[27]

Yet possibly because of an imperfect knowledge of Greek, Augustine did not refer to the Septuagint very often when faced with conflicting Latin texts. This brings us to which Latin translations he employed, and they varied throughout his Christian life. "Augustine indeed deplored the multiplicity of translations circulating in Africa and recommended the *Itala* as being superior to other versions....It [the *Itala*] would appear to have been a European version of the Old Latin translation used in North Africa in Augustine's time...."[28] After about 400, Augustine started to use portions of Jerome's *Vulgate* but still considered as authoritative, texts based on the inspired Septuagint. In this regard Bonner rightly emphasizes that "...for Augustine, it is not so much the words of the Bible themselves as the doctrine underlying the words which is important."[29]

The Cardinal Principle of Interpretation

It is essential to understand Augustine's cardinal principle, the purpose for which one tries to discover the meaning of the scriptures. Augustine formulates his cardinal principle in a negative fashion: "Whoever, therefore, thinks that he understands the divine Scriptures or any part of them so that it does not build up the double love of God and of neighbor does not understand it at all."[30] Apart from a dependency on the great commandments of the Gospels, how does the Bishop of Hippo arrive at this over-arching principle?[31] "Augustine begins by making a distinction between *use* and *enjoyment*. To enjoy a thing is to cleave to it for its own sake; to use it is to employ it as a means to obtaining what one desires to enjoy."[32] "These things which are to be enjoyed are the Father, the Son, and the Holy Spirit, a single Trinity, a certain supreme thing common to all who enjoy it...."[33] "...All other things are to be used to obtain that enjoyment, including the holy scriptures, which should be used to build up the supernatural virtues, Faith, Hope, and Love."[34] Indeed, Augustine stated that individuals do not need the scriptures if they are already in possession of these three virtues. The only need they might have of them is in the instruction of others. [35] "Therefore, when anyone knows the end of the commandment to be charity 'from a pure heart, a good conscience, and unfeigned faith' (I Tim. 1:5), and has related all of his understanding of the Divine Scriptures to these three, he may approach the treatment of these books with security."[36] Augustine also stated that charity alone will remain more certain and more vigorous in eternity.[37] This completely rules out any "mere" academic study of the scriptures and puts Augustine's basic purpose for his hermeneutical principles in contrast to many modern biblical studies. "Nevertheless, for the proper understanding of scripture with a view to increasing Faith, Hope, and Love, some knowledge is necessary and it is the character of such knowledge which is the theme of the *De Doctrina Christiana*."[38]

Knowledge: Things and Signs

Such knowledge is knowing the distinction between things and signs. Augustine begins his discussion of this important conceptual framework in a deceptively simple manner: "All doctrine concerns either things or signs, but things are learned by signs. Strictly speaking, I have here called a 'thing' that which is not used to signify something else....There are other signs whose whole use is in signifying, like words....They are things used to signify something."[39] There are two types of signs: natural and conventional. Natural signs, without any "...intention of signifying, make us aware of something beyond themselves, like smoke which signifies fire."[40] "Conventional signs are those which living creatures show to one another for the purpose of conveying...the motion of their spirits or something which they have sensed or understood."[41] Conventional signs include the scriptures. As we have seen above, words are signs and even holy scripture was conveyed in words, indeed in specific languages. Because of the Tower of Babel, languages were multiplied and now scripture had to be translated into many other tongues.[42] "But many and varied obscurities and ambiguities deceive those who read casually...."[43] These ambiguities and obscurites cause misunderstandings, but if one would follow the educational and spiritual guidelines set forth by Augustine, then he believes these difficulties could be overcome.

Brown takes up this sign theme, depicting the Bible as Augustine saw it "...as a single message in an intricate code..." and a "...communication that was intrinsically so far above the pitch of human minds that to be made available to our present senses at all, this 'Word' had to be communicated by means of an intricate game of signs...."[44] As far as the obscure signs are concerned, I think that Brown's terminology is quite appropriate; these signs had a hidden, veiled meaning that had to be decoded. But perhaps it would be more appropriate to call the Bible a puzzle of signs, rather than a game since Augustine got quite upset at Jerome when Jerome wrote that they were *playing* in the field of the scriptures.[45] We should also remember that Augustine believed that hardly anything was written in obscure passages that was not stated quite clearly elsewhere,[46] so that we are actually dealing with a very small group of passages.

"There are two reasons why things written are not understood; they are obscured by either unknown or ambiguous signs. For signs are either literal or figurative."[47] In the group of conventional signs, called words or languages, especially in the scriptures, we then have a subdivision of categories that if applied properly will help to elucidate the text. In determining whether a locution is literal or figurative, Augustine gives the following method in *On Christian Doctrine* Book II, Chapter 10: "...Whatever appears in the divine Word that does not literally pertain to virtuous behavior or to the truth of faith you must take to be figurative." Let us now focus on the Augustinian methods for decoding figurative and literal signs.

Decoding Unknown Literal Signs: Languages

"Against unknown literal signs the sovereign remedy is a knowledge of languages."[48] Here, it is clear that Augustine is putting forth the ideal training that is desirable for a Christian exegete and not the standard that must apply to everyone.[49] This is the case especially if one applies this injunction concerning the knowledge of languages to Augustine himself. Bonner writes: "He was ignorant of Hebrew, though he had some notions of Punic, apparently still spoken in the Africa of his day, which he could apply to the elucidation of a Hebrew word."[50] His knowledge of Greek is a more controverted issue. Augustine admits in his *Confessions* that he detested the study of Greek in his youth.[51] It would appear, however, that he later acquired a limited working knowledge of Biblical and Patristic Greek.[52] Yet as was noted earlier, he very rarely put this limited knowledge of Greek to use in checking what the divinely inspired Septuagint said when he came across contradictory or corrupt Latin texts.[53] However, in a letter to Jerome he felt free to use poor Latin translations as a reason for any error in the text.[54] One modern scholar views his linguistic deficiencies with a highly critical attitude, stating that since Augustine had "...no knowledge of Hebrew and a very imperfect acquaintance with Greek, he was incapacitated for thorough and independent studies of the sacred books."[55] Although such criticism is quite justified in regard to his knowledge and use of Greek, it is misplaced concerning his lack of Hebrew since he did not recognize the Hebrew (and Aramaic) scriptures as being authoritative. The Bishop of Hippo's ideal remedy against unknown literal signs is a knowledge of the Greek and especially Latin languages.

Decoding Figurative Signs: The Limited Use of Liberal Arts

Augustine also advised the conversion of aspects of liberal arts, the *liberales disciplinae* to help Christian exegetes in their interpretation. For example, "If those who are called philosophers, especially the Platonists, have said things that are indeed true and are well accommodated to our faith, they should not be feared; rather what they have said should be taken from them as from unjust possessors and converted to our use."[56] For the interpretation of figurative signs Augustine also advised the study of other "disciplines"—history, the natural sciences, dialectic, rhetoric, as well as language and philosophy, which have already been mentioned. This, of course, in large part reflects his own background, and likely represents a realization on his part that he could not, and would not ignore his own training.[57]

TeSelle sees Augustine as championing an encounter between philosophical reflection and the study of the biblical text and characterizes Augustine's conversion of non-Christian sources as an example of H. Richard Niebuhr's "Christ transforming culture."[58] Yet the degree to which Augustine advised such a transformation of such sources needs to be specified. He wrote that "...the knowledge collected from the books of the pagans, although some of it is useful, is also little as compared with that derived from Holy Scripture."[59] He thereby thought that he had relegated the use of non-Christian philosophy to a minor, secondary state—even if we in the twentieth century see Augustine's use of Neo-Platonic philosophy as an essential, primary, although Christianized, source for his interpretations.

Augustine's Organized Methods for the Interpretation of Scripture

In *On the Profit of Believing*, which is an early work, written just after Augustine became a priest in 391, Augustine sets forth four methods for the interpretation of scripture—historical, aetiological, analogical and allegorical:

Thus (for example) it is handed down according to *history*, when it is taught what has been written, or what has been done; what not done, but only written as though it has been done. According to *aetiology*, when it is shown for what cause any thing has been done or said. According to *analogy* when it is shown that the two Testaments, the Old and the New, are not contrary the one to the other. According to *allegory* when it is taught that certain things that have been written are not to be taken in the letter, but are to be understood in a figure.[60]

Allegorical and Literal Interpretations

Augustine's use of allegory should not be over-emphasized. As we have already noted, Grant believes this allegorical method was used by Augustine as an intermediate stage, by which he was able to free himself from the literalism and materialism of the Manichees.[61] Bonner concurs: "In fact, however, Augustine diminished the allegorical element in his scriptural exegesis with the passage of years, although he never wholly abandoned it."[62] Augustine tended to follow the literal reading of the text in his later works. I consider this to be a return to the principles which he learned as a student. Having found the allegorical method an appropriate weapon to fight off the Manichaean influences, and now being in a secure position within the Church—in which he was not during his early years as a layman, priest and bishop—the mature Augustine felt confident enough to be able to discern to which texts the allegorical method could be applied.

History and Prophecy

"The characteristic feature of the development in Augustine's attitude to the Bible is this deepened sense of scripture as the history of God's saving work for man in the past, present, and the future, until the Second Coming of Christ."[63] Augustine wrote: "And whatever is so narrated [concerning the social customs of the patriarchs] is to be taken not only historically and literally but also figuratively and prophetically, so that it is interpreted for the end of charity, either as it applies to God, or to one's neighbor, or to both."[64] This is a later development in Augustine's sense of history, where history and prophecy become one.[65] In his earlier writings "...he explains that the scriptures may be expounded historically (*secundum historiam*) or prophetically (*secundum prophetiam*)."[66] This sense of the history of God's actions as seen in Scripture was a development that Christianity added to a weak area in the classical education which Augustine had received. "In terms of outlook, if not technique, Augustine represents a decisive factor in the History of Western biblical exegesis by his emphasis on the historical and typological."[67]

Typological Interpretation

Let us now turn to a method of interpretation which is also advocated in *On Christian Doctrine*: typology. There Augustine repeats, with comments,

Tyconius' *Book of Rules* for the interpretation of scripture. Tyconius was a Donatist. Because of this fact it is amazing that Augustine even considers his rules, and indeed considers them worthy enough to be included in his own thought; their inclusion emphasizes Augustine's open-mindedness in that he was willing to take from any source—even from someone he has viewed as a heretic—if he considered the thought to be true. Augustine was in no way unfamiliar with the Donatists. They were numerous in northern Africa and at one time controlled a large segment of his diocese. Brown writes: "During Augustine's episcopate, Hippo became a Christian town. Augustine drove out his Christian rivals, the Donatists...."[68] And Bonner evaluates: "Indeed we may rank Tyconius with Ambrose as the major influences upon Augustine's theory of biblical exegesis, and it seems not unlikely that, in the long run, his was the stronger influence."[69] Augustine himself wrote of Tyconius' *Book of Rules*: "When these are examined as he explains them, they are of no little assistance in penetrating what is covert in the scriptures."[70] Very briefly, the seven rules are: (1) "Of the Lord and His Body"—that Christ and the Church are one and passages in scripture often refer to both the Body and the Head; (2) "Of the Bipartite Body of the Lord" or "The Mixed Church"—that there are both true believers and hypocrites, and that the latter still appear to be in the Church; (3) "Of Promises and Laws" or "Concerning the Spirit and the Letter"—that people are given faith so that they can endure the suffering through which they must go for Christ; (4) "Of Species and Genus"—to which group passages of Scripture are applicable; (5) "Of Times"—understanding the part by the whole or the whole by the part or by "legitimate" numbers (special numbers divinely designated for certain groups); (6) "Recapitulation"—that scripture may not follow strict chronological order; (7) "Of the Devil and his Body"—which parallels Christ and His Body.[71] Concerning these rules, Augustine summarizes: "All of these rules except one, which is called 'Of Promises and Law', cause one thing to be understood from another, a situation proper to figurative locutions."[72] Bonner provides an extremely sympathetic appraisal of these rules: "The greatness of Tyconius' achievement lay in his typological interpretation of scripture with a fixed pattern of thought...."[73] He also notes that by following Tyconius' *Book of Rules* Augustine could avoid both excessive literalism and allegorism.[74] Augustine had finally found a system of interpretation—typology—in which he could incorporate his life in the Church with his work on the scriptural texts. The effect can be quite significant. Bonner continues: "An impressive example is provided by his treatment of the Good Samaritan, which he originally understood as a simple allegory [*De Gen. c. Man.* 11.10, 13] but later came to regard as typifying the whole story of man's fall and redemption, with Christ Himself as the Samaritan and the wounded traveller as Adam."[75]

The *Sacramenta*

Another aspect of Augustine's interpretation is his fascination with the *sacramenta*—the hidden meanings within Scripture. Augustine uncovered these *sacramenta* throughout the Bible: in personal and place names; in the titles of the Psalms, which are more numerous in the Greek (and Latin) than in the Hebrew Bible; and especially in any biblical number. Apparently, most of Augustine's contemporaries, both pagan and Christian, also had this fascination. Numerology ran rampant and Augustine must be seen as a rather well versed student of the art. It would take someone of Augustine's creativity to come up with some of the theories that he did (e.g., the 153 fish of John 21:11 symbolize the elect: confirmation—3 (the Trinity) times 50 (Pentecost) equals 150, plus 3 (Trinity) equals 153, the number of fish). Bonner assures us that Augustine's numerological activities were quite common for his age.[76] It is somewhat surprising, however, that at another point the Bishop of Hippo warns against superstition and astrologers,[77] but perhaps here I am using my modern historical position to unfair advantage.

Inerrancy

When considering how Augustine applied his hermeneutical principles, it is important to note whether he believed the Scriptures could ever err or be in contradiction to one another. The main primary sources are *Letters* 28 and 82, both to Jerome, and both concerning the veracity of Galatians 2:11-21. According to Augustine, Jerome wanted to read that text as a deliberate lie; i.e., Paul wanted to rebuke the Judaizers in the Christian party, so in Galatians Paul staged a rebuke of Peter for trying to make Christians first Jews. Augustine replies, "I think that it is extremely dangerous to admit that anything in the Sacred Books should be a lie; that is that the men who have composed and written the Scriptures for us should have lied in their books."[78] And at another place, he states, "...I will read the Holy Scriptures with complete certainty and confidence in its truth, founded as it is on the highest summit of divine authority...."[79] As we have seen, Augustine was quite prepared to admit that there were ambiguous and obscure passages in Scripture; indeed his main purpose in writing *On Christian Doctrine* was to provide the principles and methods necessary to discover the meanings of these passages. However, he could not accept any talk about there being any deliberate lies in these writings. To quote again from one of his letters: "...it is from these books alone of the Scriptures, which are now called canonical, that I have learned to pay them such honor and respect as to believe most firmly that not one of their authors has erred in writing anything at all."[80] Yet we must underline the context of this statement: his dispute with Jerome was over a supposed deliberate lie. As far as possible contradictions go, Bonner observes: "Augustine fully recognized that discrepancies may exist between authors, that reported conversations may report general tone rather than the actual words of the speakers, and that individual authors, even if inspired, may differ in the order of narration."[81] This understanding of Augustine's belief in inerrancy, that is that there are no deliberately deceitful errors, is in contrast to some modern readings of Augustine;[82] for example, Loretz (citing Sasse) asserts:

> According to Augustine, who on this point is under the influence of pagan theories of inspiration, inspiration is to be understood as meaning 'that man is only the instrument of the Holy Spirit and the latter alone determined the content and the form of scripture. From this, it follows as a general rule that the Bible is free from mistakes, error and contradictions even in its smallest details'. [83]

This view can be countered by one example: Augustine was aware that the verse *mistakenly* attributed to Jeremiah in Matt. 27:9 was actually a paraphrase of Zechariah.[84]

The Diversity within Scripture

It has been seen that in terms of modern biblical studies, Augustine possessed neither the technical equipment nor the scholarly patience [85] required of an exegete, but this did not stop Augustine from taking a serious, systematic approach in his exegetical works. TeSelle astutely observes that Augustine matched his methods of interpretation to the diverse literary forms with the Christian canon:

> ...Repeatedly, he engaged in a systematic study of particular passages—the Sermon on the Mount, the creation narrative, the Psalms, the Pauline epistles, the gospels, the Johannine writings—with an awareness of the *diversity* within Scripture, interpreting each writing in a way suited to its literary genre and the meanings he thought it conveyed, sometimes literal (as in Paul), sometimes metaphorical (as in the creation narrative), sometimes allegorical(as in the Psalms).[86]

TeSelle's understanding contrasts with the position put forth by Brown: "For Augustine and his hearers, the Bible was literally the Word of God. It was regarded as a single message in an intricate code, and not as an exceedingly heterogeneous collection of separate books...."[87] I do not believe that these scholars' views can, or should be reconciled. In my limited reading of Augustine's works, I would align myself with TeSelle and Bonner who believe Augustine interpreted scripture as a diverse document.

Interpreting Scripture within the Church

A fundamental point of Augustine's exegesis, which could be added as a principle second only to the primary purpose of interpreting scripture (the enjoyment of God), is interpreting the Bible in the light of Christian doctrine and the life of the Church. We have already seen that it is the Church that sets and recognizes the canon of the sacred books. It follows for Augustine that the Bible had to be read and understood within the framework of the life and doctrine of the Christian community and not interpreted by mere private judgment, no matter how learned.[88] This is the impact of Augustine's typological method: all scripture could be harmonized within the life and growth of the Catholic community. By looking for types and anti-types of behavior, conditions, actions, people and institutions within the received scriptures, Augustine could constantly update the Bible for his church. We must always remember that Augustine was a Christian priest, bishop and *church*man first and an exegete only in instructing others in his ecclesiastical duties.

Augustine's Influence

The influence of Augustine's hermeneutical principles was great, especially in the Medieval Period. McNally writes: "In the eyes of the Carolingians St. Augustine was the most revered of the Latin Fathers. This evaluation was in accord with tradition in the West."[89] McNally then presents a long list of exegetes and theologians on whom Augustine had a direct bearing. Bonner also affirms the unparalleled position that Augustine held in the Middle Ages: "With Jerome, Gregory the Great, and the Venerable Bede he was one of the four greatest authorities, and would probably have been reckoned the greatest of the four."[90] His influence was so great that it would be extremely tedious even to list the effect of this one work, *On Christian Doctrine*, directly on theologians and exegetes, or indirectly on the art, literature and education throughout the Medieval Period.

Conclusion

The value of Augustine's hermeneutical principles as seen especially in *On Christian Doctrine* is at least fourfold: (a) in themselves as the mature and admittedly complex principles of one of the greatest Doctors of the Church; (b) in their application to specific pieces of exegesis in his other writings (some of his works have been described as a virtual mosaic of scriptural texts[91]); (c) in locating a relatively open way of combining various methods of interpreting the Bible within the early Christian community; and (d) in their great influence on the Western Church during later periods. As has been seen many times throughout this paper, Gerald Bonner characterizes the Bishop of Hippo as a biblical interpreter much more eloquently than I ever could:

> Augustine's power, both as a preacher and as an exegete, lies in the fact that he was, in Fredrick van der Meer's fine phrase, 'an unconditional Christian.' It is this which makes him, more that fifteen centuries after his death, supremely worth reading as a guide to the understanding, and still more to the application, of holy scripture.[92]

Gordon Hamilton was born and raised in Vancouver, B.C. After attending Brown University where he concentrated in the History of Christian Thought and Biblical Studies, he attended The Hebrew University of Jerusalem. In 1985 he received his doctorate in Near Eastern Languages and Civilizations from Harvard University. From 1985–88 he held postdoctoral fellowships at The Calgary Institute for the Humanities and the Religious Studies Department of The University of Calgary. He has been Professor of Old Testament Language and Literature at Huron College, an affiliate college of The University of Western Ontario, since 1988. His research interests range from inscriptions of the ancient Near East to Old Testament studies to the history of biblical interpretation.

NOTES

1. This paper was prepared during postdoctoral fellowships at The Calgary Institute for the Humanities and the Department of Religious Studies, The University of Calgary. It is dedicated to L. Fraser and L. Newman.

2. *On Christian Doctrine* 1.25–26, trans. D.W. Robertson (New York: Liberal Arts, 1958)—hereafter cited as *On Christian Doctrine* plus book and chapter numbers.

3. G. Bonner, "Augustine as Biblical Scholar," in *The Cambridge History of the Bible*, Vol.1, eds. P.R. Ackroyd and C.F. Evans (Cambridge: Cambridge University, 1970), 562—hereafter cited as Bonner plus page number.

4. Bonner, 561.

5. Bonner, 562.

6. Bonner, 562.

7. Bonner, 551.

8. Bonner, 552.

9. Bonner, 551.

10. R. Grant, *A Short History of the Interpretation of the Bible* (New York: Macmillan, 1963), 102—hereafter cited as Grant plus page number.

11. Grant, 110.

12. Grant, 110.

13. Bonner, 551 (based on *Confessions* VII.9, 13, 14).

14. Bonner, 552.

15. Bonner, 543.

16. Bonner, 551.

17. Grant, 102.

18. Bonner, 551.

19. Grant, 110.

20. Bonner, 543.

21. See Robertson's comments on p. ix of *On Christian Doctrine*.

22. *On Christian Doctrine*, III.35-37.

23. For a complete listing, see Bonner, 544.

24. Bonner, 544.

25. *On Christian Doctrine* II.8.

26. Bonner, 544.

27. Bonner, 546.

28. Bonner, 545.

29. Bonner, 547.

30. *On Christian Doctrine* I.26.

31. Cf. J. Wilkinson, *Interpretation and Community* (London: Macmillan, 1963), 165.

32. Bonner, 548.

33. *On Christian Doctrine* I.5.

34. Bonner, 548.

35. *On Christian Doctrine* I.39.

36. *On Christian Doctrine* I.40.

37. *On Christian Doctrine* I.39.

38. Bonner, 548.

39. *On Christian Doctrine* I.2.

40. *On Christian Doctrine* II.1.

41. *On Christian Doctrine* II.2.

42. *On Christian Doctrine* I.5.

43. *On Christian Doctrine* II.6.

44. P. Brown, *Augustine of Hippo: A Biography* (London: Faber and Faber, 1967), 252—hereafter cited as Brown plus page number.

45. *Saint Augustine: Letters*, Vol. 1. trans. W. Parsons, in *The Fathers of the Church* (Washington, DC: The Catholic University of America, 1951), *Letter* 82—hereafter cited by letter number.

46. *On Christian Doctrine* II.6.

47. *On Christian Doctrine* II.10.

48. *On Christian Doctrine* II.11.

49. Bonner, 550.

50. Bonner, 550.

51. *Saint Augustine: Confessions*, trans. V.J. Bourke, in *The Fathers of Church* (Washington, DC: The Catholic University of America, 1953), I.13.

52. Bonner, 550.

53. Bonner, 546.

54. *Letter* 82.

55. M. Terry, *Biblical Hermeneutics* (Grand Rapids: Zondervan, 1964), 657.

56. *On Christian Doctrine* II.40.

57. Cf. E. TeSelle, *Augustine: The Theologian* (New York: Herder and Herder, 1970), 58: "Augustine, who had earlier identified himself with the world of classical literature and philosophy and shared its goals even when he thought they could be attained only by following the way indicated by Christianity, now affected ignorance of and distaste for classical writers, in the typical ecclesiastical manner, lest he seem to recommend classical culture in its entirety, including its mythology, and its spectacles."

58. *Ibid*; see H.R. Niebuhr, *Christ and Culture* (New York: Harper and Row, 1951), 190-217, for a fully-nuanced examination of this difficult subject. Niebuhr himself considered Augustine to be less than a complete conversionist. To quote from p. 216 of *Christ and Culture*:

Why the theologian whose fundamental convictions laid the groundwork for a thoroughly conversionist view of humanity's nature and culture did not draw the consequences of these convictions is a difficult question. It may be argued that he sought to be faithful to the Scriptures with its parables of the last judgment and the separatist ideas in it. But there is also a universal note in the Scriptures; and faithfulness to the book does not explain why one who otherwise was always more interested in the spiritual sense than in the letter, not only followed the letter in this instance but exaggerated the literal sense. The clue to the problem seems to lie in Augustine's defensiveness.

I am grateful to Professor H. Gordon Harland for this reference.

59. *On Christian Doctrine* II.42; see especially C.N. Cochrane, *Christianity and Classical Culture: A Study of Thought and Action from Augustus to Augustine* (London: Oxford University, 1944), 476. I would like to thank Professor H. Gordon Harland for this reference as well.

60. *On the Profit of Believing*, translated by C.L. Cornish, Vol. 3 in *The Nicene and Post-Nicene Fathers* (Buffalo: The Christian Literature Company); emphasis added.

61. Grant, 110.

62. Bonner, 552.

63. Bonner, 553.

64. *On Christian Doctrine* III.12.

65. Bonner, 554.

66. Bonner, 554.

67. Bonner, 554.

68. Brown, 194.

69. Bonner, 555.

70. *On Christian Doctrine* III.30.

71. *On Christian Doctrine* III.30 –37.

72. *On Christian Doctrine* III.37.

73. Bonner, 554.

74. Bonner, 555.

75. Bonner, 560.

76. Bonner, 559–560; indebted for the whole paragraph.

77. *On Christian Doctrine* I.21.

78. *Letter* 28.

79. *Letter* 82.

80. Ibid.

81. Bonner, 556.

82. Cf. Brown, 252.

83. O. Loretz, *The Truth of the Bible*, trans. D. Bourke (New York: Herder and Herder, 1968), 5, quoting Sasse, "Sacra Scriptura—Bermerkungen zur Inspirationslehre Augustins", 262–73, in *Festschrift Franz Dornseiff*, the original of which was unavailable to me.

84. Bonner, 562 (citing *De Cons. Evang.* III.7.29).

85. TeSelle, *Augustine: the Theologian*, 346.

86. *Ibid.*, 345.

87. Brown, 252.

88. Bonner, 561.

89. R. McNally, *The Bible in the Early Middle Ages* (Westminster, MD: Newman), 42.

90. Bonner, 561.

91. Bonner, 544.

92. Bonner, 562–563.

AUGUSTINE ON MUSIC

AUGUSTINE ON MUSIC

William Jordan

Allusions to music may be found in many of Augustine's works. For example, in the *De Trinitate*, he likened the relationship between the God the Father and God the Son to the musical octave, which is obtained by dividing a vibrating string in half. And in the *Confessions* he compared our human ability to imagine a piece of music in one brief moment with God's knowledge of past, present and future. In numerous other instances music provided him with metaphor and simile, helping to clarify his arguments with respect to theological and philosophical matters.

Augustine also provided us with a treatise on music itself, and the philosophical and theological considerations found therein were employed to elucidate musical matters, rather than the other way around. Augustine's *De Musica* was distinctive among Medieval treatises on music insofar as it was concerned primarily with rhythm and metrics rather than harmonics. In this paper I propose to present what I take to be the heart of this treatise, and to show the importance it had for the music and philosophy of the later Middle Ages. As regards music, I would like to indicate how Augustine's treatise provided the theoretical framework for the rhythmic polyphony of the *Ars Antiqua* of twelfth century Paris. As regards philosophy, I would like to illustrate its influence on the writings of St. Bonaventure. I shall begin with a brief discussion of the philosophical and aesthetic precursors of this treatise in order to establish a sense of the intellectual context in which Augustine worked.

Many centuries before Augustine, Plato had been heavily influenced by Pythagoreanism, a music-based philosophy which held that numbers, and specifically musical ratios, lay at the base of everything in the universe. To the Pythagoreans, what was important about music was the mathematical structure they found in it, which they used as the basis of their cosmology. As we shall see, Augustine learned his number theory from the Pythagorean school. Shortly after Plato, Aristotle had put forward an alternative philosophy, the implications of which for music were formulated by his pupil Aristoxenus. Very generally, this Aristoxenian view held that what was important about music was its power to refine the sensibilities of Greek youth. The Platonic view survived in the *Timaeus*, which became the cornerstone for much Medieval speculative philosophy. The Aristoxenian view became the framework for a variety of rhetoricians, poets and scholars who today might be called aestheticians, people who concerned themselves with music as an artform rather than as the ground of a philosophical system. At the time Augustine wrote his treatise on music, both of these traditions were still competing for the attention of philosophers. Many of Augustine's near contemporaries can be observed choosing between the two. Augustine's treatise is important in this respect because in it, he presents a third choice, a view of music which subsumed both of these traditions under a new theory.

Other treatises from this period that bear the mark of the Pythagorean view (such as the *De Musica* of Boethius) seem to accept the reasoning of Plato's *Timaeus* in a straightforward way: music is a science of harmonics, and the numerical calculations of proportions have to do with pitch, or tuning theory. For example, the perfect fifth is obtained by dividing a string in the ratio 3:2, the whole tone is obtained by the ratio 9:8, and the semitone, or "Pythagorean comma" is obtained by a ratio of 256:243. But Augustine's use of the Pythagorean number theory was different, because he applied it to time lengths rather than to string lengths. His reason for doing this may be inferred from a passage near the end of the treatise, where he tells us that "the form changeable only in time is prior to that changeable both in time and place,"[1] or, in other words, rhythm is prior to extension. The consequences of Augustine's approach to Pythagorean thinking were twofold; 1) he was able to preserve a vast body of pagan lore, specifically the names grammarians give to poetic feet (which are found in Books II through V of the *De Musica*) and 2) he was able to invent a psychology based on continuity between perception, memory and judgment that is rooted in time and change, thereby enabling it to transcend the conventions of Hellenistic culture and speak to us today as clearly as it did to Bonaventure.

However distinctive it may be, Augustine's treatise was also clearly within the canon of Medieval treatments of music, for he regarded music as useful for uncovering vestiges left by the hand of the Creator, and saw the hierarchy of the chain of being as the model within which to conduct his search for them.

According to the canonical medieval view, all material manifestation below the sphere of the moon subdivided the celestial motion, which in turn flowed from the unity of the everlasting. Hence we experience years, months, days, hours, minutes and moments. Augustine believed that from the "short interval lengths which delight us in singing and dancing,"[2] it was possible to infer the larger cosmic cycles of universal order beyond the moon, where "the rational and intellectual numbers of the blessed and saintly souls [the angels] transmit the very law of God"[3] which no falling leaf breaks and by which the hairs on our heads are numbered. The proper end of the study of music was therefore to discover evidence of divine order as implied in the variety of ratios between time-lengths.

At the very outset of his treatise, Augustine distinguished between music and grammar, acknowledging that the names of musical rhythms were received from the grammarians. He did this by dismissing from consideration the acute accent, relegating it to the grammatical side of metrics, and by taking the names of rhythmic feet (pyrrhic, trochaic, iambic and the like) as descriptive of quantitative ratios, equally applicable to words and to the beats of a drum. Music he defined both as an art and as a science. For practical purposes, music is the business of measuring ratios between times. This is an art insofar as it requires an imitative movement on the part of the person taking the measurements, and therefore, insofar as it is an art it can be understood as the art of moving "in such a way that the movement is desired for itself, and for this reason charms through itself alone."[4] But because it is also a science, it must be based in reason, and not in mere imitation. The sense in which music is based in reason is explored in the remainder of the treatise. This "scientific" status which music must have is usually obscured because, for the most part, the music we hear is the result of mere imitation, practiced for long hours by professionals who seek praise for their skill rather than wisdom for themselves. There is, then, a science of music as well as an art, and Augustine takes great pains to distinguish them.

In his discussion of the science of music, Augustine first introduced his number theory, which forms the basis of the rest of the argument in the treatise. He first distinguished between tempo and ratio, arguing that "fast" and "slow" are not analogous to "for a short time" and "for a long time," because the latter pair can be quantified and subject to ratio.[5] The fallacy here would have been evident to him if he had had access to the modern metronome, a device that establishes precise ratios for "fast" and "slow" by determining beats per minute. But his point was not to quibble over terms; his conclusion is that "measure and limit [are] preferred to infinity and immeasurableness."[6] Taking this conclusion as his basic premise, he then worked through a number theory which he inherited directly from his Pythagorean forebears, introducing the theory of proportion based on aliquot parts, snubbing his nose at fractions or remainders, and distinguishing between connumerate, dinumerate, sesquate and complicate ratios. Continuing the Pythagorean protocol, he examined the relationship between the first four integers (one, two, three, and four) and their sum (ten). In the course of this discussion, he uncovered the basis of mathematical analogy in the progression from one to three, i.e., one plus three equals two squared, or the sum of the extremes equals the square of the mean. Ultimately, the point of all this was to rationalize the use of base ten as the operating system for mathematics without resorting to counting fingers. The conclusions were foregone, and the argument would have been very familiar to anyone who had delved into Pythagoreanism but for the fact, noted above, that Augustine was here discussing time-lengths and not string-lengths. The first book of his treatise concluded with the admonition that the study of music should proceed by examining the ratios implicit in poetry and language in order to find numerical proportion there.

Books Two through Five of Augustine's treatise are concerned with the analysis and naming of the huge variety of rhythmic feet known to the Hellenistic grammarians. This account is as thorough as it is uninteresting, but reading through it does give one a sense of the vastness of pagan culture in this period. At the outset of the sixth book of the treatise, Augustine himself dismissed all that had come before (Books I through V) as trivial and unimportant. However, it was precisely these five books of his treatise that were most influential on the musicians of twelfth-century Paris at the time of the invention of rhythmic polyphony. Looked at from the perspective of such composers as Leonin and Perotin, Books Two through Five of Augustine's treatise consist of a catalogue of rhythmic relationships. Augustine had analyzed Latin verses in terms of long and short time-lengths, and assigned quantitative ratios to rhythmic feet. The names given to these feet by the grammarians of the Hellenistic period were no longer important, but Augustine's labour was, as we shall now see.

The situation of the composer in the twelfth century was roughly as follows: there existed a huge body of plainchant which was notated as regards pitch, but not as regards rhythm. The notes which were placed over the words told the singers which pitch to sing, but the rhythm of plainchant was largely determined by convention. Furthermore, it had become the fashion in Paris and at other centers to perform elaborate tropes, or musical commentaries, on the original plainchant. This fashion was in keeping with the general scholastic tendency to gloss a text. The way it worked musically was as follows: while one singer or choir performed the original plainchant melody, another different melody was performed by a second singer or choir. This could be made to work fairly well, as long as there was a one-to-one relationship between the two voices. But in time, as the fashion caught on, composers felt the need to make their glosses more and more elaborate. The one-to-one relationship between the two parts was abandoned, and the problem of coordinating them became acute. For example, in any given piece of melismatic organum (the name given to such "tropes" of plainchant) there might be different numbers of notes performed over different syllables of the original plainchant melody; over the "vi-" of *Viderunt* there might be only two notes of "trope", while over the "der-" there might be three or more. In order to surmount this problem, composers had recourse to Augustine's treatise. They developed the different rhythmic modes, each based on the repetition of a different rhythmic foot conceived quantitatively. In this way they were able to control musical rhythms by directing a sequence of proportions, which is a very different way of going about it than the abstract system of meter and beat that we use today. Subsequent developments issuing from this breakthrough include Franco of Cologne's *Ars Cantis Mensurabilis*, which is the first full-blown treatise on rhythmic notation, and the whole of the *Ars Nova*, a philosophical mathematics which was based on the theory of numbers inherent in proportional musical rhythm. Ultimately, the whole polyphonic tradition in Western Europe can be traced back to the pioneering efforts of the composers of twelfth-century Paris, and their work in turn was based on Augustine's treatise. But Augustine had not conceived his treatise as a technical discussion of musical rhythm. The sixth and final book of the treatise remains for our consideration, and at the outset of that book the following prophetic passage occurs:

> If by chance the crowd from the schools, with tumultuous tongues taking vulgar delight in the noise of rhythm-dancers, should chance upon these writings, they will either despise all or consider these first five books sufficient. But this (the sixth) book, the very fruit of those is found in, they will either throw aside as not necessary, or put off as over and above the necessary.[7]

We have seen how books one through five were indeed taken up by musicians of a later period. We shall now undertake an exposition of Book Six, and see how it was influential in the later philosophical tradition.

In the course of Book Six, Augustine leads the reader through three general areas of discussion, which I propose to call musical psychology, musical aesthetic and ethic, and musical cosmology. The first of these discussions is by far the lengthiest and most complex, as well as the most influential on later thinkers. It presents a psychology which, to my knowledge, has no precursors. The discussion of musical aesthetic and ethic is couched in terms of the familiar virtues and vices, although there is in this discussion an admixture of neo-Platonic concern for beauty which deepens the argument considerably. The discussion of musical cosmology, although of great importance to later thinkers, is here treated rather briefly in ways which resonate with other works by Augustine, specifically the *Confessions*.

Augustine's musical psychology is an elaborate hierarchy of six levels of musical ratio and an explanation of the interconnections of this hierarchy. It is presented (as is the entire treatise) in dialogue form, and it is in this presentation that the dialectical procedure is most difficult to summarize, mainly because Augustine keeps revising the names of his categories. Rather than attempting a summary (and run the risk of confusion), I shall present the system that is more or less arrived at in the discussion in the hope that what is lost in dialectical persuasiveness is made up for in clarity. Some of the revisions in terminology will come to the surface when we examine the presentation of this hierarchy in the writings of Bonaventure.

The lowest echelon of musical ratio is that of the sounding numbers, proceeding from the instrument or the body. They serve as stimuli, but are characteristically imperfect and unequal. Next in the order of musical ratio are the memorial numbers, which reside in the memory but are brought forth to act in much the same way as the sounding numbers. These two types of ratio serve as the raw material of music, and are important only as such. The third category of musical ratio is that of the reacting numbers, which form in the soul in response to sounding or memorial numbers. The reacting numbers are the basis of recognition and identification of a familiar rhythm or melody held in the memory; when confronted with an unfamiliar, new piece of music, the reacting numbers are disposed in a new way, which is then committed to memory. The next category of musical ratio is that of the advancing numbers. They are produced by the soul as a structure for actions of all kinds; examples include breathing, heartbeat, scratching, chewing, digestion, dancing and singing. The advancing numbers are so named in order to distinguish them from the reacting numbers, which are formed passively in the soul. Augustine holds the advancing numbers to be the highest form of musical ratio involved in actual music, on the grounds that it is better to make music than to listen to it (things-making are better than things-made).

The four levels of Augustine's hierarchy so far discussed are sufficient to account for musical experience up to a point. Sounding ratios occur, we hear them and react to them, we commit them to memory and recall them, and we can produce them ourselves if we wish. But there are two more levels to Augustine's hierarchy which have to do with judgment, and it is on these that he spends the greater part of his argument. His discussion of judgment centers on the distinction between what we might call "style" and "truth," considering the issue from the modern vantage point. The importance of this distinction for Augustine stems from his rejection of the predominantly pagan character, or "style" of his world, and brings to mind his continuing war with the grammarians of the time.

Augustine frames the issue in the following way: when we hear a piece of music, we bring a judgment on what we hear that is informed by convention, fashion and taste. Judgments informed in this way enable us to distinguish what is good from what is bad, what is ugly from what is beautiful, etc., according to the criteria inherited from our culture. The numbers that regulate these judgments may be called the judicial numbers. But, as he reminds us, culture is ephemeral:

> It is not for nothing that custom is called a sort of second and fitted on nature. For we see new senses in the judging of this kind of thing, built up by custom, by another custom disappear.[8]

The sixth category, also concerned with judgment, is introduced as follows, in a passage I shall quote at length because of its eloquent summary of the entire hierarchy:

> When the verse *Deus Creator Omnium* is sung, we hear it through reacting numbers, recognize it through memorial numbers, pronounce it through advancing numbers, are delighted through judicial numbers, and appraise it by still others, and in accordance with these more hidden numbers we bring another judgment on this delight, a kind of judgment on the judicial numbers.[9]

> Therefore, if, as it is one thing to be moved to those things the body is passive to, and this is done in sensing; another, to move oneself to the body, and this is done in operating; another, to hold in the soul what is gotten from these motions, and that is to remember; so it is one thing to accept or reject these motions either when they are first produced or when revived by the memory, and this is done in the delight at the fitness or in the distaste at the absurdity of such movements or affections; and another thing to appraise whether they delight rightly or not, and this is done by reasoning—if all this is true, then we must admit these last are of two kinds. And if we have been right in our judgment, the very sense of delight could not have been favorable to equal intervals and rejected perturbed ones unless it itself were imbued with numbers; then too, the reason laid upon this delight cannot at all judge of the numbers it has under it without more powerful numbers. And if these things are true, it appears five kinds of numbers have been found in the soul, and when you add to these those corporeal numbers we have called sounding numbers, you will see six kinds of numbers in rank and order.[10]

Augustine's hierarchy of musical ratios is now complete. The sixth category of musical ratio, which he calls the numbers of reason, is constituted by pure number, the highest eternal form of number known only to reason. It is on the basis of this category that he holds out to us the prospect of transcending our culture. The whole reason for inventing a musical psychology was to lead the reader to an understanding of the fact that music can have an anagogic function. The contemplation of music leads us to the contemplation of the eternal.

Having established a psychology of music, Augustine proceeded to discuss what I have chosen to call musical aesthetic and ethic, which are indistinguishable in his presentation. Throughout the discussion, his concern for the beauty of music is balanced by his concern for the action of the cardinal virtues, which are discussed at length. He begins with a definition of prudence, which he calls "a motion of the soul by which it understands eternal things and counts temporal things below them even within itself."[11] This definition of prudence is followed by a description of what happens when prudence is overwhelmed by the seductiveness of music:

> Then the love of acting on the stream of its bodily passions turns the soul away from the contemplation of eternal things, diverting its attention [to] the care of sensible pleasure; it does this with reacting numbers. But the love of operating on bodies also turns it away, and makes it restless; this it does with advancing numbers. The phantasias and phantasms turn it away; these it does with memorial numbers. Finally, the love of the vainest knowledge of such things turns it away; this it does with sensible numbers, where lie rules of an art, as if glad in their imitation. And from these is born curiosity, by its very care an enemy of peace, and in its vanity impotent over truth.[12]

There follows a general discussion of pride and power, vices which obtain from preferring to imitate God rather than to serve him. As a result of this preference, the soul ends up enslaved by lower things which may be very beautiful.

Next, Augustine distinguished between ratio and mere order, and maintained that ratio can serve as the very basis of order when it is judged with reference to pure number. This distinction between ratio and order, although discussed very briefly in the treatise, was fundamental to the difference Augustine perceived between music and grammer in his time. As we have seen, musical ratio could be conceived scientifically, "rationally" if you like, according to models that seemed timeless and transcendental. To Augustine, this made musical ratio seem far superior to the arbitrary, alphabetic orderings favored by the grammarians. In the background of his distinction between ratio and order, then, lies Augustine's continuing war with the thinking of the grammarians, whose preoccupation with order rather than number, with grammar rather than music, seemed to Augustine to deny the immortal, transcendental capacity of the soul.

Finally, Augustine defined three virtues; temperance, fortitude, and justice, which along with prudence constitute the cardinal virtues. He defined temperance as the action of the soul by which it "extracts itself from the love of an inferior beauty by fighting and downing its own habit that wars against it." He defined fortitude as the disposition of the soul "when it advances along this way, divining eternal joys but not quite grasping them," undeterred by loss of temporal things, or deaths. Justice was "this ordering itself [of the soul], according to which it desires to be co-equal with only the purest souls and to have dominion only over animal and corporeal nature."[13] These three virtues, guided by prudence, serve the soul in its battle against the sins of pride.

In the final pages of his treatise, Augustine discusses what I have called musical cosmology. This discussion is an amplification of the passage quoted earlier in this paper, i.e., "the form changeable only in time is prior to that changeable both in time and place." It is an interesting argument, for here Augustine returns to his basic premises with respect to creation and time. He gives two analogies for creation, that of the carpenter and that of the tree. The carpenter works rhythmically, through the rhythms of his habit informed by the "numbers of reason" which lie behind his art. That is to say, he works in time-spans, and only by doing so can he "fashion visible forms in wood numbered with place-spans."[14] As for the tree,

> The time numbers of a tree must precede its place numbers. For there's no stem that does not in fixed time measures spring up to replace its seed, germinate, break out into the air, unfold its leaves, become strong, and bring back either fruit or, by very subtle numbers of the wood itself, the force of the seed.[15]

These two analogies are followed by a recapitulation of the Pythagorean progression from one to four, enumerating as follows; first, the indivisible point, second the length, or line, third the breadth, and fourth the height to complete the extended body. The final phase of the argument maintains that,

> All these things we have enumerated with the help of the carnal senses, and all things in them, can only receive and hold local numbers (place numbers) seemingly in a kind of rest, if temporal numbers, in motion, precede within and in silence.[16]

In effect, then, Augustine's line of argument in his musical cosmology is to demonstrate that extension depends upon temporality, that time is logically and existentially prior to space. If in view of this we consider the eternal nature of the creator-God, it becomes clear that our universe was made out of nothing, which is the point Augustine wanted to make all along. The eternal God does not suffer time; rather, time is a part of creation, from which springs the extended cosmos. According to Augustine, it could not be otherwise.

This line of reasoning became commonplace in Medieval thought, and it is tempting to dwell here at length on parallel passages between Augustine's *Confessions* and Bonaventure's *Breviloquium*, particularly those passages which use music as a metaphor for cosmic order, describing the universe as a poem or song. But my point in bringing Bonaventure into this paper has to do with the influence of Augustine's treatise on music itself, so I shall restrict my discussion to that area.

In the *Itinerarium Mentis in Deum* Bonaventure turns to the classical Medieval idea that things regarded in terms of their weight, number and measure provide insight into vestiges of divine will and order. But the *Itinerarium* does not regard all of the mathematical sciences found in the *quadrivium* equally; musical science is singled out as the source of the primary vestiges, for the world according to Bonaventure is essentially rhythmical. The emphasis on music is framed within a direct allusion to Augustine's *De Musica*, and provides the best evidence of the force of this treatise in the later Middle Ages.

> For he [Augustine] says that numbers are in bodies and especially in sounds and words, and he calls these sonorous. Some are abstracted from these and received into our senses, and these he calls heard. Some proceed from the soul into the body, as appears in gestures and bodily movements, and these he calls uttered. Some are in the pleasures of the senses which arise from attending to the species which have been received, and these he calls sensual. Some are retained in the memory, and these he calls remembered. Some are the bases of our judgments about all these, and these he calls judicial, which, as has been said above, necessarily transcend our minds because they are infallible and incontrovertible. By these there are imprinted on our minds the artificial numbers which Augustine does not include in this classification because they are connected with the judicial numbers from which flow the uttered numbers out of which are created the numerical forms of those things made by art. Hence, from the highest through the middle to the lowest, there is an ordered descent. Thence do we ascend step by step from the sonorous numbers by means of the uttered, the sensual, and the remembered.

> Since, therefore, all things are beautiful and in some way delightful, and beauty and delight do not exist apart from proportion, and proportion is primarily in number, it needs must be that all things are rhythmical. And for this reason, number is the outstanding exemplar in the mind of the Maker, and in things it is the outstanding trace leading to wisdom. Since this is most evident to all and closest to God, it leads most directly to God. It causes Him to be known in all corporeal and sensible things while we apprehend the rhythmical, delight in rhythmical proportions, and through the laws of rhythmical proportions judge irrefragably.[17]

We recognize in this passage all the elements of Augustine's musical psychology; the sounding numbers, the reacting, or heard numbers, the advancing or uttered numbers, the numbers of convention and fashion (which we called the judicial numbers), called by Bonaventure the sensual numbers, the numbers in the memory, and those numbers that Bonaventure called the judicial numbers (which we called the numbers of reason), which in their perfection transcend our imaginations. Bonaventure, however, is comfortable adding a seventh category, which he calls the artificial numbers. This seventh type of number channels the highest judicial numbers, the numbers of reason, through the labour of the artisan into the finished work of art. Because of this seventh category, Bonaventure is able to look at the artworks of his time and find in them not simply vestiges, but actual images of divine reason. Whereas Augustine had consigned the pagan artworks of his time to a low status, that of seductive diversion from true number, Bonaventure welcomes the Christian icons of his world as exemplars of the same true number. The difference may be no more than the difference between the two men, but it may also be a difference in the times. After all, Augustine was up against a pagan culture he wished to supplant, while Bonaventure was comfortable in a Christian culture he wished to conserve.

By way of a conclusion, I should point out that Augustine's treatise has not fared so well since the end of the Middle Ages. Two parallel developments seem to have conspired to relegate it to a position of relative nonimportance for both musicians and philosophers. In the first place, the very development of rhythmic polyphony, which this treatise facilitated so enormously, eventually led to what Augustine would have considered a perverse preoccupation with sonorous numbers; polyphony after the demise of the *Ars Antiqua* and *Ars Nova* became rhythmically simpler and considerably more luscious and sensual. In two giant steps we may survey this development; the first is to the style of Palestrina, the so-called "Counter-Reformation" style, the second is to the music of late Romanticism, for instance the tone poems of Richard Strauss. Along with this development of the sheer sound of the music came a lowered sense of its value as an indicator of something else. Palestrina's church music is very beautiful, but what it indicates is the presence of voices singing in a space as empty as that seen in a doll-house Renaissance painting. Strauss's tone-poems convey a revelling in sensuality unthinkable prior to the development of very sophisticated harmonic processes which themselves are based on considering music as a spatial art, extended within our imaginations. The philosophical developments that have contributed to the neglect of this treatise are better known; although it is true that some forms of Pythagorean thinking survived into the seventeenth century (Kepler's *Harmonices Mundi* is the last great example), by and large the business of wishing to see the universe in terms of musical numbers had given way to the more instrumental designs of the modern period by the time the Renaissance was over.

But the beauty of Augustine's treatise is that in reading it today, we can see into the mind of the early Middle Ages with great clarity. Anyone who can count from one to four can follow the argument, and it brings together the great mysteries—time and the universe—with simple, familiar experiences of music.

Dr. William Jordan, composer, comes from Georgia. He received his Bachelor of Music degree from the University of Georgia in 1971. After a summer with Nadia Boulanger at Fountainbleau (1971), he studied composition at the University of Pennsylvania with George Crumb and George Rochberg (M.A. 1973). He continued his studies at Florida State University, where he completed a Ph.D. degree in Music Theory (1976) under the direction of Alan Thomas. He is currently an Associate Professor of Music Theory and Composition at the University of Calgary, where he has taught since 1978. He has composed a large number of works, including music for solo piano, dance, an opera *The Injustice Done to Tommie Tucker*, sacred and secular choral works, music for strings, winds, guitar, works for chamber ensembles, three large works for band and over thirty songs. His orchestral works include a piano concerto, pieces for string orchestra, the concert *Children's Games*, and *Symphonic Fantasy*, a large symphonic work.

NOTES

1. VI, 44. All references are to Augustine, *De Musica*, trans. Robert Catesby Taliaferro (New York: The Fathers of the Church, 1947).

2. I, 28.

3. VI, 58.

4. I, 3.

5. I, 13.

6. I, 15.

7. VI, 1.

8. VI, 19.

9. VI, 23

10. VI, 24.

11. VI, 37

12. VI, 39.

13. VI, 50.

14. VI, 57.

15. VI, 57.

16. VI, 58.

17. *Itinerarium Mentis in Deum*, 19.

LOVE AS RHETORICAL PRINCIPLE: THE RELATIONSHIP BETWEEN CONTENT AND STYLE IN THE RHETORIC OF ST. AUGUSTINE

LOVE AS RHETORICAL PRINCIPLE: THE RELATIONSHIP BETWEEN CONTENT AND STYLE IN THE RHETORIC OF ST. AUGUSTINE

Christine Mason Sutherland

The importance of St. Augustine in the history of rhetoric can hardly be over-estimated. Originating in Sicily in the fifth century B.C., rhetoric soon became a popular study in Athens—popular enough to engage the attention of Plato, and also of Aristotle, who put it on a firm theoretical base. Isocrates, who opened what became a highly prestigious school of rhetoric, developed a sound curriculum of rhetorical studies; and it is largely owing to him that the art survived the decline of Athens to be taken over later by the Romans and made an important part of their educational system. By the time of Cicero, most of the theories of classical rhetoric had been established. For example, the three modes of persuasion, first identified by Aristotle: ethos, the character of the speaker; logos, the rational arguments; and pathos, the emotional appeal. Since the time of Aristotle, rhetoric had become an art with five clearly distinguished parts: inventio, the selection of content; dispositio, organization or arrangement; elocutio, or style, the choice of words and sentence structures; memoria, the art of remembering the prepared speech; and finally, pronunciatio, the art of delivery.

In Augustine's time, the study of rhetoric was inseparable from the study of the great works of classical literature, both Greek and Roman. And of course this characteristic inevitably meant that it was regarded with some suspicion by certain Christians. St. Jerome, for example, perceived his delight in pagan literature as temptation to be resisted. In the epistle to Eustochium, he records the dream in which he finds himself before the judgement seat: he pleads that he is a Christian, but is told: "You lie. You are a Ciceronian, not a Christian." Part of Jerome's problem is that he thinks of pagan literature as the work of devils: "We ought not," he says, "to drink both the cup of Christ and that of devils." But there is a more insidious problem too: after the polished style of Cicero, he finds the style of the prophets revolting.[1]

Moreover, the Christians were not at all sure that the human study of eloquence was legitimate. For example, in I Corinthians 2:4, St. Paul says: "My speech and my preaching was not with enticing words of man's wisdom, but in demonstration of the spirit and of power." And in Mark 13:11, Christ is recorded as having said: "But when they shall lead you and deliver you up, take no thought before hand what ye shall speak, neither do ye premeditate: but whatsoever shall be given you in that hour, that speak ye: for it is not ye that speak, but the Holy Ghost."

Considering these reservations about the acceptability of rhetoric, it is remarkable that it survived the collapse of the Roman empire and the passing of the pagan culture. It is largely owing to the influence of Augustine, himself a professor of rhetoric before his conversion, that it did survive, and indeed became an important part of the trivium. Many of its theories were retained not only throughout the middle ages, but even into the nineteenth century. It may therefore be said that Augustine prolonged the life of rhetoric by some fifteen hundred years—no mean achievement. And with its revival in this century, his influence is again being felt. For example, Kenneth Burke's *The Rhetoric of Religion: Studies in Logology* is in large part a study of the rhetoric of Augustine.[2]

Yet what Augustine believed and taught about rhetoric has often been misunderstood ever since his own time. For example, George Kennedy in *Classical Rhetoric and Its Christian and Secular Tradition* suggests that the fourth book of Augustine's treatise, *De Doctrina Christiana*, encouraged the identification of rhetoric with style.[3] That his work was so interpreted I do not dispute. But the fact that it was is strange in view of the whole tendency of ideas about discourse as we find them not only in the *De Doctrina*, but also in the *Confessions*. For if there is one thing that emerges more clearly than anything else from these works—so far as rhetoric is concerned—it is Augustine's deep conviction that there can be no separation between style and content; such disjunction, it seems to me, was considered by Augustine to be a disunity belonging to the province of evil. The identification of rhetoric with style was characteristic, not of Augustine, but of the rhetoric of the Second Sophistic, the period in which he lived. At this time there was little opportunity for orators to influence the course of public decision–making by their speeches. They therefore turned their attention more and more to the niceties of style, and less and less to the subject matter of their speeches and to the profit that the audience might derive from them. It is this rhetoric of the Second Sophistic, in which he himself had been trained, that Augustine attacks in the *Confessions*. To quote

James Murphy (the authority on medieval rhetoric): "His firm espousal of a union between meaning and expression marks his rejection of the sophistic."[4] Yet Augustine's insistence upon the indivisibility of style and content was in fact overlooked or ignored, and his authority was used to promulgate ideas about rhetoric which run counter to everything he most deeply believed about it. To quote James Murphy again:

> It was...left to other men, without the rich personal heritage of Augustine's own familiarity with Roman education, to carry on the tradition he espoused. It is not surprising that in some ways this continuation developed in ways different from what he would have preferred, even though his name was used as a seal of approval."[5]

If it is true, as Murphy asserts, that for Augustine content and style are inseparable, how did such a profound misunderstanding arise? And perhaps even more important, why does it persist even today? For it does persist. Augustine scholars still cannot agree about the matter. In its present form, the disagreement centres upon the question of the subject of *De Doctrina Christiana*: some scholars believe that only the fourth book of this work has to do with rhetoric; others contend that the whole work is a Christian rhetoric.

For example, Gerald Fulkerson, in a footnote to an article in the summer issue of the *Rhetoric Society Quarterly*, 1985, has this to say:

> Some interpreters of *De Doctrina* refer to the whole work as a rhetoric and to Books 1–3 as Augustine's contribution to a theory of invention for the Christian preacher.... Augustine's own conception, however, is clearly different. He does not conceive of Books 1–3 as part of a theory of ecclesiastical rhetoric, partly, perhaps, because he largely restricts preceptive rhetoric to matters of style."[6]

Gerald Press, however, (to whose work Fulkerson refers in the same footnote) argues that the whole of the work is a Christian rhetoric. He bases his argument on Augustine's own use of the expression "tractatio scripturarum," pointing out that "tractatio" is "a traditional term in the vocabulary of classical rhetoric."[7]

Press's contention is, I believe, further strengthened by Augustine's own use of the term "modus inveniendi" to describe the first three books of *De Doctrina Christiana*.[8] *Inventio* is recognized by Cicero as the first part of rhetoric, and Augustine, who studied Cicero's rhetoric and indeed based much of his own upon it, cannot have missed the implication of using the expression.

Yet although Augustine sufficiently implies, I think, that he is speaking of rhetoric in the earlier books of *De Doctrina Christiana*, by his use of rhetorical terms like "modus inveniendi" and "tractatio" it is true that he uses the word rhetoric mostly, if not exclusively, when he is discussing style. Hence, perhaps, the confusion. This apparent inconsistency can, I believe, be explained if we bear in mind the audience to whom Augustine was writing. In using the word "rhetoric," Augustine had to take into account what the word meant to the audience of his own day; and to them it meant the debased rhetoric of the Second Sophistic, a rhetoric concerned almost exclusively with style. It seems, indeed, that rhetoric had two meanings for Augustine, and he rather confusingly uses both of them. First, there is his own understanding of the term, his personal definition of it. When he uses the word in this sense, he praises and defends rhetoric. But second there is rhetoric in the sense in which his audience understood it, the rhetoric of the Second Sophistic. And for such rhetoric he has nothing but contempt. This ambiguity in Augustine's own use of the word has led some scholars to assume that Augustine was against rhetoric *in toto*. But this is disproved by his own defence of it in Book 4 of *De Doctrina Christiana*. The rhetoric from which Murphy says he was converted to Christianity was sophistic rhetoric, not rhetoric proper.[9]

And it was precisely the sophistic divorce of style from content of which he felt he must repent. He tells us that his father wished only that he should have "a fertile tongue."[10] And in complaining about the immoral content of pagan literature, like Plato before him, he says of words: "They are like choice and costly glasses but they contain the wine of error."[11] Indeed, the fact that Augustine despised and disliked his profession as a teacher of rhetoric has sometimes, I think, obscured the important role played by rhetorical considerations in his conversion. The account he gives in the *Confessions* of the changes in his attitude to various philosophies and Christian heresies is closely paralleled by changes in his understanding of the nature and function of words. Rather than accepting Murphy's conclusion that he was converted from rhetoric to Christianity, I would contend that his conversion to Christianity was bound up with a concurrent conversion from the false to the true rhetoric. Often throughout the *Confessions*, the sin of which he accuses himself is a sin against words (and therefore a sin against *the* Word, the second person of the Trinity). And more often than not, it is the sin of divorcing style from meaning. His conversion may be said to have begun with his reading of Cicero. Here is what he says about it:

> It was my ambition to be a good speaker for the unhallowed and inane purpose of gratifying human vanity. The prescribed course of study brought me to a work by an author named Cicero, whose writing nearly everyone admires, if not the spirit of it. The title of the book is *Hortensius* and it recommends the reader to study philosophy. It altered my outlook on life. It changed my prayers to you, O Lord, and provided me with new hopes and aspirations. All my empty dreams suddenly lost their charms and my heart began to throb with a bewildering passion for the wisdom of eternal truth. I began to climb out of the depths to which I had sunk, in order to return to you. For I did

not use the book as a whetstone to sharpen my tongue. It was not the style of it but the contents which won me over, and yet the allowance which my mother paid me was supposed to be spent on putting an edge on my tongue."[12]

At the beginning of his search for the truth, then, he is drawn from a concern with mere words to a serious consideration of content. Yet even towards the end of his search he is still making the old mistake. Of St. Ambrose, whom he met in Milan, where he held his last post as a professor of rhetoric, he says: "I listened attentively when he preached to the people, though not with the proper intention; for my purpose was to judge for myself whether the reports of his powers as a speaker were accurate, or whether eloquence flowed from him more, or less readily than I had been told."[13] He adds that he was contemptuous of Ambrose's subject matter. Yet during his search for the truth he had already begun to learn to reject the sophistic ideas about the relationship— or lack of it—between style and content, and he attributes this change in his understanding directly to God:

> But in your wonderful secret way, my God, you had already taught me that a statement is not necessarily true because it is wrapped in fine language or false because it is awkwardly expressed.... You had already taught me this lesson and the converse truth, that an assertion is not necessarily true because it is badly expressed or false because it is finely spoken."[14]

Again and again, Augustine associates sinfulness with an abuse of words: and on nearly every occasion the abuse has to do with the divorce of style from meaning. He condemns the heretics because the names of the Father, the Son and the Holy Ghost "were always on the tips of their tongues but only as sounds which they mouthed aloud, for in their hearts they had no inkling of the truth."[15] He also condemns himself for his early view of the scriptures as "quite unworthy of comparison with the stately prose of Cicero,"[16] and complains of himself that he was "words, all words."[17] He even associates God's vengeance with his own betrayal of the powers of language: "I tried only to please and not to teach—that is why you broke my bones with the rod of your discipline."[18]

But his eventual conversion did not, as has too often been assumed, imply a rejection of words, of eloquence. God indeed put an end to his profession as a mere "vendor of words,"[18] but not to his use of eloquence.[19] That the conversion of Augustine the man involved also the conversion of Augustine the rhetorician is sufficiently implied in his phrase, "you rescued my tongue."[20]

In his final position on the nature of the relationship between style and content Augustine, as Murphy shows, avoids two possible extremes, which Murphy calls the Sophistic and the Platonic heresies.[21] It is not particularly remarkable that he avoided the Sophistic heresy, that of believing that virtue resides in style regardless of content; many other eminent Christians of his time reached the same conclusion. But it is significant that, unlike many other ecclesiastical writers of the fourth century, he did not fall into the opposite error, that content alone is the criterion of judgement and style does not matter. In itself, Augustine comes to believe, style is neutral. But it is not irrelevant. Style without content, or style that transmits immoral or untrue content, may well be vicious; but content ill expressed is feeble and ineffective. If one had to choose between content and style, one would choose content. But the point is that one does not have to choose: the content of the truth can and should be expressed in such a way as to make that truth operative. At the beginning of Book 4 of *De Doctrina Christiana*, Augustine eloquently pleads for the necessity of style as a means, not as an end:

> For since by means of the art of rhetoric both truth and falsehood are urged, who would dare to say that truth should stand in the person of its defenders unarmed against lying, so that they who wish to urge falsehoods may know how to make their listeners benevolent, or attentive, or docile in their presentation, while the defenders of truth are ignorant of that art? Should they speak briefly, clearly, and plausibly while the defenders of the truth speak so that they tire their listeners, make themselves difficult to understand and what they have to say dubious? Should they oppose the truth with fallacious arguments and assert falsehoods, while the defenders of truth have no ability either to defend the truth or to oppose the false? Should they, urging the minds of their listeners into error, ardently exhort them, moving them by speech so that they terrify, sadden, and exhilarate them, while the defenders of truth are sluggish, cold, and somnolent? Who is so foolish as to think this to be wisdom?[22]

As this passage clearly implies, Augustine's guiding principle in rhetoric, as in all else, is love. The use of eloquence is legitimate, not because it is good in itself, but because its proper use promotes faith, and faith leads to love. Towards the end of Book 1 of *De Doctrina Christiana*, Augustine gives us the principle that guides all he has to say about the interpretation of scripture and the use of pagan learning:

> The sum of all we have said since we began to speak of things thus comes to this: it is to be understood that the plenitude and end of the law and of all the sacred scriptures is the love of a Being which is to be enjoyed and of a being that can share enjoyment with us, since there is no need for a precept that anyone should love himself. That we might know this and have the means to implement it, the whole temporal dispensation was made by divine Providence for our salvation. We should use it, not with an abiding but with a transitory love and delight, like that in a road or in vehicles or in other instruments, or, if it may be expressed more accurately, so that we love those

things by which we are carried along for the sake of that toward which we are carried.[23]

This is the principle of love by which Augustine decides what in pagan culture is to be retained and what is to be rejected. It is also, I believe, the principle which he applies to rhetoric, and I want to demonstrate in some detail that this is so. But first I want to point out the implications of this principle of love on the question of the essential unity of style and content. For Augustine sees unity as an essential characteristic of goodness, and particularly of love. In the *Confessions* he writes:

I loved the peace that virtue brings and hated the discord that comes of vice. From this I concluded that in goodness there was unity, but in evil disunion of some kind. It seemed to me that this unity was the seat of the rational mind and was the natural state of truth and perfect goodness; whereas the disunion consisted of irrational life...and was the natural state of the ultimate evil.[24]

The relationship of unity specifically to love and also to discourse, to rhetoric, is made clear in the Prologue to *De Doctrina Christiana*:

Charity itself, which holds men together in a knot of unity, would not have a means of infusing souls and almost mixing them together if men could teach nothing to men.[25]

He goes on to make the point that when God wished to enlighten the Ethiopian eunuch, He did not send an angel from heaven, but Philip the Evangelist, to explain to him what was hidden in that scripture in (as Augustine puts it) "human words and discourse."[26]

So far from isolating one part of rhetoric, that is, style, and making it the whole, the effect of Augustine's work was—or at least, should have been—to give to rhetoric a consistency, a unity, which it lacked in the Second Sophistic. If we now look in some detail at Augustine's theory of rhetoric, we shall see that what he has to say about it is, at every point, guided by the principle of charity, both where he reaffirms traditional theory and where he changes it.

In the first three books of *De Doctrina Christiana* in general, and in the third book in particular, Augustine deals with the interpretation of scripture. Here he gives us a Christian version of the first part of rhetoric, inventio. In classical rhetoric, this was dependent upon, and to some extent overlapped with, dialectic. It consisted of finding arguments which would be successful in persuading a particular audience. In the work of Aristotle and Cicero, some of the advice given on this subject sounds a little cynical to modern ears. The absolute standard of truth seems to be missing. This is partly because rhetoric characteristically dealt with probability rather than with verifiable truth; nonetheless, it sometimes seems as if the ancient rhetoricians defined probability not as what is probably true, but as what will probably appeal to the audience. Much depends upon the skill of the orator in choosing convincing arguments, and much credit, therefore, reflects upon him if he makes the right choices.

For Augustine, all this is changed. The orator is not the creator of the message he gives, but only its vehicle. He is the channel along which the love of God flows out to man. Much, therefore, depends upon his power of receiving the right message in the first place. As George Kennedy points out, exegesis comes to replace dialectic in Christian rhetoric.[27] And exegesis, for Augustine, is no easy matter. In Book 12 of the *Confessions*, he argues at some length the impossibility of knowing exactly what was Moses' intent when he gave the account of Creation in Genesis 1:

> The truths which those words contain appear to different inquirers in a different light, and of all the meanings that they can bear, which of us can lay his finger upon one and say that it is what Moses had in mind and what he meant us to understand by his words?[28]

He thus anticipates certain modern literary theories by nearly sixteen hundred years.

How then is the problem of interpretation to be solved? Augustine believes that any interpretation may be acceptable if it is consistent with the principle of love:

> Whatever Moses meant in his books, unless we believe he meant it to be understood in the spirit of these two precepts of charity [love of God and of one's neighbour] we are treating God as a liar, for we attribute to his servant thoughts at variance with his teaching.[29]

Similarly, in *De Doctrina Christiana*, he give this advice:

> Therefore in the consideration of the figurative expressions a rule such as this will serve, that what is read should be subjected to diligent scrutiny until an interpretation contributing to the reign of charity is produced.[30]

Not only the message of the orator, but also his image, his *ethos*, as the classical rhetoricians called it, must be consistent with love. Unlike Aristotle, but like Isocrates, Augustine believes in the fundamental importance of extrinsic ethos, the reputation the speaker already has before he begins to speak: "The life of the speaker has greater weight in determining whether he is obediently heard than any grandness of eloquence."[31] So far as intrinsic ethos, is concerned—that is, the character of the speaker as it emerges in the course of the speech itself—Augustine does not so much bring a new idea into rhetorical theory as rediscover an ancient one and raise it to an altogether higher level. In classical rhetoric, it was felt to be important that the orator should appear to have intelligence, integrity, and goodwill towards his audience: he would then be listened to attentively, receptively and benevolently. And according to Quintilian, the best way to *appear* to have these qualities was *genuinely* to have them.[32] Apparently this noble ideal had become somewhat corrupted by Augustine's time in the Second Sophistic; Augustine himself seems to believe that most orators of his time were motivated by nothing more admirable than a desire to overwhelm their audiences by a flood of eloquence, and thus gain glory for themselves. Nevertheless, the ideal of benevolence, a genuine concern for the welfare of the audience, had been present in classical theory.

But the benevolence of the classical virtues is only a pale foreshadowing of the principle of love as preached by Augustine. Mere well-wishing in terms of worldly advantage is as nothing compared with the intensity of divine love which motivates the Christian orator. For this love—the love of the neighbour—though it is felt by the orator for his audience, does not originate with him; it derives from God.

This deep concern for the welfare—the eternal welfare—of the audience informs everything that Augustine has to say about the relationship between the speaker and those who hear him. It is responsible for many of the changes that he makes in classical theory, and also for a new kind of emphasis, a redistribution of priorities.

For example, the question of correctness: correctness of diction was of paramount importance for the classical rhetoricians. Although it strictly belonged to the province of the grammarian rather than to that of the rhetorician, it was important enough for Quintilian to pay attention to it, and to recommend that parents who wished their son to achieve the heights of oratory should be careful to choose for their child a nurse who spoke excellent Latin, so that he might never have anything but the best models of speech from the cradle.[33] But for Augustine, with his concern for his audience, correctness is of less importance than clarity. "Good teachers have such a desire to teach that if a word in good Latin is ambiguous or obscure, the vulgar manner of speech is used, so that ambiguity or obscurity may be avoided and the expression is not that of the learned but the unlearned."[34] Correctness must not be allowed to become an end in itself: "What profits correctness in a speech which is not followed by the listeners, when there is no reason for speaking, if what is said is not understood by those on whose account we speak?"[35]

Concern for the welfare of the audience also governs the principle of concession. The theory itself is retained, but the reasons for its use are turned upside-down. In classical rhetoric, concession was a way of spiking the guns of the opponent, of rendering his arguments innocuous by anticipating them and refuting them in advance. Augustine too believes in refuting opposing arguments in advance, but not so that the orator may win his case or humiliate his opponent; rather, lest an objection occur to one "who is silent about it so that he goes away with less benefit."[36]

Augustine's concern about the silent learner is also evident in the comments he makes about feedback, and about the fourth part of rhetoric, *memoria*:

> In a conversation anyone may ask questions. But where all are silent that one may be heard, and all are intent upon him, it is neither customary nor proper that anyone inquire about what he does not understand. For this reason the teacher should be especially careful to assist the silent learner. However, an attentive crowd eager to comprehend usually shows by its motions whether it understands, and until it signifies comprehension, the matter being discussed should be considered and expressed in a variety of ways. But this technique may not be used by those who have prepared what they have to say and memorized it word for word.[37]

More important than fluency, which may gain admiration for the orator, is flexibility, ongoing accommodation to the needs of a particular audience.

The passage I have just quoted makes clear Augustine's attitude to *copia*, the glory of the Ciceronian orator. *Copia* is to be used only in so far as it contributes to understanding, and not for mere display. "A speaker who insists on what is already known is burdensome, at least to those whose whole expectation depends on a solution of the difficulties in the matter being discussed."[38]

This last comment illuminates for us the fact that it is not only the purpose, and therefore the practice, of the orator which have changed; the expectations of the audience have changed too. *Copia* was thought to delight ancient audiences because of its display of the fertility of the orator's powers of invention. It moved the audience to delight in sheer eloquence for its own sake. But the Christian audience has a more serious purpose. Not only the Christian speaker, but also the Christian audience, is dominated by the love of God. Those who listen do not wish to be merely pleased, or even persuaded; above all, they want to *know*. Because they love God, they want to know more about him. This has obvious implications for the Augustinian theory of style, which I shall discuss later. But it also has implications for the Christian theory of the relationship between the speaker and the audience and to pathos, the emotional appeal. Again, we see the transcendence, almost the apotheosis, of the old theory: that an orator who demonstrates benevolence to his audience will stimulate benevolence towards himself among his hearers. Now we are dealing not with mere benevolence, but with Christian love. And so important is this love that it becomes the prerequisite for communication. As Augustine says in the *Confessions*: "Although I cannot prove to [my readers] that my confessions are true, at least I shall be believed by those whose ears are opened to me by charity."[39] And later in the same passage: "Charity which makes them good tells them that I do not lie about myself when I confess what I am, and it is this charity in them which believes me."

If it is at least in part the love of God operating in the audience which gives the speaker his credibility, it is also the love of God, rather than the love of eloquence, which motivates the listeners to attend. And it is this change in the motivation of the audience, together with the speaker's answering love for them, which is the principle behind Augustine's total reorganization of the classical theory of style.

Traditionally, since before the time of Cicero, three styles had been recognized by classical rhetoricians: the high, or grand style; the middle or temperate style; and the low or subdued style. Which of them the speaker used in any given passage depended on the subject matter. The grand style was used for important matters; it was also used for outright persuasion, when the audience was to be moved to take action. The low style was used for trivial or subsidiary matters, such as money, and the temperate for those in between, particularly for attributing praise or blame. But in Christianity, the grounds for deciding what is trivial have wholly changed. Indeed, Augustine argues in the fourth book of *De Doctrina Christiana*, that for the Christian preacher, nothing—nothing, that is, that he will consider it appropriate to preach about—can be designated trivial:

> In legal questions, those things are called small which are concerned in cases involving money; they are called great when they have to do with human welfare or life.... Among our orators, however, everything we say, especially when we speak to people from the pulpit, must be referred, not to the temporal welfare of man but to his eternal welfare and to the avoidance of eternal punishment, so that everything we say is of great importance, even to the extent that pecuniary matters....should not be considered small when they are discussed by the Christian teacher."[40]

He goes on to quote St. Paul in the first Epistle to the Corinthians, 6: 1–9, where the apostle is, as he says, "speaking of worldly cases," which are in themselves small things. But, as Augustine points out, he speaks of them in the grand manner:

> Dare any of you, having a matter against another, go to law before the unjust, and not before the saints? Do ye not know that the saints shall judge the world? And if the world shall be judged by you, are ye unworthy to judge the smallest matters? Know ye not that we shall judge angels? How much more things that pertain to this life? If then ye have judgments of things pertaining to this life, set them to judge who are least esteemed in the church. I speak to your shame. Is it so, that there is not a wise man among you? No, not one that shall be able to

judge between his brethren? But brother goeth to law with brother, and that before the unbelievers. Now therefore there is utterly a fault among you, because ye go to law with one another. Why do ye not rather take wrong? Why do ye not rather suffer yourselves to be defrauded? Nay, ye do wrong and defraud, and that your brethren.

Why did St. Paul use the grand style in this passage? According to Augustine, "he did this on account of justice, charity and piety, which are great, even in the smallest things."[41]

This almost total lack of trivial matter for the ecclesiastical orator does not, however, imply that he should confine himself to the grand style. Far from it. For of the three styles, it is the subdued which is the most appropriate for teaching, and, for the Christian, teaching is by far the most important of the three reasons for making a speech, as they were understood in classical theory: to teach, to please and to persuade. Thus Augustine effects a complete reversal of the status of the three styles. The grand style had been the particular favourite of the classical orators, not only because it was used to speak of the most important matters, but also because it allowed full scope to their rhetorical skills, rather like a cadenza in a concerto. But for the Christian, it is not the most important style; indeed, ideally it will not be necessary to use it at all. It will not be necessary because what moves the Christian is not eloquence, but truth; not the style but the content of the speech.

Perhaps when necessary things are learned they [the audience] may be so moved by a knowledge of them that it is not necessary to move them further by greater powers of eloquence....Sometimes when the truth is demonstrated in speaking, an action which pertains to the function of teaching, eloquence is neither brought into play nor is any attention paid to whether the matter or the discourse is pleasing, yet the matter itself is pleasing when it is revealed, simply because it is true.[42]

In this way, language can become pleasing not because of the stylistic devices used, but because the delight of the message is associated with the words in which the message is heard: "The very language in which this is demonstrated to be true delights."[43] And the style "excites such acclamations that it is hardly recognized as being subdued."[44]

But this ideal situation does not always, or indeed, often obtain. It is therefore necessary for the ecclesiastical orator to use the temperate or even the grand style when the audience, having understood the message, is not yet moved to put it into practice. And so we come back to love—the love of the Christian preacher for those who listen to him, and his concern that they shall both understand and put into practice the love they hear him preach. So great is the necessity for such teaching that Augustine defines communication in terms of it: "I hear your voice, O Lord, telling me that only a master who really teaches us really speaks to us; if he does not teach us, even though he may be speaking, it is not to us that he speaks."[45]

And it is this principle of consideration of the audience that governs the use of the higher styles. "What does the orator desire but to be believed? And who would wish to hear him unless he could retain his listener with some sweetness of discourse?"[46]

It may appear at first glance that this passage contradicts the earlier one in which Augustine argues that the truth itself is sufficiently moving without the powers of eloquence. But in fact he is considering different audiences. For the fully sanctified Christian, eloquence may indeed not be necessary. But already in Augustine's time, and increasingly throughout his life, there were also nominal Christians, those who found it advantageous from a worldly point of view to adopt the faith. For these too Augustine is concerned, and for them he is prepared to advocate the use of all the resources of eloquence, should these be necessary.

So we come back to love; and we also come back to unity—unity not only of style and content, but unity also among the three styles so sharply distinguished in classical rhetoric. Different though they may be in form, they have now a common purpose:

> Now when it is necessary to move and bend the listener by means of the grand style (which is necessary when he will confess that the speech is true and agreeable but will not do what it says should be done), one must undoubtedly speak grandly. But who is moved if he does not know what is being said? Or who is held attentive that he may hear if he is not delighted? Whence also in this style, where the hard heart is bent to obedience through the grandness of the diction, if what is heard is not heard intelligently and willingly, it cannot be heard obediently."[47]

Mere eloquence will never be enough. Even the grand style must take on the function of the subdued style, which is to teach, if it is to be of any use to the Christian preacher. Thus the indissoluble union of the subject matter and style implies a new unity in the three styles themselves:

> Thus those three ends which we described above for a man who speaks wisely if he would also speak eloquently, that is, that he should so speak that he is heard intelligently, willingly, and obediently, are not to be taken so that one of the three styles is attributed to each one so that the subdued style pertains to understanding, the moderate style to willingness and the grand style to obedience; rather, in such a way that the orator always attends to all three and fulfills them all as much as he can, even when he is using a single style.[48]

Far from suggesting that style is the whole of rhetoric, Augustine obviously considers that rhetoric consists of a marriage between content and style. His conversion involved not a rejection of rhetoric in favour of Christianity, but a turning away from mere words to the Word. In rescuing his tongue, God did not take it from him. What he did take from him was a false division between words and the truth, between form and content, between style and matter. Words become for him a means instead of an end, the end unattainable without the means, the means empty without the end. And this unity of ends and means is part of that greater unity which is love. That Augustine should be perceived as having sanctioned the divorce of style from the other parts of rhetoric is an ironic and unhappy accident which can be explained only by the very low and limited meaning of rhetoric in his own time.

Christine Mason Sutherland was educated at Oxford and McGill. From 1978 to 1983, she was Director of the Effective Writing Programme at the University of Calgary. Since 1983, she has been teaching in the Communications Major in the Faculty of General Studies, for which she has created three courses. In 1986, she was appointed Assistant Professor. Her publications include articles on the history of rhetoric, particularly as it concerns education and Christianity. She is currently working on the rhetoric of seventeenth century women, and recently gave a paper on Mary Astell (1666–1731) at the conference of the International Society for the History of Rhetoric in Gottingen, West Germany.

NOTES

1. George A. Kennedy, *Classical Rhetoric and Its Christian and Secular Tradition* (Chapel Hill: The University of North Carolina Press, 1980), 147.

2. Kenneth Burke, *The Rhetoric of Religion: Studies in Logology* (Berkeley: University of California Press, 1970).

3. Kennedy, 158.

4. James J. Murphy, *Rhetoric in the Middle Ages* (Berkeley: University of California Press, 1974), 158.

5. Murphy, 64.

6. Gerald Fulkerson, "Augustine's Attitude Towards Rhetoric" in *De Doctrina Christiana*: The Significance of 2.37.55," *Rhetoric Society Quarterly*, 15, No. 3–4 (Summer and Fall 1985): 108–111.

7. Gerald Press, "'Doctrina' in Augustine's *De Doctrina Christiana*," *Philosophy and Rhetoric*, 17 (Spring 1984): 98–120.

8. Murphy, 60. See also Augustine, *De Doctrina Christiana* 4.1.1 in Vol. III of *Sancti Aurelii Augustini Hipporensi Episcopi, Opera Omnia* (Paris: Gaume Fratres, 1836) 111: "Quia ergo de inveniendo multa jam diximus, et tria de hac una parte volumina absolvimus, Domini adjuvante, de proferendo pauca dicemus."

9. Murphy, 51.

10. R.S. Pine-Coffin, trans., *Saint Augustine, Confessions* (Harmondsworth, England: Penguin Books, 1961), 2.3.

11. *Confessions*, 1.16.

12. *Confessions*, 3.4.

13. *Confessions*, 5.13.

14. *Confessions*, 5.6.

15. *Confessions*, 3.6.

16. *Confessions*, 3.5.

17. *Confessions*, 4.15.

18. *Confessions*, 6.6.

19. *Confessions*, 9.5.

20. *Confessions*, 9.4.

21. Murphy, 60.

22. D.W. Robertson, Jr., trans., *St. Augustine, On Christian Doctrine* (Indianapolis: Bobbs-Merrill, 1958), 4.2.3.

23. *De Doctrina*, 1.35.39.

24. *Confessions*, 4.15.

25. *De Doctrina*, Prologue, 6.

26. *De Doctrina*, Prologue, 7.

27. Kennedy, 153.

28. *Confessions*, 12.24.

29. *Confessions*, 12.25.

30. *De Doctrina*, 3.15.23.

31. *De Doctrina*, 4.27.59.

32. John Selby Watson, trans., *Quintilian, Institutes of Oratory* (London: George Bell and Sons, 1907), 12.1.1–33.

33. *Quintilian*, 1.1.4.

34. *De Doctrina*, 4.10.24.

35. *De Doctrina*, 4.10.24.

36. *De Doctrina*, 4.20.39.

37. *De Doctrina*, 4.10.25.

38. *De Doctrina*.

39. *Confessions*, 10.3.

40. *De Doctrina*, 4.18.35.

41. *De Doctrina*, 4.18.36.

42. *De Doctrina*, 4.12.28.

43. *De Doctrina*, 4.12.28.

44. *De Doctrina*, 4.12.56.

45. *Confessions*, 11.8.

46. *De Doctrina*, 4.26.56.

47. *De Doctrina*, 4.26.57.

48. *De Doctrina*, 4.26.56.

RELIGION AND SOCIETY
IN THE AGE OF THEODOSIUS

RELIGION AND SOCIETY IN THE AGE OF THEODOSIUS

Timothy D. Barnes

The title "Religion and Society in the Age of Theodosius" deliberately evokes the title of a volume of essays by Peter Brown who, through his biography of Augustine and many other studies, has transformed our understanding of Augustine and the age in which he lived and has, for more than twenty years, inspired a generation of younger scholars and historians with enthusiasm for Late Antiquity.[1] My intention is to ask how Brown's work and that of others has altered our picture of the society in which Augustine grew to maturity, underwent conversion, and then discovered his vocation as a bishop and theologian. For during recent decades much has changed in the scholarly landscape against which we view Augustine of Hippo and his conversion.

Let me begin, as the present occasion perhaps demands, with an ancient after-dinner conversation. Macrobius' *Saturnalia* used to be almost universally regarded by modern scholars as first-hand evidence for paganism in the highest echelons of Roman society in the late fourth century. The *Saturnalia* shows pagan aristocrats and scholars discoursing learnedly on Roman religion and philosophy at the Saturnalia of 384, and it was assumed that Macrobius wrote the work not long after 384, that he belonged to the same cultural milieu as the protagonists in his dialogue, and that he could be used unguardedly as primary evidence to reconstruct that milieu.[2] In 1966, Alan Cameron proved that Macrobius was writing after 430, at a distance of half a century from the dramatic date of his *Saturnalia*.[3] It follows that his picture of the *saeculum Praetextati*, the age of Vettius Agorius Praetextatus, is an idealised, retrospective panegyric of a bygone age, not the depiction of a living ideal. The wider consequences of this redating are enormous: they compel a more differentiated approach to

157

paganism in the late fourth century Rome—an approach evident in much recent work on the period, particularly that of John Matthews.[4]

I must confess a personal motive in choosing to tackle my topic as I have. My own work on Constantine and the Constantinian period has led me to a number of novel, even heterodox or idiosyncratic views. These include a conviction that the Roman Empire became Christian earlier, and in the fourth century became more thoroughly Christian than has normally been supposed by academic historians of the last hundred years.[5] Of late I have been endeavouring to apply my interpretation of the reign of Constantine to the career of Athanasius under his sons. I hope to show that there is little or nothing in the later fourth century which is not consonant with my picture of the age of Diocletian and Constantine. Unfortunately, the subject is so large that I must be highly selective. I shall of necessity say a great deal, perhaps too much, about the senatorial aristocracy and the imperial court (since our evidence for them is fuller and more explicit than for other segments of society), but I shall try to allow due weight to the immense local variety which existed within that fictitious legal unity, the Later Roman Empire.

In theory, the Roman Empire was an *indivisum patrimonium* with the same laws and government from Hadrian's Wall in Britain to the Euphrates, from the mouth of the Rhine to the cataracts of the Nile. In fact, for almost all the fourth century, there were two quite separate Roman Empires, in East and West. Constantine came to power in 306 in Britain, Gaul and Spain. In 312 he added Italy and Africa, in 316/7 most of the Balkans and Greece. It was only in 324 that he conquered Asia Minor and the East, and it was only there that he had the political opportunity to make the sweeping changes in established religion which Eusebius of Caesarea describes. From 324 onwards, therefore, the religious situation in East and West was very different. In the West, Constantine had come to power as a champion of religious tolerance and hence, despite his conversion in 312, he was committed to allowing pagans equal freedom of worship with Christians. From 312 he began to bestow endowments, favours and privileges on the Christian church and its clergy, but it was politically unwise, probably impossible, to attempt to repress long established non-Christian ceremonies. And the same picture, I believe, obtained for the territories which Constantine conquered in 316/7, including Greece—where a still unpublished inscription shows the praetorian prefects in 342 reaffirming the privileges of the priest of Apollo at Delphi.

In 324, however, Constantine conquered the East in a war which he fought as a Christian crusade, and in the immediate aftermath of that war he had the opportunity to carry through a religious reformation. I believe that he used it.[6] First, those who had supported Licinius' persecution of the Christians were killed, presumably most or all of them lynched by the relatives and friends of their victims. Second, all the ill-effects of Licinius' policies were undone, and Constantine restored confiscated Christian property without compensation to the subsequent owners. Third, pagans were forbidden to consult oracles, erect new cult-statues or to sacrifice at all, and.Constantine renewed the prohibition when protests were made. He allowed pagans to retain their temples and shrines as places of prayer, but the sacrifices which were an integral part of pagan worship were now illegal. Finally, commissioners toured the eastern provinces confiscating all the precious metals to be found in temples and shrines—not just dedications, but doors, ceilings and even cult-statues.

Imperial policy was clear. But enforcement was uneven and erratic. Constantine destroyed a few cult-centres which were notorious, for moral or propaganda reasons. In general, however, local conditions determined whether pagan temples continued to exist unmolested or were pillaged and destroyed. An excellent article has recently documented the role of eastern bishops such as Mark of Arethusa in this long process of sporadic suppression throughout the fourth and early fifth centuries.[7]

Such was the situation in the East. What of the West? I am inclined to think that Constantine's prohibition of pagan sacrifice was not merely not enforced, but probably not even promulgated in the West. I would see the reiteration of the prohibition by Constans in 341 in a constitution addressed to the *vicarius Italiae* as not only the first attempt seriously to enforce the prohibition in Italy, but also probably the first formal proclamation of Constantine's policy there.[8] Of course, Constantine never expressly restricted the application of his prohibition of 324/5 to the East; he simply extended the familiar practice of enforcing universally binding legislation in only part of the Roman Empire. (The clearest examples of this are Diocletian's price edict of 301 and his fourth persecuting edict of early 304, neither of which was ever promulgated in the West.) Moreover, the diatribes of Firmicus Maternus in his *De errore profanarum religionum*, written in 343, make it clear that temple treasures had not been confiscated in the West.[9] It has been customary to play Firmicus Maternus against Eusebius in order to convict the latter of lying or exaggeration;[10] I prefer to accept both witnesses as basically truthful in reporting what each of them knew. The discrepancy is striking testimony to the real, and in some areas enormous, differences between East and West.

Between the death of Constantine in 337 and the death of Theodosius in 395, the Roman Empire had a single emperor and single administration for a total of approximately seven years out of fifty-eight, viz.

354/5   between the deposition of Gallus and the proclamation
                   of Julian as Caesar

361–364   between the death of Constantius and the proclamation of Valens as Augustus

388–391, 394/5   while Theodosius was in the West after defeating Magnus Maximus and Eugenius (Valentinian II during the earlier period and Arcadius, who was left in Constantinople in 394, were young and totally without political independence or authority of their own.)

I emphasise this fact because, despite his Spanish origin, Theodosius was primarily an eastern emperor—and his religious policies reflect the difference between East and West. In the East, he could be aggressive towards the practice of paganism; in the West, it was still politically unwise gratuitously to offend the religious sentiments of prominent pagans in the Roman aristocracy.

The reign of Theodosius marks an important stage in the Christianisation of the Roman Empire. When Constantine assumed the title of Augustus long before his conversion, he automatically took the title *pontifex maximus* and regarded himself, *qua* emperor, as head of the college of *pontifices* and in charge of traditional Roman cults.[11] Constantine did not drop the title in 312, and his Christian successors also took the title of *pontifex maximus*—until Theodosius. It has now been demonstrated that Theodosius was the first emperor to renounce the title and that he declined to accept it at his accession in January 379.[12] Eastern pagans knew what was likely to follow. Nicomachus Flavianus the younger might be appointed proconsul of Asia, as he was for 383/4; the sophist Himerius might greet Flavianus rapturously as he travelled through Greece; and the *consularis* of Crete might conspicuously honour pagan as well as Christian Roman aristocrats.[13] But when Maternus Cynegius toured the East as praetorian prefect between 384 and 388, he went on a rampage against pagan shrines wherever the opportunity offered.[14] Theodosius not only reiterated the prohibition of pagan sacrifice, which had been rescinded by Julian and probably not reinstated by Jovian, Valentinian or Valens, but withdrew imperial protection from temples and similar buildings.[15] That was not entirely an innovation: although Constantine and Constans had forbidden their destruction, Constantius ordered temples to be closed and access to them prevented—thereby disproving an ancient and modern *canard*, frequently repeated, that Arians were softer on paganism than catholics.[16] Theodosius in 391/2 forbade anyone to enter temples or shrines, and set out to enforce the prohibition by laying down precise penalties. At the same time he officially encouraged the destruction of pagan cult-centres, most conspicuously the Serapeum in Alexandria.

Within the church, Theodosius took an equally strong line. In 380 he defined "catholic" not in neutral or platitudinous terms, but as denoting Christians whose beliefs coincided with those of Damasus, the bishop of Rome, and

Peter, the bishop of Alexandria: he stigmatised all who refused to accept the Nicene creed as heretics and forbade them to own churches, or even to meet for worship inside cities. It is perhaps anachronistic to complain that Theodosius was the "first of the Spanish Inquisitors."[17] But it is important to stress that his personal piety, and that of the Gauls and Spaniards who accompanied him to Constantinople and staffed the highest positions in his administration, created a welcoming framework for the development of asceticism, the cult of the saints and the pursuit of relics.[18]

In the reign of Constantine, the true cross could be discovered by the bishop of Jerusalem. In the reign of Theodosius, it had to be an empress— though those who manufactured the familiar legend in the late 380s could not agree whether to attribute the discovery to Helena, the mother of Constantine, or to "Protonice," a wife of the emperor Claudius unknown to history.[19]

The precise religious situation in the East varied in accordance with local factors. In a backward area like Greece, pagan rites and rituals proved very tenacious.[20] On the other hand, in the prosperous villages of the hinterland of Antioch, Christianity already permeated peasant society and created fertile ground for the growth of the holy men so lovingly brought to life by Theodoret and Peter Brown.[21] And of course there were pagan intellectual centres in Athens and Asia Minor, which we know relatively well and which have attracted much recent attention.[22] But the variations cannot mask the fact that the eastern Roman Empire integrated the Christian church into its social, political and economic fabric earlier and more effectively than the West. That is probably due largely to its more urbanised structure. But there was also a cultural barrier. Since the middle of the second century, it had been possible for Greek writers like Justin, Clement, Origen and Eusebius to expound Christianity in terms easily understandable to non-Christians through the medium of Middle Platonism.[23] Somehow, it seems to me, there was no similar common intellectual currency among those who thought in Latin until Augustine developed his theological language, initially on the basis of Marius Victorinus' translations of some treatises by Plotinus.[24] The dependence of Ambrose on Philo, Origen and Athanasius' ascetical writings indicates the lack of a living Latin tradition of philosophical theology.[25] But here I stray into territory that belongs to others. Let me turn now to the political and social framework of the western empire between 379 and 395. It is complicated.[26]

When Valentinian died suddenly in November 375, he left two sons: Gratian, aged sixteen and an Augustus since 367, and Valentinian, a boy of four whom the generals at once proclaimed Augustus. After an obscure period of political intrigue with several executions of high officials, including the general Theodosius, Gratian established some sort of ascendancy with an administration led by his elderly tutor Ausonius. In 378, however, came the disaster of Adrianople in which Valens perished. Gratian recalled the younger Theodosius, who became Augustus of the East in January 379, either on Gratian's initiative or, more probably, because Gratian accepted a proclamation by the troops under Theodosius' command.

Relations between Theodosius and the sons of Valentinian were never very warm, not even, I suspect, after Theodosius fell in love with and married Galla, the sister of Valentinian II. The order to execute his father at Carthage in the winter of 375/6 had been issued in the names of Gratian and Valentinian II—and Magnus Maximus, who supplanted Gratian as ruler of Britain, Gaul and Spain in 383, was a relative of Theodosius. Theodosius recognised Maximus as a legitimate emperor and colleague. We cannot avoid asking ourselves what Theodosius' policy would have been in 387 if he had not been a widower and if Justina had not possessed an attractive daughter to ensnare him. Would he have rescued and restored the Arian Valentinian II, whose name authorised his father's death-warrant, at the price of war against a good catholic kinsman? I personally doubt it very much. Consequently, I am tempted to explain Theodosius' lenient treatment of Maximus' noble supporters in Rome, like Symmachus, less by a need to conciliate a politically powerful pagan party in the aristocracy than by a sincere recognition that, since Maximus was not a normal usurper, their support of him was not as criminal as it seemed in retrospect after his defeat. It is a pity that we do not have the panegyric which Symmachus delivered before Maximus: I suspect that it was very flattering to Theodosius.

The political background impinges vitally on the religious policies of the western emperors from 379 to 395. I should like to consider them in an order which is not quite chronological: first Maximus, then Gratian and Valentinian, then Theodosius, and finally Eugenius, who was proclaimed Augustus in Gaul in May 392 and defeated by Theodosius in September 394.

Maximus in many ways exemplifies the predicament of the usurper who, whatever his personal predilections, must seek political support wherever he can find it. When Maximus invaded Italy in 387, he tried to conciliate pagans without offending Christians by offering private subsidies to replace the public ones recently suspended, and he made the grave political mistake of ordering a Jewish synagogue in Rome which had been burnt down in a riot to be rebuilt. However, the most famous episode associated with Maximus' name arose from his need to satisfy the catholic bishops of Gaul by showing that he would not tolerate what they perceived as a heretical challenge to their authority. The execution of Priscillian of Avila is not the first execution of a Christian for heresy, nor is it the first execution of a bishop by the secular authorities for an ecclesiastical offence. Although the case of Priscillian is complicated and controversial, it seems clear that he was a layman condemned for magic and probably also immorality.[26]

The sources for the career of Priscillian are unsatisfactory: mainly the eleven tractates, some by Priscillian himself, discovered by Schepss at Würzburg in 1885, and Sulpicius Severus, whose main concerns seem to be to defend and magnify Martin of Tours, and to belittle and calumniate the episcopal enemies of Priscillian, in each case as a means of attacking the prosperous and spiritually flabby bishops of Gaul with whom he was at odds.[28] Given the state of the evidence, it is difficult, though not impossible, to unravel the course of events. The crucial point is that Priscillian was a layman.[29] A synod at Saragossa in 380 condemned his teaching, which had Gnostic affinities, and his ascetical practices. In the following year, the two bishops who had supported him consecrated him bishop of Avila, but the consecration was clearly invalid: the Council of Nicaea had made the consent of three bishops, including the metropolitan bishop of the province, a necessary condition for a valid consecration and had implicitly provided that provincial councils of bishops decide disputed cases. His opponents, therefore, held that Priscillian was not a bishop and never had been—and by normal criteria they were correct. Priscillian and his supporters then sought support in Italy and with some success at the court of Gratian. Magnus Maximus, however, convened a council of bishops to try the case at Bordeaux in 384/5: there Priscillian made the ultimately fatal mistake of appealing to the emperor, and his appeal was allowed by the council precisely because he was a layman not a bishop. Finally, despite the opposition of Martin, Priscillian was tried at Trier by the praetorian prefect of Maximus and executed together with some of his supporters. The ill-feeling which this provoked in certain quarters has unfortunately misled many modern scholars: even the normally judicious Henry Chadwick depicts Priscillian throughout as a bishop and brushes aside any doubt with the assertion that it is improbable that the Nicene rulings about the consecration of bishops were understood to be force in Spain.[30]

The case of Priscillian tells us a great deal about Christianity in Spain and Gaul, but it is not the striking precedent which some have seen. In the context of the 380s the real innovation came from Gratian, under the influence of Theodosius. In 382, he ordered the altar of Victory to be removed from the senate-house in Rome, and public subsidies for ancient Roman cults to be discontinued. Constantius had removed the altar when he visited Rome in 357; Julian had restored it; Valentinian made no change in the *status quo*. In 382, Gratian acted and when the Senate sent an embassy to protest, he renounced the title of *pontifex maximus* too. The rest of the story of the altar of Victory is familiar and need not be repeated.[31] The altar became a symbol and Ambrose won a symbolic victory in 384 when, after Gratian's death, he persuaded

Valentinian II to deny a formal request for the restoration of the altar from the *praefectus urbi* Symmachus representing the Roman Senate. One issue perhaps deserves consideration here. Both Symmachus and Ambrose claimed to have the majority of the Senate on their side. How can that be? I suspect that Ambrose was thinking of the whole senatorial class, whereas Symmachus refers only to the majority at a particular meeting. It would be bad method to discount Ambrose, then to take Symmachus as evidence that the Roman Senate was still predominantly pagan in 384. Our evidence consistently gives us only a minimum for estimating the number of Christian senators, not an accurate count. This point needs emphasis because the two are often confused. For example, when it was recently and convincingly argued that the first Christian *consul ordinarius* was Ovinius Gallicanus, consul in 317, that was subsequently construed as proving how few Christians there were in the Roman aristocracy under Constantine.[32] But the earlier article never addressed that question, and so far as I can see, the majority of non-imperial consuls between 317 and 337 were probably Christians.[33] When the emperor Julian accused Constantine of making barbarians consuls, he did not mean Germans, as Ammianus Marcellinus thought: he meant non-Hellenes, i.e., Christians.[34]

No biography of Ambrose of Augustine can omit the struggle between the bishop of Milan and Justina over whether Arians should be allowed a church in the city in which to worship.[35] In the present context, therefore, I can content myself with singling out two aspects of the struggle for comment. First, it is extremely misleading to talk of "the persecution of Justina." Ambrose, like Athanasius in Alexandria, was determined that the Arians should have no church for worship. If the term "persecution" is to be used at all, the Arians were the victims. Second, although the Arian Auxentius held the see of Milan from 355 to 374, the sentiment of the Christian populace of the city was probably solidly catholic by the 380s. Ambrose would not have been able to win by using techniques of passive resistance if there had been serious opposition to him in the city. The Arians who needed a church were primarily Gothic troops—as in Constantinople in 400 when the inhabitants slaughtered the followers of Gainas. We already see signs of the socio-religious differentiation which was to prevent the development of the barbarian kingdoms of the fifth century into enduring states: the Gothic and Germanic invaders, the Franks excepted, had a different religion from the existing population and remained socially distinct. At the end of the fourth century, it is not surprising that Arianism was strongest in Pannonia, that is, in an area where the population contained a high proportion of "barbarians."

Valentinian fled to Theodosius when Maximus invaded Italy in 387. Acceptance of Nicene Christianity was a condition of his restoration. Theodosius defeated Maximus in 388, then resided in Italy until 391 with the intention of organising the government of the West under his hegemony on a permanent basis. In Milan he confronted Ambrose, who won two symbolic victories over the emperor.[36] First, in 388, he compelled Theodosius to rescind an imperial order that the Christians of Callinicus on the Euphrates rebuild a Jewish synagogue and a conventicle of the Valentinians which they had burned down under the leadership of their bishop. Second, in 390, he compelled Theodosius to perform penance after he ordered a punitive massacre in Thessalonica, where the people had murdered a barbarian general. In both cases, Ambrose exerted moral pressure of a type only possible because Theodosius was a baptised Christian. He had been baptised in 380 when ill. He was not the first emperor to be a baptised Christian: that distinction belongs to Constans (or possibly to his older brother Constantinus).[37] But Theodosius was the first Christian emperor who was forced publicly to confront the dilemma which Constantine and Constantius had avoided by postponing baptism: can a Christian rule without committing serious sin? Constantine clearly did not think so: when he received the catechumen's robe, he laid aside his imperial insignia. Augustine moves in a different world, where bishops often act as judges and magistrates—and are perhaps present when witnesses are tortured. Before he left Milan in 391, Theodosius shattered any impression which he might have given of sympathy towards paganism: he banned all sacrifices, public and private, and prohibited access to temples.[38]

Theodosius' arrangements for the government of the West did not last long after he returned to the East. Within a year Valentinian II was dead, either murdered or, more probably, by suicide, and the general Arbogast had put up Eugenius as emperor of the West. The revolt of Eugenius has received an enormous amount of modern attention as the last pagan revival in the West, and the issues of interpretation which it raises are so important that they deserve a careful analysis. I should like to concentrate here on what seem to me to be the two basic problems, which lie at each end of a spectrum. At the highest level of generality, the nature of late Roman paganism is in dispute; at the most specific level, the date and target of the anonymous poem normally known as the *Carmen contra paganos*. Let me take the general issue first.

Two approaches must, I think, be rejected outright. First, the cynical view that Symmachus and his friends had no real religious opinions, only social prejudices and a financial stake in official subsidies for the traditional cults.[39] Their snobbery and financial interests cannot be denied, but they can hardly be the whole story. It was too easy in the 380s to join the bandwagon, and prosper by being a Christian. When Praetextatus said "Make me bishop of Rome and I will become a Christian," he was voicing a jocular criticism of Damasus' behaviour, not revealing his deepest convictions. However, when Symmachus proclaimed that "Not by a single route can one penetrate so great a mystery," he was voicing a view widely espoused by pagans confronting intolerant Christianity—and which may derive from Porphyry. Secondly, we should reject the view that paganism was no more than old-fashioned antiquarianism with no political overtones at all, or at least, to quote the proponent of this view, that after 384 "the very slight tendency toward organised resistance and action which [Praetextatus] represented among the pagan aristocracy disappeared."[40] Despite the eloquence with which this view has been argued, I believe that there is too much evidence for pagan support of Eugenius to explain away. Moreover, the plausible suggestion has recently been made that Prudentius wrote the first book of his *Contra Symmachum*, not in 402/3 when he wrote Book Two, but in 394/5, immediately after the Battle of the Frigidus.[41] The poem depicts Theodosius as converting the Roman Senate after his defeat of Eugenius.

If we discard these two approaches, we can see three main, and successive, interpretations. First, the view which D.N. Robinson stated in 1915, and to which Herbert Bloch gave classic expression: that there were two pagan parties in the Roman aristocracy of the late fourth century, viz. the traditionalists, led by Symmachus, who were concerned to preserve the traditional cults of ancient Rome (Vesta, Jupiter, the Altar of Victory), and the orientalists, led by Praetextatus and then the elder Flavianus, whose religious emotion was attached to oriental cults and practices like the taurobolium and the cults of Cybele, Isis and similar deities.[42] This view was subjected to searching scrutiny by John Matthews in a long study of the religion of Symmachus. His argument is complex, but its conclusion can be summarised as follows: first, the nature of Symmachus' letters is such that we could not expect him to say much, if anything, about Oriental cults, whatever his personal beliefs were; second, the epigraphical and other evidence which attests the devotion of other aristocrats to Oriental cults is of a type which we lack for Symmachus himself; therefore, third, for all that we know, Symmachus may have been a *tauroboliatus* himself.[43] Matthews' view is carefully formulated with a keen eye for the precise value and import of evidence, and with a proper emphasis on the cultural context. However, much of the same evidence has been marshalled into a significantly different pattern by Lelia Cracco Ruggini. She adopts a very political interpretation of late Roman paganism, in this siding with Bloch against Matthews.

Ruggini argues that the death of Praetextatus in 384 deprived Roman pagans of their leader and began an ebb-tide for their cause, and that the cause itself changed significantly: whereas the generation of Praetextatus had practised every sort of cult, with a predilection for the Oriental and exotic, the generation of Flavianus and Symmachus, though only a few years younger, was exclusively Roman and traditional in its religious loyalties.[44] I have to

confess that that sort of argument has an innate appeal for anyone who reflects
on the differences between the two generations of students that came of age in
the late 1960s and early 1980s. But the strength of Ruggini's case, and the impetus to her conclusions, come from a consideration of the date of the *Carmen
contra paganos*—the very specific problem so germane to any overall interpretation of Roman paganism.

The so-called *Carmen contra paganos* is a poem of one hundred and twenty-three hexameters transmitted anonymously in a sixth century manuscript of
Prudentius (Paris, Bibliothèque Nationale, Fonds Latin 8084). The poem has
been edited several times, and is now translated into English.[45] It attacks a
prominent Roman pagan aristocrat who has recently died at the age of sixty.
Ruggini revives the suggestion made in 1868 by the despised Robinson Ellis
that the target of the poem was Vettius Agorius Praetextatus.[46] This suggestion
was eclipsed in 1870 by Mommsen's identification of the prefect and consul
whom the poem lampoons as Nicomachus Flavianus the Elder, consul in
394.[47] So strong indeed was the influence of Mommsen's authority that when
John Matthews in 1970 published an article entitled "The Historical Setting of
the *Carmen contra paganos*," he considered and decisively rejected G.
Manganaro's proposal to identify the prefect as the *praefectus urbi* in 408/9,
but never even mentioned the claims of Praetextatus.[48] And I must add a *mea
culpa*: twice in recent years I have accepted Matthews' conclusions and built
on them.[49] Let me now announce a repentance, perhaps even a conversion.
Since this is not the context in which to assess all the details of an often
obscure text, let me make five central points. First, the man attacked in the
Carmen contra paganos is described as both prefect and consul: that rules out
all identifications except two, viz. Praetextatus, who died as praetorian prefect
of Italy, Illyricum and Africa in late December 384 a few days before he was
due to take up the *fasces* as ordinary consul on 1 January 385, and Flavianus,
who served Eugenius as praetorian prefect in Italy and ordinary consul in 394.
Second, what is said about the prefect's death is difficult to square with
Flavianus' suicide, and I no longer think that any of the other personal details
necessarily favour Flavianus over Praetextatus. Third, a point made by Ruggini: the *Carmen* has no obvious or detectable allusion to the political and
military *débacle* of 394, whereas anyone ridiculing or satirising the dead
Flavianus would surely have made that a central part of his indictment. Fourth,
a medieval catalogue from the Benedictine Abbey of Lobbes describes a poem
which can hardly be anything other than the *Carmen contra paganos* as
"Damasi episcopi versus de Praetextato praefecto urbis."[50] Damasus was too
competent a versifier to have written the halting hexameters of the *Carmen*, but
the identification of its target as Praetextatus must be taken seriously. Fifth,
and last, a strong *prima facie* case has now been made for believing that
Proba's introduction to her Virgilian cento retelling Biblical stories uses and

adapts a phrase from *Carmen contra paganos*. If this is so, then for reasons to do with the textual transmission of Proba's cento, the *Carmen* must have been written some years before 395, i.e., before the death of Flavianus.[51]

I must apologise for being so technical in a general exposition. But the problem of attribution has wide ramifications. I have already commented on the change of perspective which Alan Cameron's redating of Macrobius' *Saturnalia* brought about. A similar change comes with redating the *Carmen contra paganos*. To change the metaphor, we have a somewhat different matrix into which to fit the rest of our evidence. Overall, I think, pagans in the reign of Theodosius were less powerful than the traditional view held, but more embittered. Peter Brown has emphasised the peaceful aspects of the "Christianisation of the Roman aristocracy."[52] I do not wish to deny those aspects which he emphasises, but he seems to me to downplay the religious tensions and even hostility between Christians and pagans which surfaced not infrequently. The issue of how important paganism was still remains to be settled. Roman historians have sometimes discounted too heavily the religious significance which Augustine around 413 read into the Battle of the Frigidus; we come closer, I think, to the spirit of the reign of Theodosius when we read Robert Markus on the triumphal phase of Augustine's thinking about history. Under the impact of contemporary events, Augustine briefly accepted a providential view of history as leading towards the victorious Christianity of the reign of Theodosius.[53] The later Augustine reacted strongly against such optimism. Therein lay both his genius and his originality: everyone else, pagan and Christian alike, saw God's hand actively assisting the course of history to ensure the success of his true worshippers. Hence the pagan argument, formulated by Eunapius in the East, but also perhaps perceptible in Ammianus, that the disaster of Adrianople in 378 was the consequence of the conversion of the Roman Empire to Christianity. Christians replied, at lease in part, by stressing the piety and the victories of Theodosius.

An adequate discussion of religion and society in the reign of Theodosius would require a book rather than a lecture. With a broad canvas, I could begin to develop the theme of local variations. For it is obvious, to take only cities associated with Augustine, that Thagaste was not like Carthage, Rome was not like Milan, nor Ostia Hippo—any more than Calgary is like Edmonton. As it is, I must leave that theme largely unexplored, and conclude with something which I, as a Roman historian, tend to take for granted. It is not only our approach to religion and society which has changed in the last generation, it is our approach to the Later Roman Empire as a whole.

An earlier generation approached the fourth century in a censorious spirit:

The administration of justice in the least civilized kingdom of modern Europe seems ideal in comparison with the system which obtained during the fourth century in the Roman Empire.

Thus the Roman world was already in decay. The population was steadily dwindling. Hundreds of thousands of acres formerly cultivated had returned to waste. The middle class, crushed by over-whelming financial burdens and degraded by the caste-system to a condition resembling serfdom, was ruined and fast disappearing. The bureaucracy, from top to bottom, was incorrigibly corrupt. The army, packed with barbarians, was in a state of chaos. Justice was in abeyance; political freedom was non-existent. In short, the fabric of the Empire, though still imposing in appearance, was rotten to the core. A series of shocks from without could hardly fail to bring about a complete and final and irremediable collapse.[54]

That is Homes Dudden setting the stage for Ambrose's career as a bishop of Milan from 374 to 397. He was writing in the early 1930s—a man with a secure well-paid job in the great depression.

After the Second World War, a more positive note begins to be sounded. Let me quote (in translation) the concluding lines of André Piganiol's *L'empire chrétien*, published in 1947 and reflecting the spirit of a renascent France:

It is false to say that Rome was decadent. Pillaged, disfigured by the barbarian invaders of the third century, she was rebuilding her ruins. At the same time was being accomplished, at the cost of a grave crisis, a work of internal transformation: there was forming a new concep-tion of the imperial power, that of Byzantium, a new conception of truth and beauty, that of the Middle Ages, a new conception of collec-tive and joint labour in the service of social ends. All the ills from which the empire suffered, stifling taxation, the ruin of fortunes and social classes, have their origin not in this fertile work of transforma-tion, but in the perpetual warfare carried on by the unorganised bands of these Germans who, on the frontiers of the empire, had succeeded in living for centuries without becoming civilised.

It is too easy to pretend that when the barbarians arrived in the Empire "everything was dead, it was a worn out body, a corpse stretched out in its own blood," or even that the Roman Empire of the West was not destroyed by a brutal blow, but just fell asleep.

Roman civilisation did not die of its own accord. It was assas-sinated.[55]

There speaks the spirit of the French Resistance. Yet most who now write about the age of Theodosius accept Piganiol's principal assertion that Augus-tine grew to manhood in a society which was changing, alive, vibrant. That perception inevitably affects the way all of us think about Augustine himself and his conversion.

Timothy D. Barnes is the author of the following publications: *Tertullian: A Historical and Literary Study*, 1971, 2nd ed. 1985; *The Sources of the Historia Augusta*, 1978; *Constantine and Eusebius*, 1981; *The New Empire of Diocletian and Constantine*, 1982; and *Early Christianity and the Roman Empire*, 1984.

NOTES

The present paper is a superficially revised and lightly annotated version of the lecture delivered in Calgary on Halloween 1986, and prepared for publication in the following year. I am most grateful to the organisers, Hugo Meynell and Shadia Drury for inviting me to participate in a most successful colloquium—and for persuading me to venture in print some assertions which I probably could not prove to the satisfaction of my academic peers.

1. See especially *Augustine of Hippo. A Biography* (London 1967); *The World of Late Antiquity* (London 1971); *Religion and Society in the Age of Saint Augustine* (London 1972); *Society and the Holy in Late Antiquity* (Berkeley and Los Angeles 1982).

2. e.g., S. Dill, *Roman Society in the Last Century of the Western Empire*, 2nd ed. (London 1899) 92 ff., 154 ff., dating the work to "the first quarter of the fifth century."

3. Alan Cameron, "The Date and Identity of Macrobius," *Journal of Roman Studies* 56 (1966): 25–38.

4. See J. Matthews, *Western Aristocracies and Imperial Court A.D. 364–425* (Oxford 1975), 1 ff., 370 ff.

5. *Constantine and Eusebius* (Cambridge, MA., 1981), 191 ff., 210 ff., 245 ff. For a fuller statement of the thesis, see "The Constantinian Reformation, The Crake Lectures 1984" (Sackville, N.B., 1986), 39–57. The principal evidence is provided by Eusebius, *Life of Constantine* 2, 19–60, 3, 54–59; *Panegyric of Constantine*, 8.1 ff. In formulating the thesis around 1980 I drew a conscious analogy in my own mind with the situation in Iran immediately after the fall of the Shah.

7. G. Fowden, "Bishops and Temples in the Eastern Roman Empire A.D. 320–435," *Journal of Theological Studies*, N.S. 29 (1978): 53–78.

8. *Theodosian Code*, trans, C. Pharr (Princeton 1952), 472 (16.10.2).

9. Firmicus Maternus, *De err. prof. rel.* 16.4, 28.6 ff. For an English transla-
    tion of the relevant passages, see C.A. Forbes, *Firmicus Maternus: The
    Error of the Pagan Religions (Ancient Christian Writers 37, 1970), 77 f.,
    110 ff. I have argued for the precise date of 343 in American Journal of
    Ancient History* 3 (1978): 75, n. 100.

10. For a recent example of the traditional disparagement of Eusebius, see
    H.A. Drake, *In Praise of Constantine: A Historical Study and New Trans-
    lation of Eusebius' Tricennial Orations* (Berkeley 1976), 65, 150. In his
    defence on this issue, "Constantine's Prohibition of Pagan Sacrifice,"
    American Journal of Philology 105 (1984): 69–72.

11. On this aspect of an emperor's function, F. Millar, *The Emperor in the
    Roman World (31 B.C.-A.D. 337)* (London 1977), 355 ff.

12. Alan Cameron, "Gratian's Repudiation of the Pontifical Robe," *Journal of
    Roman Studies* 58 (1968): 96–102.

13. See now "Himerius and the Fourth Century," *Classical Philology* 82
    (1987): 206–225.

14. J.F. Matthews, "A Pious Supporter of Theodosius I: Maternus Cynegius
    and his Family," *Journal of Theological Studies* 18 (1967): 438–446.

15. *Theodosian Code* 16.10. 3–12; 16.1.2. The interpretation of Theodosius'
    policy offered by N.Q. King, *The Emperor Theodosius and the Estab-
    lishment of Christianity* (London 1961), 71 ff. is unfortunately unsatisfac-
    tory.

16. Stated in its most extreme form by H.M. Gwatkin, *Studies of Arianism,*
    2nd ed. (London 1900), 273: "Arianism was an illogical compromise. It
    went too far for heathenism, not far enough for Christianity."

17. H. Trevor-Roper, *The Rise of Christian Europe* (London 1965), 36.

18. J.F. Matthews, *Western Aristocracies* (1975), 131 ff.; E.D. Hunt, *Holy
    Land Pilgrimage in the Later Roman Empire A.D. 312–460* (Oxford
    1982), 135 ff., 155 ff.

19. Constantine's letter to Macarius alludes to the discovery of the cross *(Life
    of Constantine* 3.30.1) and wood from the cross soon found its way to
    remote areas of North Africa: see Yvette Duval, *Local Sanctorum Africae*
    1 (Rome 1982), nos. 157, 167. On "Helena-History and legend" see E.D.
    Hunt, *Pilgrimage* (1982), 28 ff. However, Hunt builds too much on the
    silence of Eusebius, which must be regarded as deliberate rather than
    probative. I am inclined to explain Eusebius' silence by his detestation of

Macarius, the bishop of Jerusalem; for a more complicated explanation in terms of his attitude towards Constantine, see H.A. Drake, "Eusebius on the True Cross," *Journal of Ecclesiastical History* 36 (1985): 1–22.

20. T.E. Gregory, "The survival of paganism in Christian Greece," *American Journal of Philology* 107 (1986): 229–242.

21. Theodoret's *History of the Monks (Philotheos historia)* has been edited critically with a French translation by P. Canivet and A. Leroy-Molinghen, *Théodoret de Cyr: Histoire des Moines de Syrie (Sources chrétiennes* 234, 1977; 235, 1979): this text is now excellently translated into English by R.M. Price, *Cistercian Studies Series* 88 (Kalamazoo 1985). On the historical background, see G. Tchalencko, *Villages antiques de la Syrie du Nord* (Paris 1953-1958); P. Brown, "The Rise and Function of the Holy Man in Late Antiquity," *Journal of Roman Studies* 61 (1971): 80–101, reprinted in *Society and the Holy* (1982): 103–152.

22. For a conspectus, see G. Fowden, "The Pagan Holy Man in Late Antique Society," *Journal of Hellenic Studies* 102 (1982): 33–59, esp. 40–48.

23. H. Chadwick, *Early Christian Thought and the Classical Tradition* (Oxford 1966); T.D. Barnes, *Constantine and Eusebius* (1981), 86 ff., 181 ff.

24. See the still important paper by P. Henry, "The *Adversus Arium* of Marius Victorinus, the first systematic Exposition of the Doctrine of the Trinity," *Journal of Theological Studies* N.S. 1 (1950): 42–55.

25. A systematic modern exploration of this important topic seems to be lacking: for a bibliography of work before 1930 and a summary of its results, see F. Homes Dudden, *The Life and Times of St. Ambrose* (Oxford 1935), 113 f.; on Ambrose's use of Philo, H. Savon, *Saint Ambroise devant l' exégèse de Philon le Juif* 1 (Paris 1977); "Saint Ambroise et saint Jérome, lecteurs de Philon," *Aufstieg und Niedergang der Römischen Welt* II. 21. 1 (1984), 731–759. G. Nauroy, "La structure du *De Isaac vel anima* et la cohérence de l'allégorèse d'Ambroise de Milan," *Revue des études latines* 63 (1985): 210–236, rightly stresses Ambrose's originality and creativity as a biblical exegete, while incidentally confirming that the texts and hermeneutical traditions on which he draws are exclusively Greek.

26. The following exposition owes much to my pupil John Vanderspoel, whose thesis *Themistius and the Imperial Court* (Diss. Toronto 1989), Ch. 7, suggests some significant modifications in standard narratives of Theodosius' reign, such as that offered by J.F. Matthews, *Western Aristocracies* (1975), 55 ff., 173 ff., 223 ff.

27. The affair of Priscillian has been discussed many times: one of the best introductions is by A.R. Birley, "Magnus Maximus and the Persecution of Heresy," *Bulletin of the John Rylands Library* 66 (1982/3): 13–43.

28. On these two sources of information, see respectively, H. Chadwick, *Priscillian of Avila* (Oxford 1976), 57 ff; C. Stancliffe, *St. Martin and his Hagiographer. History and Miracle in Sulpicius Severus* (Oxford 1983), 278 ff.

29. Best demonstrated (in German) by K.M. Girardet, "Trier 385. Der Prozess gegen die Priszillianer," *Chiron* 4 (1974): 577–608.

30. H. Chadwick, *Priscillian* (1976) 111 ff. (the trial and its political context), 33 f. (the validity of Priscillian's consecration).

31. The main sources are collected and translated by B. Croke and J. Harries, *Religious Conflict in Fourth-Century Rome* (Sydney 1982), 30 ff.

32. E.J. Champlin, "Saint Gallicanus (consul 317)," *Phoenix* 36 (1982): 71–76, cf. Averil Cameron, *Journal of Roman Studies* 73 (1983): 185.

33. Between 317 and 337 there are twenty-nine *consules ordinarii* other than emperors, among whom I count seven certain and seven probable Christians, three certain and two probable pagans, and ten men whose religious adherence is uncertain: see "Christians and Pagans in the Reign of Constantius" *Entretiens Hardt* 34 (1989): 301–337.

34. Ammianus Marcellinus 21.10.8, cf. *Constantine and Eusebius* (1981), 403, n. 3.

35. F.H. Dudden, *St. Ambrose* (1935), 270 ff.; P. Brown, *Augustine* (1967), 81 f.

36. For a sensible account of these two episodes, F.H. Dudden, *St. Ambrose* (1935), 371 ff.; on their symbolic significance, G.W. Bowersock, "From Emperor to Bishop: The Self-conscious Transformation of Political Power in the Fourth Century A.D.," *Classical Philology* 81 (1986): 298–307.

37. Athanasius, *De Fuga* 7, implies that Constans had been baptised long before 350: there seems to be no explicit evidence.

38. *Theodosian Code* 16.10.10.

39. Voiced in English by J.A. McGeachy, *Q. Aurelius Symmachus and the Senatorial Aristocracy of the West* (Chicago 1942), and, more recently, in French by F. Paschoud, "Réflexions sur l'idéal religieux de Symmaque," *Historia* 14 (1965): 215–235.

40. J.J. O'Donnell, "The Demise of Paganism," *Traditio* 35 (1979): 45–88.

41. J. Harries, "Prudentius and Theodosius," *Latomus* 43 (1984): 69–84. It is not necessary to believe, however, that Symmachus ever published or circulated Book One separately.

42. D.N. Robinson, "An Analysis of the Pagan Revival of the Late Fourth Century, with Especial Reference to Symmachus," *Transactions of the American Philological Association* 46 (1915): 87–101; H. Bloch, "A New Document of the Last Pagan Revival in the West, 393–394 A.D.," *Harvard Theological Review* 38 (1945): 199–244; "The Pagan Revival in the West at the End of the Fourth Century, in A.D. Momigliano, *The Conflict between Paganism and Christianity in the Fourth Century* (Oxford 1963), 193–218. The view was by no means novel in 1915: see S. Dill, *Roman Society* (1899), 74 f.

43. J.F. Matthews, "Symmachus and the Oriental Cults," *Journal of Roman Studies* 63 (1973): 175–195.

44. L. Cracco Ruggini, "Il paganesimo romano tra religione e politica (384–394 D.C.): per una reinterpretazione del "Carmen contra paganos,"" *Memorie dell' Accademia Nazionale dei Lincei*, Classe di Scienze Morali, storiche e filologiche, Serie VIII 23 (1979), 3–141.

45. B. Croke and J. Harries, *Religious Conflict* (1982), 80–83. The most recent edition is by D.R. Shackleton Bailey, *Anthologia Latina* I.1 (Leipzig: Teubner, 1982), 17–23; the two most important earlier editions are by M. Haupt, *Hermes* 4 (1870): 354–358 (an edition often misattributed to T. Mommsen despite his clear statement: "ipsum carmen Hauptius sic constituit") and A. Riese, *Anthologia Latina* I.1 (Leipzig: Teubner, 1894): 20–25.

46. R. Ellis, "On a recently discovered Latin poem of the Fourth Century," *Journal of Philology* 1.2 (1868): 66–80.

47. T. Mommsen, "Carmen Codicis Parisini 8084," *Hermes* 4 (1870): 350–363, reprinted in his *Gesammelte Schriften* 7 (Berlin 1909): 485–498. Flavianus had already been identified as the target of the poem by C. Morel, "Recherches sur un poème latin du IVe siècle," *Revue archéologique*, N.S. 17 (1868): 451–459; 18 (1868): 44–55.

48. J.F. Matthews, *Historia* 19 (1970): 464–479.

49. *Revue de l'Université de Ottawa* 52 (1982): 69, n. 37; *Phoenix* 37 (1983): 257.

50. F. Dolbeau, "Damase, le *Carmen contra paganos* et Hériger de Lobbes," *Revue des études augustiniennes* 27 (1981): 38–43.

51. D.R. Shanzer, "The date and identity of the centonist Proba," *Revue des études augustiniennes* 32 (1986): 232–248.

52. P. Brown, *Religion and Society* (1972), 161 ff., 183 ff.

53. R.A. Markus, *Saeculum: History and Society in the Theology of Saint Augustine* (Cambridge 1970), 22 ff.

54. F.H. Dudden, *St. Ambrose* (1935), 106.

55. A. Piganiol, *L'Empire chrétien* (Paris 1947), 421–422.

THE BACKGROUND TO AUGUSTINE'S DENIAL OF RELIGIOUS PLURALITY

THE BACKGROUND TO AUGUSTINE'S DENIAL OF RELIGIOUS PLURALITY[1]

John Vanderspoel

Near the end of his life, Augustine felt the need to reexamine statements that he had made in earlier writings. Published as his *Retractions*, these reassessments can reveal important changes in Augustine's thought or attitudes. One of his remarks about his *Soliloquies* reads as follows (*Retract.* 1.4.3):[2]

> Again, my statement, "Union with wisdom is not achieved by a single road," does not sound right, as if there were another way apart from Christ, who said "I am the way." Therefore this offence to religious ears ought to have been avoided. Although that one universal way exists, there are however other ways about which we sing in the psalm, "Make known to me your ways, Lord, and teach me your paths."

It would be pointless to discuss at length the intent of the second part of Augustine's remark. For the record, the bishop was entirely human, in that he is attempting to explain or excuse his earlier lapse. He cites a passage of Scripture that could in theory support his earlier statement, though even a cursory reading of the *Soliloquies* suffices to reveal that the psalm is irrelevant to the statement later retracted. The ways or roads in question are entirely different.

More interesting for the present purpose are the statement "Union with wisdom is not achieved by a single road" from the *Soliloquies* and Augustine's later reaction: "This offence to religious ears ought to have been avoided." On the surface, the offence in the statement is readily apparent. Like a number of others, Christianity is by nature an exclusive religion, permitting only a single road to God. Any suggestion that more than one way was possible could not help but give offence to many of Augustine's contemporaries. Although to this point in the *Soliloquies* Augustine has not yet specifically equated wisdom, *sapientia* in the Latin, with God, the work is a written record of his thoughts, soon after his conversion, in his search for wisdom and God, taking the form of a dialogue between Reason and Augustine himself. It was natural enough, therefore, for his audience to make the connection.

The offence, however, is much more serious than the obvious interpretation would suggest, on two counts. In the first place, *sapientia* is a loaded word, with important implications for Augustine's thought immediately after his conversion. Secondly, the number of roads to wisdom or God was by no means a settled point when Augustine wrote the *Soliloquies* in the winter of 386/7. This will become clear shortly. First, however, a brief treatment of Augustine's other remarks on some of the issues involved.

As he himself states at the end of Book 10 of the *City of God*, Augustine devoted the first ten books of that work to the destruction of pagan views.[3] After remarking that the entire first part of the work was designed to refute those who preferred their own gods to the founder of the holy city, he continues (CD 10.32):

> Of these ten books, the first five were written against those who think that they ought to worship the gods for good things during earthly life; the second five, moreover, against those who think that the worship of the gods ought to be preserved for the sake of the life that will occur after death.

In other words, Augustine directed the first quintet against traditional Roman religion and the second against a variety of views that promised life after death, mostly the views of philosophers and their schools. Books 9 and 10 address questions raised and solved to their own satisfaction by the Neoplatonists,[4] with Plotinus and Porphyry singled out for special attention. The bishop reserves his final remarks for Porphyry, and the last chapter of Book 10 treats the Neoplatonist philosopher's views on the universal way to the liberation of the soul. In this chapter, Augustine says nothing about the concept of a single road to wisdom, emphasising instead the error of Porphyry's view in a treatise the bishop calls the *de regressu animae*, (*On the Return of the Soul*). This work of Porphyry is no longer extant, except for the quotations and paraphrases in the *City of God* and possibly a few elsewhere.[5] The fragments and the title, however, clearly indicate that Porphyry discussed the return of the soul to God after death, in other words, the union of the soul with God, or salvation.[6] It is almost impossible to believe that the Neoplatonist philosopher did not also discuss the number of ways to God, and the indirect evidence suggests that the topic was included.

Augustine does not mention this, but attempts to show that Porphyry did not in fact believe what he said he believed. In the *de regressu animae*,

Porphyry had stated that he had not committed himself to any specific sect because none of those known to him offered the universal way to the liberation of the soul. Augustine goes to work on that statement, with somewhat greater attention to rapier logic than to accurate representation of the philosopher's views. The bishop argues that Porphyry was implicitly confessing that a universal way existed, since he had accepted this as a criterion for adherence to a specific sect or religion. Naturally too, Augustine seizes upon the examples offered in Porphyry's work. The philosopher's inability to accept the view that the Brahmins of India or the Chaldaeans offered a universal way to the liberation of the soul helps Augustine to reject these as well (*CD* 10.32), on Porphyry's authority. Augustine does not stop with these successes, suggesting that Porphyry implicitly recognised that his own philosophy was inadequate, since no view known to him offered a universal way.

Augustine has seriously prejudiced the outcome of his own argument with his misrepresentations of Porphyry's views. The bishop chooses to omit the fact that the Neoplatonist had also rejected Christianity, which the philosopher knew very well. He had written the treatise *Against the Christians*, which drew an early refutation from Eusebius. The philosopher's knowledge of Christianity is clear from the fragments of that work, since he proved that the Book of Daniel was written later than it pretends to have been written. In fairness, it may be noted that he elsewhere also proved that the Book of Zoroaster was a forgery.

More important than Augustine's sin of omission in this regard is his sin of commission. The bishop unilaterally condemns Porphyry to an unrequited search for the universal way to the liberation of the soul, a search whose existence the philosopher did not himself quite recognise. The naiveté ascribed to Porphyry is not credible, and an alternate reason for his refusal to commit himself to a specific sect or religion must be found. The solution is simple. Porphyry recognised that different sects or religions offered different ways to God and he allowed each a certain legitimacy because each offered some truth. In short, Porphyry accepted the concept of religious plurality and promoted that view in at least some of his works. Undoubtedly, part of the impetus for the promotion of the concept was the philosopher's desire to combat the exclusivity claimed by Christianity. Nevertheless, his discovery that some religious works were forgeries indicates that his main preoccupation was the search for truth, historical, religious and philosophical. Whether or not his views were or are correct is, to some extent at least, irrelevant, as it is more important to determine why Augustine fulminated against them.

Before leaving Porphyry, however, some other remarks are in order. It is interesting to note that, in the *City of God*, Augustine focusses on two works of the philosopher, though he mentions others. The first of these is the treatise *On the Return of the Soul*, discussed in some detail in Book 10. The other is the work *On Philosophy from Oracles*, the target of some of Augustine's criticisms in the last books of the *City of God*. Extensive fragments of this work, in the original Greek, are extant.[7] In this work, Porphyry cites oracles and draws philosophical, as well as religious, conclusions. Conspicuous by its complete absence from the *City of God* is the work *Against the Christians*. Augustine's reasons for passing by this work are not entirely clear. Presumably, however, he regarded the treatise as unimportant for his purposes in the *City of God*. That interpretation ought not to occasion surprise. The treatise directly attacked Christianity, and Augustine perhaps thought it unnecessary to refute a polemic that offered no alternative.[8] The treatises *On the Return of the Soul* and *On Philosophy from Oracles* did, on the other hand, offer another view. As has been seen, the first of these probably promoted the concept of religious plurality, among other things. The second treatise was perhaps even more dangerous to Christianity. With his quotation and exegesis of oracles from a variety of sources, Porphyry was in effect compiling Scripture (or divine revelation) for the religious elements in Neoplatonism. These two treatises might thus have had a greater impact on Augustine's contemporaries, both pagans and Christians.

It must also always be kept in mind that Augustine wrote the *City of God* in the context of the sack of Rome by Alaric in 410, while a Christian emperor who credited his victories to the Christian God occupied the throne.[9] Pagans had had their worst fears confirmed, while some Christians began to question their beliefs.[10] Some may even have begun to look elsewhere for salvation. As an alternative to Christianity, Neoplatonism was by far the most important for intellectuals in the fourth and fifth centuries. Moreover, at the end of the fourth century, in the West at any rate, the brand of Neoplatonism that Porphyry contributed, with his edition of Plotinus and his own work, was almost exclusive. It is not surprising, then, to discover that Augustine devotes the ends of both parts of the *City of God* to a refutation of the views of Porphyry.[11] Be that as it may, Augustine certainly pays considerable and emphatic attention to Porphyry.

To return to the *Soliloquies*. It will by now be reasonably clear that the offence to religious ears in the statement "Union with wisdom is not achieved by a single road" lies primarily in the fact that Augustine's words sound too Neoplatonic and too much like Porphyry. Similarly, the concept of wisdom or *sapientia*. The term is in fact the Latin equivalent for the idiosyncratic Neoplatonic Greek term Nous, the World-Mind, or the very concept of intelligence itself. That makes Augustine's statement doubly suspect, as both the union with wisdom and the plurality of roads to that union echo Porphyry and Neoplatonism.

While the recognition that Augustine's statement has a definite Neoplatonic sound is easy to determine, his intent in this regard is slightly more difficult to analyse. As noted earlier, the *Soliloquies* is a dialogue between Augustine and Reason. The offending statement is made by Reason, and not by Augustine himself. Nevertheless, the entire work is shot through with Neoplatonic concepts, as are many of the other works written in the immediate interval after his conversion. The structure of the argument, the questions raised and the answers given are cast in Neoplatonic terms throughout, including the excessively long prayer that follows the brief introduction. Indeed, Augustine's very search for *sapientia* and God reflects the Neoplatonic quest for union with Nous and the One.

Augustine himself offers evidence that he was influenced by Porphyry when he wrote the work, or rather, he states emphatically that the view that he was following the Neoplatonist was a misinterpretation. He retracts another statement in the *Soliloquies* as follows (*Retract.* 1.4.7):

> And in the place where it was said, 'Those sensible things ought entirely to be avoided," I ought to have been on guard, lest I be thought to hold to the opinion of the false philosopher Porphyry, when he said that the whole body ought to be shunned. However, I did not say all sensible things, but those, that is, the corruptible. But I ought rather to have said this specifically; moreover, such sensible things will not exist in the new heaven and the new earth of the future age.

Though Augustine manages to show how his statement was not entirely reminiscent of the view of Porphyry, he cannot hide the fact that the similarities are evident enough to require correction. In both of the retractions quoted, Augustine remarks that he ought not to have said what he did, which indicates either carelessness or a change of view between the original and the retraction. As many have seen, his views on these and other issues changed through time as his pagan education receded further into the past. In particular, his thought became less Neoplatonic, until he achieved the ability to argue strenuously against this particular pagan view. This is not to suggest that Augustine was a Neoplatonist philosopher during the first period after his conversion. Rather, the views that he expressed at this time were heavily influenced by Porphyry and others, and the Christianity in his early writings is little more than a veneer, a veneer that in time replaces the old material.[12]

It is clear, then, that when Augustine permitted a variety of roads to union with wisdom he was under the influence of Porphyry, who had held, perhaps originated, the concept. Since the Neoplatonist philosopher had been dead for almost a century when Augustine wrote the *Soliloquies*, it will be useful to trace the concept of religious plurality through the fourth century, where it fortunately appears on a few occasions. The discussion, which will necessarily be selective, will clarify the reason for Augustine's vigour when he attacks the concept by calling it an offence to religious ears.

Porphyry's promotion of the concept of religious plurality reflects a change of status for Christianity in the last part of the third century. Previously, pagans had argued against Christianity on different grounds, focusing on some of the problems and inconsistencies that they saw in the upstart religion. Christianity nevertheless increased in popularity to the extent that many pagans felt a threat of religious extinction. New weapons were necessary to combat the influence of the new religion that claimed to have an exclusive road to God and salvation. Porphyry selected the claim to exclusivity as one of the more vulnerable tenets of Christianity and began to promote the concept of religious plurality. In doing this, he doubtless hoped to coalesce opposition to Christianity by the many other beliefs available during this period. Many of these were threatened and many promoted a preferred highway, rather than an exclusive road, to God and salvation. The period of transition can perhaps be defined specifically as the working period of Porphyry's life. As has been seen, the Neoplatonist philosopher wrote a treatise *Against the Christians*. This appears to have been a polemic of traditional technique, but was argued more effectively, more completely and more intelligently than previous efforts. It also seems to have been the basis for Julian the Apostate's treatise *Against the Galilaeans* written in the early 360s. Porphyry also wrote a treatise that promoted the concept of religious plurality and perhaps attempted to create pagan Scripture with his *On Philosophy from Oracles*.[13] The dates of these works have been endlessly disputed, and it has been suggested that *On the Return of the Soul* is the same work as *On Philosophy from Oracles*, since Augustine discusses them in similar terms, referring to the first with a Latin, the second by its Greek, title. Problems exist, therefore, but the important conclusion is that a transition appears during the lifetime of Porphyry.[14]

Pierre Courcelle has shown that Porphyry's work and ideas were very influential in the Latin West on both pagan and Christian authors of the fourth century and beyond.[15] One vehicle for the diffusion of that influence was Marius Victorinus, a grammarian, rhetorician and Neoplatonist philosopher who became a Christian. The date of his conversion is a matter of some dispute, but a date around 350 has emerged as the most likely. Much of his work is no longer extant, though some grammatical works, as well as treatises written after his conversion, are available for those who care to read them. The most serious losses are the philosophical works, including translations of some works of Plotinus and Porphyry into Latin, which introduced many intellectuals in the West to the ideas of Porphyry. Augustine's knowledge of Porphyry, particularly during the earlier part of his career when he could not read Greek very well, almost certainly derives from these translations, which were perhaps part of the curriculum at the later stages of literary and philosophical education. As might be expected, the Christian writings of Victorinus are heavily influenced by Neoplatonism, though, to return to my ostensible subject, he apparently stops short of stating that there is more than one way to God.[16]

Early direct evidence for the popularity of Porphyry's concept of religious plurality among pagans occurs in a panegyric written and delivered in the East by Themistius, a pagan philosopher, politician and orator who spent his working life at Constantinople. His extent philosophical works are *Paraphrases* of works of Aristotle, and not surprisingly he is normally considered to be a philosopher of Aristotelian inclination. Other preserved works include a good many orations, of which nineteen are panegyrics of emperors from Constantius to Theodosius. These speeches reveal Aristotelian and Platonic influences throughout. What has not generally been recognised, however, is that Neoplatonic ideas have occasionally slipped into the speeches. One speech in particular is relevant to the present discussion.[17]

On 1 January 364, Themistius delivered a panegyric of Jovian, the successor to Julian the Apostate. The speech is at its core a plea for religious tolerance.[18] During the previous reign, Julian had actively championed the cause of paganism with measures such as the prohibition of the teaching of non-Christian authors by Christian teachers and the return of lands, buildings and subsidies to pagan cults. Naturally, most pagans were pleased that the favoured position granted to Christianity by Constantine had fallen by the wayside, though not all, including Themistius, were happy with the vigour displayed by Julian. Arab sources report that Themistius wrote to Julian in an effort to turn the emperor away from persecution of Christianity. That letter, if it ever was written, is no longer extant, unfortunately, because it would reveal much about Themistius' thought and about negative pagan reaction to Julian.

The accession of the Christian Jovian reaffirmed the position of Christianity as the religion of the imperial court. Zealous Christians soon began once again to attack and destroy pagan temples. Jovian himself may not have condoned these activities, since he was very cautious in his actions on religious matters during the first few months of his reign. This is not at all surprising. He had laid claim to the throne after the death of Julian, by means that can best be described as semi-legitimate. In addition, he had inherited a court that was largely pagan. After those first few months of hesitation, Jovian began to take stronger measures on behalf of Christianity and against paganism. Themistius' panegyric of the emperor was delivered in this context, about six months after Jovian took the throne.[19]

The first half of the speech addresses a variety of problems, including the question of Jovian's legitimacy as emperor which the author naturally answers in the affirmative. In the second part, Themistius pleads with Jovian for religious tolerance and for the peaceful co-existence of a variety of religions. The philosopher's key argument is the desirability of religious plurality, based on the diversity created in the world by God. In other words, God had created differences within mankind and consequently wanted to be worshipped in different ways by different peoples. In effect, more than one road to God was possible.

With great intelligence, Themistius uses as his point of departure a statement that the emperor himself had made. At this period, Christianity had split into a number of disputing factions, in particular the followers of Athanasius and the adherents of Arius. When Jovian was besieged by these warring factions of bishops, each of which wanted him to favour its view, he remarked that, while he himself followed Athanasius, he had no intention of outlawing the other group. Themistius understood this to mean that Jovian was permitting a variety of religious persuasions within Christianity and pleads for equal consideration for pagans on the same basis. Jovian's statement was tantamount to a decree, since the emperor was Law Incarnate in the philosopher's view, and Themistius desired an extension of that decree to include all religions, including pagans.

The nature of his arguments will become more clear from the following quotations from the panegyric. On the emperor's statement that he would allow all forms of Christianity, he remarks (5.68a):

> You decree that all have a share in divine worship, thereby emulating God, who made the predisposition to piety a common characteristic of human nature, but left the manner of worship to the will of each individual. He who applies compulsion takes away the freedom of choice which God has allowed.

After some other brief remarks, the orator states that diversity is healthy, because it creates a rivalry that strengthens piety. The emperor, Themistius intimates in his continuing praise of Jovian's statement, was aware of this (68d-69a):

> For this reason, you do not prevent the good strife of piety; for this reason you do not dull the goad of zeal for the divine, rivalry with one another and emulation. Just as all runners go to the same distributor of prizes, not however all for the same race, but some for one, some for another, and the unrewarded loser not at all, so you understand that there is one great and true director of the contest. It is not, however, a single road that leads to him, but there is a road that is barely passable, a broader way, a rough road and a level one. Nevertheless, they all stretch toward that one same haven. Our rivalry and zeal stem from nothing except the fact that all do not walk the same road. If you permit only a single road, you will cut off the others, and you will block off the open space of the contest.

Finally, Themistius comments on the diversity of mankind. Noting that the emperor's army consisted of many types of soldiers, with different tasks, and that the empire consisted of many kinds of men, such as farmers, orators, city-dwellers and philosophers, he remarks that all are dependent on their emperor. He then gives Jovian some advice (70a):

> Think that the founder of all also takes delight in this diversity. He wants the Syrians to be one variety of citizen, the Greeks another variety, and the Egyptians another variety still. Even the Syrians themselves are not homogeneous, but are in fact broken down into small units. Indeed not one single person understands things in exactly the same way as a neighbour, but one in this way and another in that. Why then then do we force what cannot be put into practice?

Clearly, Themistius holds the view that religious plurality is appropriate and desirable. He employs the concept of different roads to God and salvation, and it is arguable that his thought on this topic shows the influence of Porphyry, even if he has added some elements of his own. In passing, it may be worth noting another possible influence of Porphyry on Themistius. In a eulogy, the orator describes the return of his father's soul, which had been incorruptible while on earth, to a reunion with God, whence it had come. This sounds rather like it derives in part from Porphyry's *On the Return of the Soul*. In the present context, the most important point is this: a leading pagan intellectual in the East *publicly* promoted the concept of religious plurality in a speech to a Christian emperor. This should be some indication of the importance of the concept in pagan thought.

Themistius undoubtedly used many of the same arguments in another speech no longer extant. Valens, the successor to Jovian in the East, was an ardent follower of Arius and made life miserable for the adherents of Athanasius. In 376, Themistius, who was disturbed by the disharmony and the resulting disorder, pleaded with Valens for religious toleration within Christianity, on the grounds that different branches of Christianity differed less from each other than from paganism. The ecclesiastical historian Socrates, who reports the speech, also summarises some of its arguments. One has been mentioned. He describes some of the others as follows (*HE* 4.32): "With regard to worship from compulsion, great discord results. God therefore wants to be worshipped in different ways, in order that each individual might reverence his majesty all the more, because he has not come to knowledge of him easily." Socrates reports that Themistius had some success with his arguments, since Valens became less harsh.

The concept of religious plurality emerges again in a well-known letter of Symmachus to the emperor Valentinian II. In this letter, he pleaded with the emperor for the restoration of the Altar of Victory to the senate-house. This altar had had a chequered history during the fourth century. Constantius removed it, Julian restored it and Gratian removed it once again. In addition to the altar itself, pagans were concerned about the loss of state subsidies to pagan cults, in the belief that official recognition validated these cults. The Altar of Victory was the symbol of this dispute.

Shortly after the death of Gratian, Symmachus, as the official representative of the Senate at Rome, wrote *Relation* 3. He held the city prefecture in 384, and, as such, was the appropriate choice to perform the task. The letter itself, which is an official letter from city prefect to emperor,[20] discusses a number of topics and uses a variety of arguments in support of the requests. These include the benefits that the state cults had conferred throughout the course of Roman history and the practice of other emperors, including those Christian rulers who had continued the subsidies. He uses other arguments as well, arguments that show the influence of Porphyry and perhaps Themistius.

At one point, he writes (*Rel.* 3.8):

Everyone has his own customs, his own religious practices; the divine mind has assigned to different cities different religions to be their guardians. Each man is given at birth a separate soul; in the same way each people is given its own special genius to take care of its destiny.

A little later, he remarks (3.10):

It is reasonable that whatever each of us worships is really to be considered one and the same. We gaze up at the same stars, the sky covers us all, the same universe compasses us. What does it matter what practical system we adopt in our search for truth? Not by one avenue only can we arrive at so tremendous a secret.

Symmachus' plea in these statements is that religious plurality be allowed, and he uses many of the arguments also found in Themistius. To what extent the orator from the East influenced Symmachus is unknown. In any case, the argument itself goes back to Porphyry,[21] and both writers have accepted the Neoplatonist philosopher's view. Both also use terminology that is similar to that of each other and to the terminology that Porphyry seems to have used. Nevertheless, it may be worth mentioning that some of Themistius' philosophical work was known in the West. Boethius informs us that a contemporary of Symmachus, the influential pagan Vettius Agorius Praetextatus, translated into Latin some of Themistius' *Paraphrases* of Aristotle. In addition, Themistius visited Rome in 376 to deliver a panegyric of Gratian, and he almost certainly came into contact with leading intellectuals in the West.[22] Part of Symmachus' argumentation may thus derive from Themistius, rather than directly from Porphyry.

Once again, the concept of religious plurality appears as a cornerstone of pagan arguments for religious toleration. Christian reaction to Symmachus was swift and strong. Before he had even seen the letter, Ambrose wrote to the emperor, warning him not to accept the arguments and requesting a copy that he could refute point by point (*Ep.* 17). Shortly thereafter, he wrote the refutation in another letter to the emperor. The detailed reply (*Ep.* 18) does not always discuss the arguments themselves. Rather, Ambrose at times prefers to ridicule the statements made by Symmachus, though he pays tribute to the eloquence of his opponent. He does not discuss the diversity created in the world, as Symmachus had done, and his remarks on the number of roads to God are unsatisfactory, since he merely states his own opposing view without further discussion (*Ep.* 18.8):

> Not by one avenue only, he says, can we arrive at so tremendous a secret. What you do not know, we know from the voice of God. And what you search for with merely conceptions, we have discovered with absolute certainty from the very wisdom of God and from truth. Your views, therefore, do not sit well with us.

On that last point, Symmachus presumably had no doubt. Twenty years later, in the context of another attempt by Symmachus to secure religious toleration, his letter to Valentinian was refuted again, this time in a long poem by the Christian poet Prudentius. About the same time, the pagan poet Claudian wrote a short poem (*carm. min.* 50) in which he replies to Jacobus, a Christian general who had disputed claims that Claudian had made about a battle against the Goths in 402. Claudian had given credit for the so-called victory to the traditional pagan gods, while Christians, including Prudentius and apparently Jacobus, felt that the Christian God was responsible. Jacobus in fact openly attacked Claudian's views. The poet responded, with the argument "You may have your saints and apostles to help you, Jacobus, but whatever you do, do not attack my poetry." Claudian expresses this view in a poem that is best seen as a sarcastic attack on the Christian reliance on saints.[23] Nevertheless, he allows Jacobus to have his own religious views, but expects the same courtesy in return.

The plea for religious plurality, watered down in Claudian but with full force in Porphyry, Themistius and Symmachus, became, during the fourth century, one of the leading arguments used by pagans to promote their own cause, and if they truly believed in plurality, pagans were more content to tolerate opposing views than was Christianity. Augustine recognised the danger. The reason for the vigour of his attack on the concept and the reason for his retraction of an earlier statement are now clear. The bishop was responding to a key element of pagan, Neoplatonic thought, even if that idea was largely a matter of self-defence for pagans. In the early years after his conversion, Augustine was still under the influence of that thought. Later, he attempted to set the record straight.

In 1961, Norman King reacted to the letter of Symmachus as follows:[24]

The well-known plea of the pagan Symmachus is really only for the remnants of Roman paganism to be allowed to co-exist with Christianity. The old man's thinking does not reach fundamentals.

Augustine was considerably more perceptive. He recognised that the dispute over the number of ways to God was a dispute over fundamentals. If salvation is the goal, what could be more fundamental than the road or roads to that goal? Augustine's accurate recognition of the prominence and importance of the concept in pagan thought spawned his vigourous denial of religious plurality.

John Vanderspoel has been Assistant Professor in the Department of Classics at the University of Calgary since 1985. He holds degrees from Calvin College (B.A., 1980) and the University of Toronto (M.A., 1981; Ph.D., 1989). His interests include the history of the Roman Empire, especially during the later period, and the relationship between Christianity and other religions in Late Antiquity. He has published a number of articles on the history and intellectual history of Late Antiquity in leading classical journals in North America and Europe. He is, with two others, a founding co-editor of the *Ancient History Bulletin*.

NOTES

1.   Only minor changes and the correction of typographical errors distinguish the present version of the text from that read at the Conference. I have added some annotation, designed to indicate my debt to others, to provide some basic bibliography for those who wish to read further, and to clarify points raised in the text of the paper. The notes are in no way exhaustive and should not be regarded as such. Translations, except where otherwise noted, are my own.

2. I translate from the text of A. Mutzenbecher, *Sancti Aurelii Augustini Retractationum Libri II* (= CCL 57).

3. Augustine discusses his goals and the plan of his work elsewhere as well: *CD*. 6. praef.,1; *Ep.* 184A; *Ep. ad Firmum*; *Retract* 2.69.

4. I use what has become the standard term for students of and adherents to Platonic philosophy from Plotinus onward, even though it is difficult to speak of a school of philosophy with a single emphasis during the late third and early fourth centuries.

5. Those from the *City of God*, Book 10, are conveniently collected in an appendix by J. Bidez, *Vie de Porphyre* (Gand and Leipzip 1913), 25*–44*. J.J. O'Meara has attempted to show that *Philosophy from Oracles* is the same work and has argued for additional fragments in the *City of God* and elsewhere in *Porphyry's Philosophy from Oracles in Augustine* (Paris 1959) and *Porphyry's Philosophy from Oracles in Eusebius' Praeparatio Evangelica and Augustine's Dialogues of Cassiciacum* (Paris 1969) (reprinted from *Recherches Augustiniennes* 6 [1969], 103–139). Few have accepted his views, and P. Hadot, "Citations de Porphyre dans Augustine," RÉAug 6 (1960): 205–244, disposes of most of them.

6. An accurate understanding of Porphyry's thought is difficult to achieve, because so few of his works are extant. Detailed discussion on matters of this sort would be out of place here and is, in any case, beyond my competence. I therefore city only those works which I found useful in the present paper. As a general discussion, R.T. Wallis, *Neoplatonism* (London, 1972) is helpful, though often very brief. A. Smith, *Porphyry's Place in the Neoplatonic Tradition* (The Hague 1974) devotes much of his attention to a discussion of Porphyry's view of the soul and related topics. He notes the philosopher's concern with salvation (e.g. 144ff.) and discusses the peculiarly Porphyrian view on the liberation of the soul from the cycle of reincarnation (56ff.,65ff.) In the first of the two works cited in the previous note, O'Meara (23–27) discusses Porphyry's *de regressu animae* and the views on the soul implicit in the fragments.

7. Collected and edited by G. Wolff, *Porphyrii de philosophia ex oraculis haurienda Librorum Reliquiae* (Berlin 1856; repr. Hildesheim 1962).

8. T.D. Barnes has reminded me that the work was banned by Constantine (Soc. *HE* 1.9.30; cf. *CTh* 16.5.66) and was probably unavailable to Augustine, who shows no knowledge of the treatise anywhere.

9. There is no point in listing all the works that discuss the historical background to the work. Most treatments of Augustine do. I therefore cite only P. Brown, *Augustine of Hippo* (Berkley and Los Angeles 1967), 287ff.

10. On the intellectual (and historical) circumstances, see the recent discussion by T.D. Barnes, "Aspects of the Background of The *City of God*," *Revue de l'Université d'Ottawa* 52 (1982): 64–80.

11. O'Meara, *Porphyry's Philosophy from Oracles in Augustine*, 101 offers similar remarks about the appearance of Porphyry at the end of both parts of the *City of God*.

12. I do not intend, of course, to question the sincerity of his conversion, but only to suggest that the structure of his thought during the early years as a Christian was largely built from Neoplatonic material. Cf. P. Henry, *Plotin et l'Occident* (Louvain 1934), 142: "Le vocabulaire d'Augustin peut n'être qu'une traduction de celui de Plotin, sa mentalité, une mentalité de néoplatonicien, son esprit est un esprit tout nouveau, c'est l'esprit de l'Évangile de l'Église du Christ."

13. Cf. the remarks of J. Geffcken, *The Last Days of Greco-Roman Paganism* (= *Der Ausgang des griechisch-römischen Heidentums*), trans. S. Mac-Cormack (Amsterdam, New York, Oxford 1978), 57–59.

14. For the view that the two works, which are extremely difficult to date, are the same, see the works of O'Meara cited in n.5 above. For the treatise attacking Christianity, T.D. Barnes, "Porphyry *Against the Christians*: Date and the Attribution of Fragments," *Journal of Theological Studies* 24 (1973): 424–442 with references to earlier treatments, suggests a date much later than most have favoured.

15. P. Courcelle, *Les Lettres Grecques en Occident* (Paris 1948) 153–182 (= *Late Latin Writiers and their Greek Sources*, trans. H.E. Wedeck [Cambridge, Mass. 1969], 165–196), for the influence on Augustine in particular. P. Henry (n. 12 above), 44–145, discusses Marius Victorinus' and Augustine's knowledge of Plotinus' thought.

16. On Victorinus, P. Hadot, *Porphyre et Victorinus* (Paris 1968) and *Marius Victorinus. Recherches sur sa vie et ses oeuvres* (Paris 1971) are detailed treatments. Courcelle and Henry discuss the role that Victorinus played in the transmission to the West of Porphyry and Plotinus respectively, in the works already cited. Augustine's ability or inability to read Greek is a matter of some dispute; most, however, would accept the standard view that he was not a proficient reader of Greek until the mid–410s or later; cf. Courcelle, 183–194 (196–208 in the translation).

17. No full–scale, and only one lengthy, published treatment of Themistius exists in any language. G. Dragon, "L'Empire Romain d'Orient au IVe siècle et les traditions politiques de l'Hellénisme. Le témoignage de thémistios," *Travaux et Mémoires* 3 (1968): 1–242, discusses only some elements of

the orator's thought and life. I have recently completed a Ph.D. thesis entitled "Themistius and the Imperial Court" (Diss. Toronto, 1989).

18. Cf. L.J. Daly, "Themistius' Plea for Religious Tolerance," *Greek, Roman and Byzantine Studies* 12 (1971): 65–79.

19. I discuss Themistius' attitude to Julian in Ch. IV and Jovian's reign in Ch. V of my thesis.

20. Cf. R.H. Barrow, *Prefect and Emperor. The* Relationes *of Symmachus A.D. 384* (Oxford 1973), 15–16. The translations of *Relation* 3 are those of Barrow.

21. P. Courcelle, "Du nouveau sur la vie et les oeuvres de Marius Victorinus," *Revue des Études Anciennes* 64 (1962): 131, drew attention to Symmachus' debt to Porphyry on this point. Before this came to my attention, I had thought that he owed the concept to Themistius, which may still be partly the case.

22. Praetextatus' translations: Boethius, *De interpret. ed. sec.* 1.289. Themistius in Rome: T.D. Barnes, "Constans and Gratian in Rome," *Harvard Studies in Classical Philology* 79 (1975): 329, and my thesis, Ch. VI.

23. Cf. J. Vanderspoel "Claudian, Christ and the Cult of the Saints," *Classical Quarterly* 36 (1986): 244–255.

24. *"Compelle Intrare* and the Plea of the Pagans," *The Modern Churchman,* n.s. 4 (1961): 113, as quoted by Daly (n.18 above), 77, who accepts the view.